Nationalism, Law and Statelessness

In 1998 a bloody war erupted in the Horn of Africa between Ethiopia and Eritrea. During the war Ethiopia arrested and expelled 70,000 of its citizens, and stripped another 50,000-plus of their citizenship on the basis of their presumed ethnicity. *Nationalism, Law and Statelessness: Grand illusions in the Horn of Africa* examines the events which led up to the war, documents the expulsions and denationalizations that took place and follows the flight of these stateless Ethiopians out of the Horn into Europe.

The core issue examined is the link between sovereignty and statelessness as this plays out in the Horn of Africa and in the West. The book provides a valuable insight into how nations create and perpetuate statelessness, the failure of law, both national and international, to protect and address the plight of stateless persons, and the illusory nature of nationalism, citizenship and human rights in the modern age. The study is one of a very few which examines the problem of statelessness through the accounts of stateless persons themselves.

This book will be of great interest to students and researchers in anthropology, law, politics, African studies and refugee studies as well as professionals and all those interested in stateless persons in the West, including Eritreans, who continue to be denied basic rights.

John R. Campbell is a social anthropologist who has undertaken fieldwork/ development consultancies in Ghana, Tanzania, Kenya, Ethiopia, Botswana and the United Kingdom. He currently teaches anthropology at The School of Oriental and African Studies, London.

Routledge Explorations in Development Studies

The Domestic Politics of Foreign Aid
Erik Lundsgaarde

Social Protection in Developing Countries
Reforming Systems
Katja Bender, Markus Kaltenborn and Christian Pfleiderer

Formal Peace and Informal War
Security and Development in the Congo
Zoë Marriage

Technology Development Assistance for Agriculture
Putting Research into Use in Low Income Countries
Norman Clark, Andy Frost, Ian Maudlin and Andrew Ward

Statelessness and Citizenship
Camps and the Creation of Political Space
Victoria Redclift

Governance for Pro-Poor Urban Development
Lessons from Ghana
Franklin Obeng-Odoom

Nationalism, Law and Statelessness
Grand Illusions in the Horn of Africa
John R. Campbell

Nationalism, Law and Statelessness

Grand illusions in the
Horn of Africa

John R. Campbell

Routledge
Taylor & Francis Group

LONDON AND NEW YORK

First published 2014
by Routledge
2 Park Square, Milton Park, Abingdon, Oxfordshire OX14 4RN

Simultaneously published in the USA and Canada
by Routledge
711 Third Avenue, New York, NY 10017

First issued in paperback 2015

Routledge is an imprint of the Taylor & Francis Group, an informa business

British Library Cataloguing in Publication Data
A catalogue record for this book is available from the British Library

Library of Congress Cataloging-in-Publication Data
Campbell, John (John R.)
 Nationalism, law and statelessness : grand illusions in the Horn of Africa / John R. Campbell.
 pages cm. — (Routledge explorations in development studies ; 7)
 1. Refugees—Legal status, laws, etc.—Ethiopia. 2. Refugees—Legal status, laws, etc.
 —Eritrea. 3. Refugees—Horn of Africa. I. Title.
 KQC567.C655 2013
 362.870963—dc23
 2013001836

ISBN13: 978-1-138-92810-7 (pbk)
ISBN13: 978-0-415-63493-9 (hbk)

Typeset in Times New Roman
by Swales & Willis Ltd, Exeter, Devon

Contents

Figures

Tables

Boxes

Case studies

Case law, international legal conventions and other legal documents

Case law

Nottebohm Case (*Liechtenstein* v. *Guatemala*) *6 April 1955*, ICJ Reports 1955, p. 4; General List No. 18.

Kelzani v. *SSHD* (7 Nov. 1978), [1978] Imm AR 193.

R v. *Secretary of State for Home Department ex parte Bradshaw* [1994] Imm AR 359.

R v. *Secretary of State for Social Security ex parte JCWI*, QBD [1996].

YL (Nationality – Statelessness – Eritrea – Ethiopia) Eritrea, CG [2003] UKIAT 00016.

BG (Removal to Eritrea of Ethiopia/Eritrea) Eritrea, CG [2003] UKAIT.

R v. *SSHD ex parte Q*, EWCA [2003] EWHC 195 (Admin).

Tedros Medhin v. *John Ashcroft*, No. 02-4247, decided 1 December 2003 in the Seventh Circuit Court of the United States.

MA and Others (Ethiopia – Mixed ethnicity – Dual nationality) Eritrea, [2004] UKIAT 00324.

R (on the application of Tewolde) v. *Immigration Appeal Tribunal*, Administrative Court, 28 January 2004.

R v. *SSHD ex parte Adam, Limbuela and Tesema*, [2005] UKHL 66.

Senait Kidane Tesfamichael; Dawit Tessea-Damate, petitioners, v. *Alberto Gonzales, US Attorney General, respondent*, No. 04-61180, S Fifth Circuit Court, 24 October 2006.

MA (Draft evaders – Illegal departures – Risk) Eritrea, CG [2007] UKAIT 00059.

FH and Ors, R (on the application of) v. *Secretary of State for the Home Department, Court of Appeal – Administrative Court, July 05, 2007*, [2007] EWHC 1571 (Admin).

EB (Ethiopia) v. *SSHD*, [2007] EWCA Civ 809.

491 F.3d 470, Hiwot Nemariam et al., appellants v. *The Federal Democratic Republic of Ethiopia and the Commercial Bank of Ethiopia, appellees*, No. 05-7178, decided on 22 June 2007 in the US Court of Appeals, District of Columbia.

Nighisti Woldemariam, Issac Ghebretnsae Beletse, petitioners v. *John Ashcroft,*

US Attorney General, No. 03-4518, decided 22 June 2007 in the US Third Circuit Court.

Dawit Tekle v. *SSHD*, in the High Court of Justice, Queen's Bench Division, Administrative Court, Case No. CO/10249/06, [2008] EWHC 3064 (Admin) 11 December 2008.

Saba Tesfamichael, Claimant v. *SSHD, Defendant*, in the High Court of Justice, Queen's Bench Division, Administrative Court [2008] EWHC 3162 (Admin) heard on 19 December 2008.

R (*on the application of Samuel Hailemariam*) v. *SSHD*, Case No. CO/5850/2008 [2009] EWHC 468 (Admin) 17 February 2009.

MA (Ethiopia), [2009] EWCA Civ 289.

R (on the Application of Rabah, Woldemichael and Saddah) v. *SSHD*, High Court, Queen's Bench Division, Case No. CO/5985/2007, 18 March 2009, [2009] EWHC 1044 (Admin).

R (on the Application of MS, AR & FW) and SSHD, Court of Appeal, Civil Division, 4 December 2009; [2009] EWCA Civ 1310.

Hanane M Seid, petitioner v. *Eric Holder, Attorney General, respondent*, No. 05-72176, US Court of Appeals for the Ninth Circuit, filed 23 December 2009.

R (on the application of ZO (Somalia) and others) (Respondents) v. *Secretary of State for the Home Department (Appellant)*, [2010] UKSC 36.

MO (illegal exit – risk on return) Eritrea, CG [2011] UKUT 00190 (IAC).

ST (Ethnic Eritrean-nationality – return) Ethiopia, CG [2011] UKUT 0025.

R (on the application of ST (Eritrea)) (FC) (Appellant) v. *Secretary of State for the Home Department (Respondent)*, [2012] UKSC 12.

Hirsi Jamaa and Others v. *Italy*, Application No. 27765/09, European Court of Human Rights, Grand Chamber, Strasbourg 23 January 2012.

International legal conventions

Universal Declaration of Human Rights (1948).

Refugee Convention (1951).

Convention Related to the Status of Stateless Persons (1954).

Convention on the Reduction of Stateless Persons (1961).

International Covenant on Civil and Political Rights (1966).

International Convention on the Elimination of All Forms of Racial Discrimination (1966).

International Convention on the Protection of the Rights of All Migrant Workers and Members of Their Families (1990).

African Charter on Human and People's Rights (1986).

Other legal documents

Constitution of the Federal Republic of Ethiopia (1994).

Preface

The fieldwork on which this book is based was funded by a grant from the UK Economic and Social Research Council (RES-062-23-0296) entitled 'Refugees and the Law: An ethnography of the British asylum system'. The grant covered fieldwork in British courts, immigration firms, barristers' chambers and in Ethiopian and Eritrean communities in London and south-east England from January 2007 to January 2009, and it allowed me to employ Dr Solomon Afework as my research officer. I owe Solomon a debt of gratitude as a colleague and as a friend. He was responsible for much of the community-based research, including the 'conversations' with failed asylum seekers which are discussed in Chapter 6.

I am especially indebted to Eric Fripp (Barrister, Mitre House), Ravi Low-Beer and David Longe (both formerly with the Refugee Legal Centre), Professor Werner Menski (School of Oriental and African Studies, London) and Mrs Alem Gebrehiwot (Director of the Ethiopian Community Centre in the UK, London) who, as members of my project advisory board, provided invaluable guidance and support.

Over the course of the project I was assisted by many Ethiopians and Eritreans in the UK, including individuals seeking asylum and community leaders in nearly 70 refugee community organizations who agreed to speak to us about their work and concerns. In addition I thank the many immigration case workers, barristers, officials and others who gave us much of their valuable time, answered our questions and directed us to others who might assist the project. I owe special thanks to Lucy Kralj at the Helen Bamber Foundation, who found individuals for me to interview. I am also indebted to many other individuals whose names do not appear in this book but who provided invaluable assistance.

Unfortunately we encountered many officials who innately distrust independent researchers. We were refused research access to the Asylum and Immigration Tribunal despite the offer of written guarantees promising anonymity and confidentiality to those who agreed to speak to us. Nevertheless, as members of the public we attended a large number of asylum, immigration and bail hearings and, via contacts with barristers and case workers, we were given access to asylum applicants and their case files. Initially we enjoyed limited access to one London-based Home Office Presenting Unit, where I was allowed to 'work shadow' Home Office Presenting Officers, interview them and discuss their casework. I am grateful to these officers for showing me how they perceive and perform their work. Unfortunately, a senior Home Office official unceremoniously withdrew my research access following a damning report on their institution by the Independent Asylum Commission.

I want to thank my partner Sarah and my children Alex, Nina and Eleanor for their patience and support while I conducted fieldwork in the UK and in Ethiopia, and during the countless months I have spent writing up my material. Sarah ensured that I had time and space to write and also made valuable comments on draft chapters.

More generally, without sufficient time to write up fieldwork – which I earned by taking up the thankless task of head of department – it would not have been possible to write this book. The burgeoning administrative work at universities, together with a decline in research funding, will make it increasingly difficult for university-based researchers to undertake fieldwork and write up their material.

In compliance with the conditions placed on my grant by the ESRC I have consistently followed the principle of informed consent in all meetings and interviews. This means that in the UK I used interview forms written in Amharic, Tigrinya, Oromiffa and English and that, where relevant, I employed trained research assistants who spoke the relevant vernacular language to interview asylum applicants. The purpose of the research was fully explained to individuals, as were the possible uses of the information that individuals provided to us. Signed consent forms were used in every case. Where possible we recorded interviews that were later transcribed. In Ethiopia, however, my informants were reluctant to be recorded, which meant that I took notes of our talks which I later wrote up. If individuals did not wish to participate in the research we left them in peace. I have anonymized all the interview data for the 26 individuals whose cases are used in this book, for the 15 'failed' asylum seekers and for officials, barristers etc.

In conducting research into the asylum system I have relied heavily on the UK's Freedom of Information Act (2000) to obtain information about the work of the UK Border Agency, the Ministry of Justice, the Asylum and Immigration Tribunal and the Treasury Solicitor's Department. Most of this information ought, by right, to be in the public domain. Without the right afforded me under the 2000 Act to demand information it would have been impossible to assess, much less understand, how key government institutions operate – particularly those who deny independent researchers access.

Even so, it is important to note that where I report data/information that derives from a Freedom of Information request and/or when the source is an official publication of the British Home Office/UK Border Agency all such data should be treated *as provisional* and subject to revision. This is owing to: (a) the late reporting of cases (a small proportion of cases are not included when the statistics are produced); (b) the results of data cleansing exercises; and because (c) subsequent publications do not accurately reconcile figures in alternative data sources (UK Home Office 2012a: 17). In addition, since 2005 the Home Office has changed the way it collects and reports some data.

In preparing this book I owe a debt of gratitude to Ned Collier at the School of

Oriental and African Studies, University of London for assisting in the production and editing of the maps, figures and appendix and to Helen Bell, the editorial assistant at Routledge for her advice and support.

Finally I would like to dedicate this book to Sarah. I also want to offer my profound thanks to Genet, Gebriel, the members of SINIT , to 'Eritreans' seeking refuge in the West and to the countless 'Eritreans' in Ethiopia, Eritrea and in transit across Africa and the Middle East. You have not been forgotten.

The value of currency

1. In 1998, Eritrean nakfa 7.36 = US$1.00
2. In 2000, Eritrean nakfa 9.63 = $US1.00
3. Between 1998 and 2000, Ethiopian birr 8.00 = $US 1.00.

Permissions

Chapter 4 is partly based on a revised version of my paper, 'The enduring problem of statelessness in the Horn of Africa: How nation-states and Western courts (re) define nationality', *The International Journal of Refugee Law* 2011; 23 (4): 656–79.

Chapter 3 is partly based on a revised version of my paper, 'Caught between the ideology and realities of development: Transiting from the Horn of Africa to Europe'. Migration Studies Unit Working Papers No. 2009/01. London School of Economics and Political Science; 2009.

I want to thank the following persons/institutions for permission to use their material in this book:

1. The Public Affairs Section, Department of Peace Keeping Operations of the United Nations to use their 'Map of the Horn of Africa' (Figure 0.1).
2. Professor Lea Brilmayer, Yale University, for releasing submissions made by her to the Eritrea–Ethiopian Claims Commission at The Hague and to reproduce Figures 1.1 and 1.2 (and the translations) from Eritrea 2002, which appear in this book as Tables 2.1 and 2.2.
3. The Permanent Commission at The Hague for permission to reproduce two maps from the final decision of the Eritrea–Ethiopia Boundary Commission in 1992, which appear in this book as Figures 2.1 and 2.2.
4. The International Organization for Migration, and Christopher Horwood, to use the maps on p. 45 and p. 47 of *In Pursuit of the Southern Dream: Victims of Necessity*' (2009), which appear in this book as Figures 3.1 and 3.2.
5. Figure 3.3 was created for me by Richard Grosse of Falconbury Design.

Introduction

'Daniel', an Addis Ababa businessman, community leader and father of three, was awakened at 5 a.m. in July 1998 by four armed policemen who forced their way into his home. Pointing their guns at him they said, 'you have to go'. At the gate of his house four more armed officers joined the escort which took him to the police station. After several hours he and 20–25 other individuals were taken to the community hall and detained. When an official photographed us on the second day we said, 'Why are you taking our pictures?' He replied, 'We have been ordered to do so. We are doing our job.' I said, 'Why are you arresting us? Tell us.' He said, 'Because you are an Eritrean.' I replied, 'I am not an Eritrean. I was born in Ethiopia. I've never been to Eritrea. If you want I can show you my passport.' On the seventh day Daniel was put onto a bus and driven, together with 1,500 others, to the Eritrean border – a war zone – which they were forced to walk across at night.[1]

Ethnic discrimination, which resulted in the mass denationalization of hundreds of thousands of individuals between the two world wars, remains a potent political issue today. In this book I provide an ethnographically informed account of the mass denationalization of Ethiopian-born ethnic Eritreans which began in Ethiopia in May 1998. As well as documenting a recent case where ethnic discrimination was the basis for denationalizing an estimated 250–300,000 persons, this study explores these individuals' continuing experiences of statelessness, which have been compounded by the West.

The structure of this chapter is as follows. In the first section, 'Sovereignty and statelessness', the principle theoretical issues underpinning the study are examined, namely the link between national sovereignty and the enduring phenomenon that is statelessness. The initial ideas of Arendt and Agamben on this issue have been modified in light of insights from anthropological fieldwork. The section entitled 'Conceptualizing the role of law' looks at the role of law, particularly Agamben's notion of the 'political exception' in everyday life. I set out a brief description of the denationalization of Jews in World War II as an exemplar for understanding the situation in Ethiopia. The situation of denationalized Jews and other Europeans provided the impetus for the creation of the Refugee Convention and the two statelessness conventions. I review the effectiveness of international protection for stateless persons and outline fundamental gaps in protection which arise from the sovereign right of states who are responsible, on the one hand, for the rapidly rising numbers of stateless persons and refugees today and, on the other hand, for their unimaginative response to the presence of stateless persons in their country, namely to detain and deport them. The final section outlines the structure of the book and ends with a discussion of the value and limitations of ethnographic research.

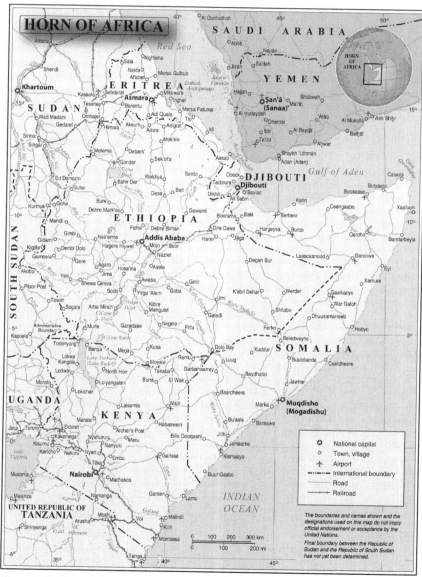

Figure 0.1 Map of the Horn of Africa. Source: United Nations Cartographic Section, Department of Field Support.

Sovereignty and statelessness

In May 1998 a costly and bloody border war erupted between Ethiopia and Eritrea (Figure 0.1) during which both states rounded up and detained enemy 'aliens' within their territories. In Ethiopia an estimated 70,000-plus Ethiopian-born ethnic Eritreans were summarily arrested, bussed to the Eritrean border and forced to walk across a war zone, and tens of thousands of others were stripped of their nationality. For its part Eritrea oversaw the flight and subsequent repatriation of an estimated 70,000 resident Ethiopians.

For reasons which will become clear I distinguish between three categories of Ethiopian-born ethnic Eritreans – the people who are the subject of this book – namely those who were arrested and forcibly expelled by Ethiopia, those who fled in fear of possible persecution and those who continued to live in Ethiopia. Individuals in the first two categories became *de jure* stateless persons, while individuals in the third category – who were stripped of their nationality and forced to apply for the right to remain – became *de facto* stateless persons. I will refer to *all* Ethiopian-born ethnic Eritreans as 'Eritreans'. The use quotation marks draws attention to the arbitrary way that 'Eritreans' were treated by Ethiopia, their country of origin. By contrast, I will refer to individuals born in the state of Eritrea simply as Eritreans (i.e. without quotation marks).

An analysis of statelessness requires me to look to history and political theory to understand the link between state power and the role of law which creates stateless persons and refugees. My approach is informed by Hannah Arendt (1968) who, in the aftermath of World War II, identified three basic forms of the 'human condition': mere biological life-forms, labouring beings and political actors. Her principal concern was with the situation of individuals made stateless in the inter-war period who were reduced to 'mere existence' by their country of origin, which had deprived them of their nationality and stripped them of political rights (p. 296). As she observed of stateless persons (p. 292):

> it turned out that the moment human beings lacked their own government and had to fall back upon their minimum rights, no authority was left to protect them and no institution was willing to guarantee them.

In analysing the impact of large numbers of refugees and stateless persons on 'civilised' states she noted the damage to national law – with its 'time honoured and necessary distinctions between nationals and foreigners' – which was unable to naturalize or get rid of them. States therefore transferred the problem of dealing with stateless persons to the police. At that time (p. 286):

> The stateless person, without right to residence and without the right to work, had of course constantly to transgress the law. He was liable to jail sentences without ever committing a crime. More than that, the entire hierarchy of values which pertain in civilised countries was reversed in his case. Since he was the anomaly for whom the general law did not provide, it was better for him to become an anomaly for which it did provide, that of the criminal.

The role of law is clearly central to the creation and enduring situation of stateless persons. In recent years Agamben has taken up Arendt's work to argue that undocumented migrants, refugees and stateless persons are reduced to the inhuman condition of 'bare life' (1998). He rejected Arendt's argument that the figure of the refugee 'embodies the rights of man par excellence' and has argued instead that the sovereign exercise of power which protects citizens also excludes non-citizens who are reduced to an inhuman condition he calls 'bare life'.

He utilized Schmidt's (1985) notion of the 'political exception' – in which state sovereignty 'must be juridically defined correctly, not as the monopoly to coerce or to rule, but as the monopoly to decide' – to characterize the rule of law in modern nation-states. For Agamben (p. 26):

> The law has a regulative character and is a rule not because it commands and proscribes, but because it must first of all create the sphere of its own reference in real life and *make that reference regular*. Since the rule both stabilizes and presupposes the conditions for this reference, the ordinary structure of the rule is always of the kind: 'If (a real case in point . . .), then (juridical consequence . . .')' in which a fact is included in the juridical order through its exclusion, and transgression seems to precede and determine the lawful case.

For Agamben the political exception *is* the defining principal of modern sovereignty because it defines the 'right' to life within the polity. For him it is not merely the right to exist that is at stake it is also the right 'to one's body, to health, to happiness, to the satisfaction of needs and, beyond all oppression or "alienation", the right to discover what one is and all that one can be' (p. 121; he is quoting Foucault 1976).

Despite the power of his argument, his approach has important limitations. First, nation-states use the political exception to redraw a number of key socio-legal boundaries. Thus, in addition to distinguishing between non-citizens and citizens, states also set criminals, black marketeers, political dissidents, terrorists and others outside the law (Das and Poole 2004). Furthermore a state can also make 'exceptions' to include and grant recognition and rights to certain types of person.

Aihwa Ong (2006) has observed that Agamben's concept of sovereignty is based on the development of the Western nation-state and shows little awareness of how sovereignty is grounded in everyday life or in politics. Her observation suggests that Agamben's focus hinders comparative analysis. How are we to understand differences and apparent similarities in the exercise of sovereignty between, say, Europe/North America, where neo-liberalism informs state policy, and Africa? How do we consider the effect of different moral discourses of human worth on the exercise of sovereignty? She cites Islam as an alternative moral discourse on humanity, to which I would add differences in political culture. Furthermore there must surely be differences in the use of the political exception between states where the 'rule of law' exists and in authoritarian states where it does not.

Secondly, for Agamben, the state's exercise of sovereign power is absolute: there is no space for negotiation, compromise or indeed defeat and thus no need to rescind or reformulate a decision. For Agamben, state power and the law is 'everywhere', whereas ethnographic research shows that there is an interplay/tension between those who exercise power and others who contest or evade the state. In short, Agamben overemphasizes the power of the state and the extent to which humans are compliant political subjects.

Third, Agamben's notion of citizenship – based on an assumption of rootedness and an unproblematic, stable link to a national territory – may be historically inaccurate and it may no longer be irrelevant because citizens no longer have guaranteed political and civil rights. Ong points to the disappearance of entitlements caused by a shrinking of the welfare state and to the effect of 'market intrusions'. The latter phenomenon has led many states in the West to create new avenues to citizenship – via the exercise of the political exception – to enable foreign entrepreneurs and skilled migrants to acquire or 'earn' citizenship. Similarly, the situation facing excluded persons is not absolute and unchanging because many placed outside the state successfully contest their legal status and sometimes compel a state to reinclude them.

The above caveats allow Ong to reconceptualize the exercise of sovereignty 'as an extraordinary departure in policy that can be deployed *to include as well as exclude*' (my emphasis; 2006: 5). As she phrases it, sovereignty can be seen as a way of exploring 'the *hinge* between neo-liberalism as exception and exception to neo-liberalism, the interplay among technologies of governing and of disciplining, of inclusion and exclusion, of giving value or denying value to human conduct' (ibid.).

Das and Poole take the idea of the exception a step further by looking at the everyday practices of officials who implement the law. Officials act to enforce the law *but* they may also blur legal boundaries by enabling individuals to cross 'the seemingly clear divide separating legal and extralegal forms of punishment and enforcement' (2004: 14). In this way, state-based practices sanction some identities (which are made secure by issuing official documents such as passports, ID, court papers, birth certificates, etc.) while punishing others by excluding them from the state and its protection (and by removing their papers and access to basic services etc.; see Collier, Maurer and Suarez-Navaz 1995). Indeed as Dauvergne (2004) has argued, the tasks of a sovereign nation include governing those who live within its territorial boundaries *and* regulating the entry – through the issue of visas, passports and enforcement of border controls – of 'aliens' into the nation. In light of increased globalization and the 'threat' of international terrorism many nations have revised migration and citizenship law and reinforced border enforcement in an attempt to reassert national sovereignty (in part by arresting and deporting aliens). In this context, as Dauvergne notes, '[m]igration law is transformed into the new last bastion of sovereignty' (p. 588).

In this book I take up the notion of the political exception and explore how it operates in Ethiopia *and* in the West where 'Eritreans' have sought refuge. Specifically I seek to explore how official practices and policies – i.e. the power of the executive, the 'practices' of officials *and* the work of law – have brought into being a category[2] of person who, in international legal terms, is stateless and who lacks political rights. Far from being compliant political subjects, however,

'Eritreans' have reassembled their lives and communities in ways which have brought them into renewed conflict with the state. As citizens of Ethiopia they were transformed into stateless persons without human and civil rights, but the 'zone of indistinction' into which they were placed by the Ethiopian state has not erased their moral claims as human beings. While Ethiopia has purged 'Eritreans' from the body of the nation, its actions provide the basis for new legal and moral claims on their behalf by its citizens, human rights organizations and courts. Indeed the activities of stateless persons – who tend to be perceived through the opaque lens of their legal status as depoliticized, politically inert individuals who have been effectively consigned to a 'bare life' – challenges dominant notions of citizenship and politics in the West.

To quote Das and Poole, 'ethnography is a mode of knowing that privileges experience' (2004: 4). I seek to understand, via participant observation, interviews and documents the experience of stateless 'Eritreans'. This task requires that I attend to history, that I grasp the significance and importance of culture, ideas of ethnicity and nationality, and that I critically analyse the role of (national and international) law to understand the 15-year odyssey of stateless 'Eritreans'.

Thus it is important to understand that violence is a key element in the arsenal of tools used by the Ethiopian state to govern. Following Scheper-Hughes and Bourgois (2004) I see violence as arising out of contested social interaction involving attempts by one party to 'harm' another. In his analysis of violence in Ethiopia/Eritrea, Abbink (1995: 130) has argued that:

> the unleashing of violence was related to the problems of modernity in Ethiopia – to the changes in the socio-economic infrastructure, social ideologies and categories, to transformations of traditional authority and power relations, and, finally to changing cultural notions of political legitimacy and social justice.

He observed that:

> In reaction to the challenges of modernization, new and aspiring elite groups seized upon violence as means to promote new goals, to bridge social or regional disparities, to forge new structures of discipline and order, and to advance what they saw as development or social cohesion.

Abbink draws our attention to state-directed forms of violence which began with policies pursued by Haile Selassie between 1940 and 1974. He traces the violence generated by a military coup in the mid-1970s that saw the emergence of the *Derg*, which dehumanized, intimidated and liquidated its enemies (see Box 0.1). To this narrative should be added the violence inflicted by guerrilla movements in their struggle for self-determination, which culminated in a *coup d'état* in May 1991 (see Table 1.1 and Box 1.1). Once in power, the Ethiopian People's Revolutionary Democratic Front (EPRDF) oversaw extensive human rights violations directed at ethnic groups and opposition political parties (Tronvoll 2008), while the People's Front for Democracy and Justice (PFDJ) in Eritrea has relied upon extreme forms of violence to control and intimidate its nationals (United Nations High Commissioner for Refugees [UNHCR] 2011b; Bozzini 2011).

Table 0.1 is a heuristic which identifies three principal forms of violence (in the left column) in descending order from forms of 'ordinary' inter-personal violence to more structural forms of violence culminating in state-directed violence. To the right of each form is a list of specific types of violence that have been documented in Ethiopia. While all three forms of violence coexist, the heuristic facilitates a focus on one type. In this book I focus on a type of state-directed violence that has violated international law. It is immediately obvious from the heuristic, however, that not all types of state-directed violence attract sanctions.

The heuristic suggests several interesting questions. First it alerts me to the fact that my focus on denationalization rests on an arbitrary distinction in which denationalization blurs imperceptibly with other types of violence, for instance ethnic cleansing, which did not attract criminal sanctions much less interest by international legal organizations. Second, the heuristic points to apparent differences from and similarities to other forms and types of violence which are also worth exploring (even if they are not examined in this book).

Third, the heuristic raises a further issue: namely why a specific form of violence is viewed by a state as criminal (and merits sanction) while other similar acts are not sanctioned. The answer must be that violence is fundamentally cultural in nature, which helps explain why acts of violence are purposeful and pervasive in Ethiopian social life (Scheper-Hughes and Bourgois 2004). Cultural norms etc. change slowly, even in the face of modern forms of justice, which may also explain why some types of violence are punished while other actions go unpunished. Even so it is remarkable that a relatively narrow range of violent actions carry a criminal sanction and it underlines the fact that despite the promise that 'all men are equal before the law', in reality the law fails to address inequality in vast areas of social life (Collier, Maurer and Suarez-Navaz 1995: 18).

Table 0.1 Forms and types of violence in Ethiopia

Forms of violence	Types of violence		
Everyday/interpersonal	Intimidation, robbery and violence Hunger	Domestic violence Bride capture/ abduction	Child abuse 'Extreme' poverty
Revolutionary	Killing of state officials	Attacks against rival political opponents	Attacks against civilians, including withholding food (famine)
State-directed	'Policing' civilians Political persecution; creation of statelessness	Human rights violations Ethnic cleansing, mass expulsions	Genocide

I use the accounts of 'Eritreans' about the violence which they have suffered at the hands of the state and its agents for two reasons. First, their accounts help us understand the nature and extent of violence in Ethiopia and how law functions as an extension of state power. In short, their accounts challenge the state's story about past events. I have also included such accounts because when an individual makes an asylum claim her experiences are stripped away by the judge in a search for the appropriate legal rule to apply to the case. In short, official and legal accounts provide a skeletonized, incomplete record of the violence suffered by stateless persons and refugees.

Conceptualizing the role of law

Agamben's notion of law as political exception is very straightforward. He appears to presume that the values, ideas and beliefs embodied in law are 'true' and that the power of law 'rests in its authority to legitimate certain visions of the social order, to determine the relations between persons and groups, and to manipulate cultural understandings and discourses' (Hirsch and Lazarus-Black 1994: 1). In short, he assumes that law speaks from a hegemonic position and that it effectively channels and directs citizens into accepting certain behaviours, values and cultural notions as correct. It is notable that this sense of law, which also promotes the idea that it is objective, impersonal, universal and necessary, is highly ideological when in fact it functions differently in other cultures.

Thus politics in the Horn of Africa is infused with distinctive cultural values – conceptions of justice and notions of entitlement based on ethno-nationalist conceptions of citizenship (see Chapter 1). Officials do not follow, much less enunciate, an ethic of impartiality and service. While officials may articulate a neo-liberal political philosophy, in fact they tend to rely on violence.

While all states make law, it is implemented by officials and imposed – by force or consent – on citizens and residents. It is analytically useful therefore to assess official practices to see where they fall on a continuum ranging from actions: (a) that accord with a strict reading of the law and a strict application of it; (b) which reflect a degree of 'discretion' allowed to those who implement it; (c) performed poorly, in error or not at all (e.g. because officials are poorly managed by their superiors); (d) which deliberately subvert the rules; and finally (e) which are illegal or involve bribery. Recognizing such distinctions may allow us to better assess how state bureaucracies, police and the judiciary treat stateless persons in Africa and elsewhere.

European history provides an apt illustration of how a state can create statelessness. During the 1930s the rise of National Socialism witnessed the creation of a state which sought to purge the body politic of non-Aryans (and others) through a program of mass denationalization and state-organized genocide. The Intergovernmental Committee on Refugees issued a memorandum entitled 'Statelessness and Some of its Causes: An Outline' (1946; quoted in Massey 2010: 3–4), which summarizes how German Jews were denationalized. The memorandum provides an exemplar against which the experience of 'Eritreans' can usefully be compared. Thus:

The racial (Nuremberg) laws of 15th September, 1935, did not provide, as is often assumed, for the en masse denationalization of German Jews.

The law introduced a new conception, namely the division of all German nationals into (a) citizens of the Reich (Reichsbuerger) and (b) other German nationals (Staatsangehoerige). Those having Aryan nordic blood were citizens with all civic rights, while Jews became mere nationals with no civic rights nor the obligation of military service.

Subsequently the notion of "Staatsangehoerige" applied to the Jews was gradually emptied of any positive content whatsoever by various persecution measures and acts of disposition and despoliation.

Mere German nationals or "Staatsangehoeright" of Jewish origin were able to leave the country with valid German passports stamped with a big "J". Up to the war and even, in some cases, up to 1941, Jews abroad were able to obtain renewal of the validity of their passport from German Consulates. However, such holders of "J" passports were otherwise denied the right to ask for German consular and diplomatic protection, so that both the League High Commission and the Intergovernmental Committee on Refugees, as well as most governments rightly considered them as persons who, in fact, did not enjoy the protection of their Government.

By October 1941, the German authorities stopped getting rid of Jews by facilitating their taking refuge in other countries and refused henceforth issue of passports or grant of exit permits.

In pursuance of the above mentioned law of the 15th of September 1935, the German Government issued on the 25th of November 1941 a decree . . . which laid down:

1. That a Jew who has his ordinary place of residence abroad cannot be a German national;
2. That the Jew loses his German nationality either on the date of issue of the decree, or from the date he has taken up his ordinary residence abroad, or at a later date, when he transfers his ordinary residence abroad.

A considerable number of Jews lost their nationality as a result of that Decree. It also provided for the confiscation of property of Jews who became stateless as a result thereof.

Thus all Jewish refugees (whether confessional Jews or Christian non-Aryans) living as refugees outside the territory of the Reich, and not having acquired another nationality (e.g. by immigration into Palestine or the USA) became stateless.

The 1946 memorandum then turned to the situation facing German Jews at the end of World War II, who were considered to be *de jure* stateless persons. Recognition of their precarious position was a first step in rebuilding Europe and finding an international resolution for the problem of denationalized, stateless Jews, which was more fully addressed in the 1951 Refugee Convention. The Refugee

Convention sought to provide protection for German Jews and millions of other stateless persons by establishing clear and fair procedures to assess individual applications for asylum that would ensure international protection for recognized refugees. The phrase 'a well-founded fear of persecution' provides the key to understand who is, and is not, entitled to recognition as a refugee (UNHCR 1992). The Convention provides a lengthy discussion of the accepted meaning of 'persecution' understood *only* with respect to individuals being persecuted for 'reasons of race, religion, nationality, membership of a particular social group or political opinion'.

At the time the Refugee Convention was being drafted preparations were also underway to develop the first International Convention on Statelessness, which was expected to define the meaning of, and rights associated with, stateless people. In the preliminary work for the 1954 Convention Relating to the Status of Stateless Persons a key distinction emerged between individuals who were considered to be *de jure* stateless – a class of persons whose rights were enshrined in the 1954 Convention – and *de facto* stateless persons, who were excluded from the Refugee Convention *and* from the 1954 and 1961 Conventions on Statelessness. Indeed the 1961 Convention merely called upon signatory states to 'consider sympathetically' the possibility of according *de facto* stateless persons the treatment which the Convention offers to *de jure* stateless people (Blitz 2009: 7).[3]

In the 1954 Convention a *de jure* stateless person was defined as 'a person who is not considered as a national by any State under operation of its law' (Art. 1[1]) and was understood to apply to individuals who had fled their country of origin *and* who were refused recognition as a national by their state of nationality. The committee drafting the two conventions wanted to prevent the possibility of individuals deliberately renouncing their nationality for 'personal convenience' (Batchelor 1995: 248). The committee also believed that 'if flight occurred, the refugee definition was broad enough to encompass all those concerned' (ibid.: 251). The definition adopted in the 1954 Convention insists that a stateless person must have an 'effective nationality' and it requires an individual to prove that neither their state of nationality nor any other state will accept them as a national (see Chapters 5 and 6; Equal Rights Trust 2009: 18–19). However, as Batchelor has argued, 'the greatest number of cases of statelessness has been created by collective denationalization on political, racial or religious grounds' (1995: 256).

In the 1954 Convention a *de facto* stateless person is understood to be a person who: (a) has a nationality; (b) is outside the state of their nationality; and (c) has been refused diplomatic and consular protection by that state (Massey 2010). Despite the very close similarity to the definition of *de jure* statelessness, the term is used to refer to individuals who continue to reside in their country of birth but who do not possess an 'effective nationality' because they lack identity documents (e.g. birth certificates) to prove their claim or they have been made stateless as a result of state succession.

Due in part to the imprecise distinction between *de jure* and *de facto* statelessness and the fact that only the former is recognized as deserving protection, *de facto* stateless persons remain unrecognized in international law even though the reasons for their situation are the same as those for refugees. The Statelessness

Convention's definition of *de facto* statelessness is thus 'too narrow and limiting because it excludes those persons whose citizenship is practically useless or who cannot prove or verify their nationality' (Weissbrodt 2008: 84). In short, stateless persons are not recognized as refugees and can be refused asylum.

Unfortunately, the failure of international humanitarian law is not limited to an ambiguous distinction between *de jure* and *de facto* statelessness. First, because only a small number of states have ratified the two conventions on statelessness their reach is geographically limited (see Table 0.2). Second, there is a plethora of contradictory legal definitions of statelessness. As Massey (2010) has argued, UNHCR has expanded the concept of statelessness into new areas 'not all of which can be fully reconciled with the traditional view' found in the two statelessness conventions. Third, UNHCR has only recently begun to monitor whether states create/reduce statelessness (Blitz 2009; Weissbrodt 2008: 104; Massey 2010: 31).[4] The most recent estimate is that there are approximately 12 million stateless persons (UNHCR 2010a): including an estimated 21,109 in Africa, 2,853,245 in Asia and 588,689 in Europe (UNHCR 2010b: Annex 7). The number is clearly an underestimate and reflects the problem of collecting statistics on a population that is largely invisible to or is actively discriminated against by governments. There are well-known cases of stateless persons, such as the Bidoon in the Middle East; Rohingya in Burma; Palestinians; Kenyan Nubians; 'estate Tamils' in Sri Lanka; Slovenes; Roma; and Crimean Tartars in Ukraine (Blitz and Lynch 2011). But there are also many other less well-documented groups.

Quite apart from the above problems, the fundamental issue and fatal weakness of international law on statelessness is that sovereign states define the criteria for citizenship and they decide who is entitled to nationality and who will be refused access to it. Thus in 1998 Ethiopia denationalized an estimated 250,000-plus 'Eritreans', and in 2004 it introduced a one-off registration of resident 'Eritreans' which allowed some to individuals to reacquire nationality while excluding many others. In effect, international law allows a state to act with impunity when it excludes and denationalizes citizens.

Table 0.2 Signatories and parties to the UN Conventions on Statelessness

Convention	Signatories and parties to Convention
1951 Convention Relating to the Status of Refugees Entered into force on 22 April 1954	144 Signatories and 145 parties (Ethiopia acceded in 1969, Eritrea has not)
1954 Convention Relating to the Status of Stateless Persons Entered into force on 6 June 1960	23 Signatories and 76 parties (neither Ethiopia nor Eritrea have acceded)
1961 Convention on the Reduction of Statelessness Entered into force on 13 December 1975	5 Signatories and 48 parties (neither Ethiopia nor Eritrea have acceded)

Source: United Nations Treaty Collection. Available at: http://treaties.un.org/Pages/ParticipationStatus.aspx (accessed 12 December 2012).

Since 1951 more than 80 international legal conventions and declarations have come into force aimed at defining and guaranteeing key human, cultural, economic and legal rights. Worryingly, the past 60 years have also seen a massive rise in the number of refugees and stateless persons, which suggests that international humanitarian law is ineffective. The international community has responded to the plight of stateless persons by identifying 'gaps in protection'. However, closing such gaps still depends upon the willingness of a state: (a) to fund and implement birth registration; (b) to change the way it defines the right to nationality; (c) to accord rights to non-national spouses; (d) to provide the right to naturalize; (e) to recognize dual nationality; and (f) to set out the criteria and define the process whereby citizenship can be removed (see Manby 2009a). In short, international solutions to the problem of statelessness naively presume that the state which today violates the human rights of its nationals can be relied upon tomorrow, when it becomes a signatory to an international convention, to protect its citizens.

The situation facing stateless persons is compounded by Western nations in three ways. First, the West fails to hold governments to account for policies/actions which contribute to or cause violence, population displacement and statelessness. Second, the West increasingly fails to commit sufficient resources to assist refugees (Vayrynen 2001). Specifically, the West has cut its funding to UNHCR and to countries which host and assist the vast majority of the world's refugees to find shelter, integrate and resettle (UNHCR 2011a: Chart 15).[5] Third, the West/international community has failed to address the problematic link between state sovereignty and state responsibility for creating and resolving statelessness (an issue which is a central concern of this book).

The West's reluctance to fund 'durable' solutions for refugees is pushing UNHCR to pursue short-term solutions, which include maintaining refugees in semi-permanent refugee camps and/or quickly (and perhaps prematurely) repatriating them to their country of origin. The insecurity and violence that is a feature of life in refugee camps in the Horn of Africa contributes to a situation where growing numbers of people leave the camps in an attempt to find refuge elsewhere.

In the West the arrival of relatively small numbers of refugees is anticipated by governments and the press in negative and sensationalist terms: everyone applying for asylum is categorized as a 'bogus' asylum seeker, economic migrant and a threat to the welfare system, despite the fact that only 5–10 per cent of all irregular migrants enter Europe clandestinely (Kaye 2001; Collyer, Duvel and de Haas 2012). As Greenslade has argued, the language of the media 'has served to reinforce and justify existing racism and prejudices' (2005: 3). Rather than allaying public concerns political parties use asylum/immigration as an election issue and seek to close international borders (to keep out unwanted 'economic migrants') and to introduce increasingly restrictive asylum and immigration policies (Boswell 2003; Khoser 2001).

Thus, as if gaps in protection, definitional ambiguity, and reliance on nation-states to bring their practices into line with international legal norms were not problematic enough, the relatively small number of refugees and stateless persons who reach the West find it increasingly difficult to obtain refugee status.

From ethnic discrimination to denationalization: The organization of this book

Chapter 1 sets out the historical context for the case study by examining key political developments in the Horn of Africa from the late 19th to the late 20th century relating to the development of ethnic and national identity. First I focus on the political understandings that underpinned the joint military operations launched against the *Derg* by the Tigray People's Liberation Front (TPLF) and the Eritrean People's Liberation Front (EPLF). Second, following their seizure of power in 1991, I address the failure of the two movements, now ruling political parties, to deal with the growing political and economic differences which culminated in war between Ethiopia and Eritrea in May 1998. I then examine Ethiopia's treatment of her ethnic 'Eritrean' nationals. I begin by setting out the experience of an estimated 75,000 persons who were arrested and expelled from the country before turning to the situation of the remaining 75–200,000 'Eritreans' who were denationalized by decree and forced to apply for permission to remain.

In December 2000 Ethiopia and Eritrea ended the war and were compelled by the UN Security Council to submit their dispute to The Hague in The Netherlands (the Security Council also created a demilitarized zone and sent UN troops to police the disputed border). Two legal processes were instituted at The Hague. First, the Eritrea–Ethiopia Boundary Commission (EEBC) considered submissions by the two states regarding their claims to their disputed boundary and simultaneously the Eritrea–Ethiopia Claims Commission (EECC) considered state claims for war reparations.

Chapter 2 analyses how The Hague examined and decided both issues. With regard to reparations, however, I look only at the question of mass expulsions, denationalization, the confiscation of private property and allegations of forcible family separation. The chapter examines the failure of the international community and The Hague to address and resolve the underlying political issues between Eritrea and Ethiopia.

Chapter 3 traces the flight of 'Eritreans' out of the Horn following the December 2000 peace treaty. The general climate of violence and insecurity in the immediate post-war period saw 'Eritreans' join refugees and migrants leaving the Horn along one of four major transit routes: west to Sudan (to Libya, Egypt and Israel), north-east to Yemen (and the Middle East), south to Kenya (and southern Africa) and by air. I trace their journeys and document the discrimination, violence, imprisonment, mistreatment and death which has been their lot. The vast majority of these sojourners remain in the region; very few reach the West.

Chapter 4 examines the political situation in the Horn for 'Eritreans' following the war. First I explore the experience of the deportees – known as *amiche* – in Eritrea who found themselves subject to considerable animosity and ethnic discrimination, which led them to flee back to Ethiopia where they were placed in refugee camps as Eritrean nationals. I then examine the situation of the estimated 75–150,000 'Eritreans' who remained in Ethiopia. These individuals were stripped of their nationality and forced to register as 'aliens'. Following the war

Ethiopia issued a number of decrees which held out the possibility that resident 'Eritreans' might reacquire their nationality and reclaim the property that had been confiscated by the state. I argue, however, that the Ethiopian government's promises are illusory and that while some individuals were readmitted into political society, others remained stateless. Very few indeed have been able to reclaim their property. In short, the idea that 'Eritreans' might return home or regain their property has proved to be an illusion.

Chapter 5 focuses on the situation facing the small number of 'Eritreans' who managed to reach the West and apply for asylum. I begin by looking at the asylum bureaucracy in the West and at problems arising from the way that the refugee authority processes asylum claims, at problems of legal representation, the difficulty posed by complex law and the problematic role of the courts. Specifically I focus on immigration law and practice in the UK and discuss how the UK's breach of its obligations under the 1954 Convention Related to the Status of Stateless Persons prevents the claims of stateless 'Eritreans' – both *de jure* and *de facto* – from being recognized. I then analyse two recent 'Eritrean' asylum claims which provide important insights into how the courts decide the asylum claims of stateless 'Eritreans'.

Chapter 6 looks at the implication for stateless 'Eritreans' of being refused asylum. Refusal of status in the West entails a circuitous descent into illegality and destitution, involving periods of time spent living on the street and being detained in immigration detention centres. Once an asylum claim is refused individuals (and their children) are stripped of their legal rights – i. e. the right to shelter, to medical care and to a minimum intake of food – and are subject to arrest and deportation. The chapter examines the deterrent nature of British policy towards failed asylum seekers and argues that this policy does not work. A careful look at how British officials implement asylum policy also reveals that the state 'produces' illegality by 'manifestly unreasonable' delays in considering fresh asylum claims, by wrongly putting asylum applicants into 'fast-track' procedures, by poor record keeping and by failing to implement key elements of government policy.

My 'conversations' with failed asylum seekers, which are discussed in Chapter 6, reveal that, contrary to official statements and the thrust of academic and newspaper accounts, existing policies are inhumane *and* ineffective. The continued presence among us of failed asylum seekers should been seen as evidence of an effective political struggle for recognition as human beings and not as evidence of law breaking. Indeed their presence poses a fundamental challenge to impoverished Western conceptions of politics and citizenship.

I conclude by drawing the different strands of my argument together under four inter-related themes: namely the illusion of nationalism, the illusion of return, the illusion of refuge and the illusion of justice/redress. The last theme compels me to anticipate the future of 'Eritreans' living in the West, which begins by looking at attempts by 'Eritreans' to use the law to obtain legal redress against Ethiopia. I then look at the effect of a 'creeping amnesty' implemented by the British Home Office and ask whether this might result in stateless 'Eritreans' obtaining status. Finally, in light of this case study, I re-examine the link between sovereignty and statelessness.

The value and limitation of ethnographic research

This study is primarily based on ethnographic research, which is to say that it is based upon participant observation in British courts and law firms, and among Eritreans and Ethiopians settled in England. In addition I have interviewed British and Ethiopian officials in the UK, and Ethiopian officials and 'Eritreans' in Ethiopia. I have also had access to extensive documentary material. My research has sought to understand the experience and perspective of stateless Eritreans and of the officials who have been responsible, in different ways, for their predicament. This study provides a rare insight into the situation of stateless persons because, as Blitz and Lynch (2009, 2011) have argued, there are relatively few comparative, empirical studies of stateless persons.[6] For instance the studies contained in both of their volumes and that of Sawyer and Blitz (2011a), while valuable in pointing out key issues and problems confronting stateless persons, are based on a small number of interviews.

By and large, stateless persons are undocumented – a situation which creates considerable problems for those who wish to study the extent and nature of statelessness (see Sawyer and Blitz 2011b). Stateless persons are 'invisible' to researchers in their country of origin and in the country where they currently reside because they are discriminated against, they may be politically disenfranchised and because they avoid contact with officials. Being invisible creates problems for researchers: how does one locate, identify and gain the consent of appropriate individuals? Given the complex legal statuses defining the entitlements of migrants, failed asylum seekers and refugees, questions about the legal identity of individuals are not easy to resolve. Indeed, many stateless persons are unaware of their precise legal status. Such problems are compounded when the subjects of one's research are illegal because they tend to be mobile and wish to remain invisible. Such problems were less difficult for me to overcome, partly because of my prior knowledge of Ethiopia but primarily because of my contacts with refugee organizations and refugee lawyers.

In the late 1990s I began to write 'expert' reports on behalf of the claims of Ethiopian and Eritrean asylum applicants. I found that my research/development work in Ethiopia in the 1980s and 1990s 'qualified' me to accept work as a 'country expert' (see Good 2004 for a discussion of country experts). I was first instructed to write reports for Ethiopians who claimed that they were made stateless by Ethiopia in 2002. Their asylum claims (and associated bundles of material linked to them) provided my initial insight into the problem of statelessness. However, I learned that the order imposed on an asylum claim by bureaucratic procedures produces a narrow focus on particular elements of a claim, which was at odds with the lived experience of individuals seeking asylum. '[T]he reasonless and orderless qualities of violence' (Nordstrom and Robben 1995: 10) experienced by refugees is reframed by lawyers and re-presented to the court in a manner that conforms with Western legal expectations of a credible account of persecution as defined by the Refugee Convention. As the case studies in this book show, however, because so much is left out of an asylum claim what remains is one-dimensional and devoid of meaning, especially to asylum applicants.

In 2007 I began a two-year ethnographic study of the British asylum system funded by the UK's Economic and Social Research Council. The project sought, in part, to identify and follow the asylum claims of Ethiopians and Eritreans through the British asylum system. I was able to follow 26 different claims through the courts, including three claims by 'Eritreans' alleging denationalization. I also collected documents on a large number of related cases I was unable to follow in person. Two cases were followed which are of particular relevance to this book, namely those of 'Medhin' and 'Solomon' (Cases 5 and 6), which are discussed in Chapter 5. Research on the British legal system allowed me to collect a wealth of documentation (case law, witness statements, interview records, court decisions, etc.), conduct interviews (with lawyers, judges, stateless Ethiopians etc.) and follow a range of asylum claims which helped me understand how asylum cases are argued and decided.

In early 2009 I wrote to the Ethiopian embassy in London requesting a meeting with officials to clarify how the embassy interviewed failed 'Eritrean' asylum seekers and to discuss a recent directive allowing deported Eritreans to reclaim their property (see Chapter 4). After several inconclusive meetings with embassy officials the Ethiopian ambassador wrote to clarify the situation (see Chapter 4 and Appendix 4.1) and he arranged for me to meet officials in Ethiopia who would, I was told, answer my questions.

I flew to Addis Ababa in April 2010 to speak with a senior official in the Ministry of Foreign Affairs, who answered some of my questions about the 2009 Directive. However, my questions regarding the legal status of resident Eritreans were deferred to immigration officials, who declined to meet me. I had anticipated that immigration officials would refuse to meet me and used contacts to identify 'Eritreans' in Addis Ababa to speak to. Some of the 'Eritreans' I spoke with suggested others and/or they brought friends and family members to talk to me. I also engaged a research assistant who located several 'Eritreans', whom I interviewed, while she conducted two interviews with particularly vulnerable 'Eritrean' women. In total, nine interviews were conducted with 'Eritreans' who had been expelled (and had returned), seven with 'Eritreans' who had lived continuously in Ethiopia and a further six interviews with Eritrean refugees who corroborated information provided by the deportees (see the list of case studies, which provides details including a breakdown by gender of the cases).

Interviewing stateless persons/refugees is problematic. Considerable negotiation took place over the phone to establish my identity, how I came to have information about them, what I wished to talk about and how I intended to use information they might give me (see Mackenzie, McDowell and Pittaway 2007). Several individuals had been contacted by family or friends about my research, but others needed assurances which meant that I did not record interviews nor did I write down information that could be used to identify them. I also had to arrange a private, safe place to meet and talk. Despite their personal concerns, however, many

'Eritreans' insisted that I should use the information they gave me to advocate on behalf of 'Eritreans' seeking asylum in the West.

Interviews lasted from 40 to 60 minutes. I began by asking individuals to tell me about their personal history (including information about their parents, siblings etc.) prior to the outbreak of war with Eritrea in 1998. I then asked about their experiences during and after the war (i.e. about their arrest, detention, expulsion from Ethiopia, arrival and life in Eritrea). I also sought information about what happened to family members during and after the war. Finally I asked about their current situation. For those who had not been expelled I sought to understand what had happened to them and their family prior to, during and after the war. The interview often took the form of a narrative of persecution and flight, which some individuals found difficult to put into words. I felt their distress as they told me their stories. To protect their identity I have used pseudonyms for each interview. I am deeply grateful for their trust and candour in speaking to me.

My understanding of the 'Eritrean' odyssey has been deeply enriched by the willingness of members of the large community of 'deportees' in England to speak with me. Their willingness to allow me to attend association meetings and to be interviewed enabled me to better understand their individual stories and their current legal status.

The principal limitation of this book arises from the fact that my fieldwork is predominately UK-based. While comparative fieldwork elsewhere in Europe or North America would have been ideal – or for that matter more in-depth field-work in Ethiopia and Eritrea – for financial reasons it was simply not possible. I have sought to use 'Eritrean' asylum claims made in other countries to provide a comparative picture of how such claims are decided outside the UK. Clearly, my understanding of the situation of 'Eritreans' in Ethiopia would have been greatly improved had officials chosen to answer my questions; their refusal to do so, how-ever, reflects their consistent denial that Ethiopia violated international law in the treatment of her nationals. Official attitudes also reflect indifference about the situation of deported 'Eritreans', including a refusal to recognize that 'Eritreans' have an entitlement to Ethiopian nationality and that their property was illegally taken and should be restored to them.

Research about refugees, as with vulnerable individuals generally, raises dif-ficult ethical issues (see Polzer and Hammond 2008). This book brings to light the injustices suffered by Ethiopian-born ethnic Eritreans. While I have adopted pseudonyms for all informants, my research nevertheless makes this category of person visible to policymakers and officials in Ethiopia, the UK and elsewhere. How might this visibility affect them? In theory Ethiopia could impose greater surveillance on 'Eritreans', but officials would find it difficult to identify such persons much less control them. Alternatively it is possible that Ethiopia (and other countries where 'Eritreans' reside) might restrict foreign researchers' access to the country.[7]

The increased visibility of 'Eritreans' in the UK is also a concern. I have made it a point of seeking informed consent from everyone I have interviewed and I have met with an association of 'Eritrean' deportees in England to inform them about my research and to answer their questions. The vast majority of 'Eritreans' I have spoken to are supportive of publication in the hope that it might embarrass Ethiopia into admitting its illegal actions and returning their property. I think it more realistic that the book might bring their plight to the attention of the public. In particular it is my hope that the book will provide additional evidence of the need to reform asylum policies and procedures in the West and for states to accede to the 1954 Convention Related to the Status of Stateless Persons.

1 Nationalism, the 1998–2000 Ethiopia–Eritrea war and the denationalization of 'Eritreans'

To understand why Ethiopia and Eritrea expelled, or created the conditions conducive to the flight of, tens of thousands of individuals from their territories it is necessary to consider the historical and political relations between the two liberation fronts who, as erstwhile comrades in arms against the *Derg*, fought a bitter war against each other between 1998 and 2000.

The first section, 'Seeing the present though the past', assesses the historical relationship between the EPLF and TPLF from the late 1980s onwards to the outbreak of war between Ethiopia and Eritrea in May 1998. I focus on the political understandings that underpinned their joint military operations against the *Derg* and their failure to deal with growing political and economic differences between 1991 and 1998, which directly contributed to war in May 1998. The second section, 'The "enemy within"', examines Ethiopia's treatment of her ethnic 'Eritrean' nationals. I begin by setting out the experience of an estimated 75,000 persons who were arrested and expelled from the country between June 1998 and March 2002; I then examine the situation of the remaining 'Eritreans' – variously estimated at 75–200,000 people – who were denationalized by decree and forced to apply for permission to remain.

Seeing the present though the past: History, nationalism and identity

Western intervention in Eritrea and Ethiopia began in earnest in the 19th century, following Egyptian attempts to control the port of Massawa on the Red Sea coast between 1820 and the late 1870s. In an attempt to curtail French ambitions Britain encouraged Italy to take over Massawa in 1885, following which Italy sought to annex land claimed by Ethiopia. Following its defeat by Ethiopian forces in 1896, Italy negotiated successive treaties with Ethiopia – in 1900, 1902 and 1908 – to establish the border between its colony (Eritrea) and Ethiopia. Italy invaded Ethiopia in 1935 and occupied it until 1941 when a joint Ethiopian–British force defeated Italian forces, thereby allowing Haile Selassie to reoccupy the throne. Following Italy's defeat, Eritrea was administered by Britain under a UN mandate until 1952 when, following a controversial referendum, the UN decided that Eritrea should be federated with Ethiopia.

In 1962 Haile Selassie formally incorporated Eritrea into Ethiopia, an act which alienated substantial sections of Eritrea's population and contributed directly to the rise of the Eritrean Liberation Front (ELF) and later the EPLF. Despite occupying Eritrea militarily from 1962 onwards, Ethiopia failed to destroy the ELF and the EPLF (despite internecine conflict between the two fronts in the 1970s and early 1980s). Ethiopia's ability to subjugate Eritrea was undermined by the rise of armed opposition movements in Tigray (the TPLF), the military overthrow of Haile Selassie in 1975, and the 1976 war with Somalia (which invaded the Ogaden in support of the Western Somali Liberation Front).

In the Horn 'history' has a Janus-like quality and has been selectively used by nationalists who have 'mined' the past – which they see as a repository of cultural exemplars (Smith 1996: 450) – to identify a 'common' language, shared symbols and values and political 'myths' to create a new 'nation' (Baxter 1994; Alemseged Abbay 1997). Ethno-nationalists in Ethiopia and Eritrea have used history as a resource and as a tool to mobilize support around their idea of the nation, which is said to possess an 'authentic' national culture that is worth defending. This process is especially evident in Tigray and Eritrea, where many individuals share a common language, kinship and culture that remains important today (Alemseged Abbay 1997, Tronvoll 1999: 105). Indeed the leadership of the two fronts are both Tigrayan and they 'issue from tightly-knit elite groups with a tradition of authoritarian rule and (ethnic) group cohesion' (Abbink 1998: 558).

The EPLF developed out of the ELF, which was a Muslim-based organization that drew its initial support from the north-western lowlands. Internal divisions within the ELF, in particular its hostility to growing numbers of recruits from the Christian highlands, lay the basis for the emergence of a secular, socialist programme by the EPLF (Firebrace, Holland and Kinnock 1984; Weldehaimanot and Taylor 2011). Growing internal political differences led the EPLF to break away from the ELF in the mid-1970s and the two fronts became embroiled in a bitter war of fratricide which forced the remnants of the ELF to retreat to the Sudan in 1981.

The bitter war between the two Eritrea-based fronts – which was being waged simultaneously with Ethiopia's attempt to occupy and administer Eritrea – required the EPLF to create and sustain its political base. Thus in addition to cultivating support from its ethnic 'heartland', the Christian highlands of Kebessa (i.e. the provinces of Akele Guzai, Serae and Hamasien) it was compelled to seek support (or effect control over) former ELF areas in the north-west and among ethnic minorities such as the Adi Caieh, Kunama and Afar (the latter two live on the border with Ethiopia and have periodically supported the Ethiopian government).

As Gilkes has noted, the Kebessa is 'largely synonymous with the area inhabited by the Tigreans of Eritrea, Tigrinyna speaking, Orthodox Christian, agriculturalists' (1999a: 12). Specifically (p. 13):

> the Kebessa had previously been an integral part of the state against which the
> EPLF was attempting to build up a nationalist agenda. This forced the EPLF

leadership to create a new past, to invent their version of Eritrea's history, indeed to fabricate a history of conflict between the Kebessa and the region of Tigray south of the Mareb river[1].

The nationalist vision of the EPLF that emerged in the 1980s was isolationist and guided by an unswerving ideological commitment to socialism based on the front's reading of history. Through political indoctrination and the struggle against Ethiopia the EPLF forged a strong political identity among several generations of *tegedalie* (fighters) who fought and died to achieve Eritrean independence.

Matsuoka and Sorenson summarize the EPLF's vision in the following way (2001: 50):

> Eritreans conceptualize their identity . . . as a hybrid produced of centuries of cultural fusion and shaped by Italian colonialism, which transformed social and economic relationships within a colonial space and established a sense of Eritrean-ness within those boundaries. This sense of national identity was then strengthened by Ethiopian repression and through the independence struggle.

There is ample evidence that the *Derg*, the military council against which the EPLF fought, committed crimes against humanity in its fight against secession-ist movements *and* against Ethiopians (Human Rights Watch 1991; Tronvoll, Schaefer and Girmachew 1999). The *Derg* committed numerous atrocities against civilians directly, through the violence inflicted by its armed forces and indirectly by the violence caused by its policies and implemented by its officials. Table 1.1 lists some of the major 'crimes' of the *Derg* that fall under the rubric of state-directed violence and have been recognized as genocide (see Box 1.1)

After Eritrean independence in 1993 public support for the EPLF began to wane. Rather than reaching out to Muslims and minority groups the party sought

Table 1.1 The *Derg's* 'crimes against humanity', 1975–1991

Year	Incident
1970–75	The massacre/murder of large numbers of civilians in Eritrea
1977–78	Killing an estimated 20,000 individuals during the 'Red Terror' in Addis Ababa, Tigray and other provinces
1982–86	Counter-insurgency operations were responsible for the deaths of 225,000 to 317,000 'famine' victims
1984–88	50,000 deaths caused by compulsory resettlement
1988	Implementation of a 'state of emergency' in Eritrea and Tigray which led to the execution of civilians, forced relocation and air raids and cluster bombing of civilians, markets etc.

Source: Human Rights Watch 1991.

to ensure support from the Kebessa and the diaspora. In particular it relied on its control of the armed forces and a policy of compulsory, indefinite conscription to control and to inculcate its version of history into new generations of Eritreans.

By contrast, the TPLF only cultivated support from Christian, Tigrinya-speaking agriculturalists in northern Ethiopia who nursed long-standing grievances against the Ethiopian state (Aregawi Berhe 2004). However, it was not until the fall of the Haile Selassie government in 1975 and the concomitant politicization of university students that political space emerged for the development of socialist-inspired ethno-nationalist movements. At this time the Tigrayan National Organization emerged and espoused 'national armed struggle' against the *Derg* and 'the right of nations to self-determination' (p. 581). The movement was forced underground and retreated to Tigray, where students used the vernacular language, Tigrinya, and their knowledge of local culture and history to recruit peasants to join an armed rebellion against the Ethiopian state.

Initially, the founders of the TPLF conceived of 'self-determination' as a call for autonomy or 'self-rule for Tigray in a democratic, poly-ethnic Ethiopia' (p. 591). By the late 1970s the TPLF's leadership reinterpreted the idea to mean 'secession for an independent republic of Tigray but this idea clashed with the political programme of the EPLF, with whom it had forged a military alliance in the 1980s. Specifically, '[T]he EPLF claimed that although Ethiopian nationalities had the right to self-determination, the right to independence was conditional on first, the nationalities previously being independent, and second, on their being economically cohesive' (Young 1996: 113). Debate and discussion between the two fronts led to a further qualification of the 'right' to succession, namely that acceptance of the EPLF's position on this issue was a precondition for the formation of a united front with them. The TPLF grudgingly accepted this condition even though it continued to promote the development of other 'nationalist' movements against the 'Amhara-dominated' *Derg*.

Though the two movements fought together against the *Derg* they remained divided on numerous issues: the TPLF relied on mobilizing rather than conscripting peasants; the TPLF relied upon guerrilla tactics while the EPLF gravitated increasingly to conventional warfare; and the TPLF kept prisoners for relatively brief periods before releasing them while the EPLF incarcerated prisoners for years (Young 1996; Abbink 1998). In the name of revolutionary justice, both movements committed major atrocities against civilians, unarmed officials and the armed forces of the Ethiopian state (Table 1.2).

Regardless of a major rift between the movements between 1984 and 1988, they submerged their differences and fought the *Derg*. Following major successes against Ethiopian forces between 1989 and 1990, the TPLF established a coalition of Ethiopian-based opposition movements, which it called the Ethiopian People's Revolutionary Democratic Front (EPRDF). In May 1991 representatives of the EPLF, the EPRDF and the Ethiopian government were invited to a US-brokered peace conference in London. During the conference EPRDF forces entered and secured control of Addis Ababa on 29 May and effectively brought the conflict to an end.

Table 1.2 Eritrean People's Liberation Front (EPLF) and Tigrayan People's Liberation Front (TPLF) acts of 'revolutionary violence', 1975–1991

EPLF	TPLF
1970–74: assassination of Ethiopian officials	1978: annihilation of the Ethiopian People's Revolutionary Party in Tigray
1987–88: multiple attacks against relief convoys and the destruction of food aid	1986: attack at Alamata, killing two World Vision employees
1988–91: assassination of hundreds of 'collaborators'	1990: 200 civilians killed in a fight against the *Derg* at Massawa
1991: ethnic 'cleansing' of 120,000 Ethiopian soldiers and their dependents	April–May 1991: EPRDF/TPLF killings of anti-EPRDF protestors in Gojjam and Addis Ababa

Source: Human Rights Watch 1991.

Issais Afeworki, the chairman of the EPLF, abruptly announced[2] that his party would 'run their own province without declaring full independence from Ethiopia' and that it would 'limit its participation' in the forthcoming multi-party National Conference scheduled for 1 July to 'discussing cooperation' with the EPRDF government. The EPRDF had no choice but to accept Afeworki's statement but it added two provisos: Eritrean independence must be supported by a referendum and Ethiopia must be guaranteed access to the port of Assab.

The 1991 National Conference agreed to establish a 'transitional government' with Meles Zenawi, chairman of the TPLF, as the head of state. A council of representatives was also established which adopted a national charter setting out basic rights and began the task of drafting a new constitution and organizing national elections.

In July 1991 the EPLF decided, with the support of the EPRDF, to cleanse Eritrea of tens of thousands of Ethiopian soldiers and their dependents – many of whom were Tigrayan – by forcing them to walk, without food or shelter, to the Ethiopian border (Box 1.1).

Following internationally supervised elections in June 1994 – which were boycotted by opposition groups – the EPRDF won an overwhelming majority of the vote and assumed power in Addis Ababa (Banks and Muller 1998). The government adopted a new federal constitution, which should have protected the rights of its 'Eritrean' citizens.[3]

Thus Art. 6 of the constitution addressed the question of Ethiopian nationality and states that:

(1) Any person of either sex shall be an Ethiopian national where both or either parent is Ethiopian;
(2) Foreign nationals may acquire Ethiopian nationality; and
(3) Particulars relating to nationality shall be determined by law.

Box 1.1 Eritrea's ethnic cleansing of Ethiopians in July 1991

'Six weeks after they lost the war, hundreds of thousands of Ethiopian army soldiers, sick and hungry, are huddling without shelter in squalid camps or slogging on foot through brutal mountain passes in a chaotic nightmare of demobilization . . . Hundreds have died of exhaustion, malaria and pneumonia.' Some men were forced to walk 200 miles from Aduwa to Mekele, where there were 'only 50 tents in this rain-drenched camp to protect more than 50,000 soldiers, some of whom were trying to carve sleeping places out of mud'. After defeating the Ethiopian army 'the Eritreans held most of them as prisoners of war. In the last several weeks they have been pushing them across the border . . . The Eritreans . . . refused to agree a proposal by the ICRC to fly some of the soldiers to the southern part of Ethiopia with the result that soldiers are strung out in camps around the city of Gondar . . . [and] in the province of Gojjam [and in] Aksum, Aduwa, Adigrat and Mekele in the province of Tigray. About 50,000 soldiers . . . escaped across the Sudan border to Kassala and 40,000 more clustered around Homera on the Sudanese border.' 'About 30,000 wives and children of the Ethiopian soldiers stationed in Eritrea have been bussed by the EPLF across the border in the last two weeks and are crowded into camps.'

Source: Perlez, J. 'Ethiopia troops battle to survive misery of peace', *New York Times* 15 July 1991. The EPRDF provided no assistance to the soldiers (or their dependents) who survived the expulsion. Also see Tekeste and Tronvol (2000: 46–7).

Art. 13(2) incorporated human and civil rights in conformity with the Universal Declaration of Human Rights, i.e. 'everyone has the right to a nationality' (Art. 15). Furthermore Art. 33(1) set out an important protection for nationals by stating that 'No Ethiopian national shall be deprived of his or her Ethiopian nationality against his or her will. Marriage of an Ethiopian national of either sex to a foreign national shall not annul his or her Ethiopian nationality.'

Art. 39 spells out the basis of a federal state in terms which directly reflect the TPLF's 1980 position on self-determination. Thus:

Sec. 1. Every Nation, Nationality and People in Ethiopia has an unconditional right to self-determination, including the right to secession.
Sec. 2. Every Nation, Nationality and People in Ethiopia has the right to speak, to write and to develop its own language; to express, to develop and to promote its culture; and to preserve its history.
Sec. 3. Every Nation, Nationality and People in Ethiopia has the right to a full measure of self government which includes the right to establish institutions of government in the territory that it inhabits and to equitable representation in State and Federal governments.

Sec. 5. A 'Nation, Nationality or People' for the purpose of this Constitution, is a group of people who have or share a large measure of a common culture or similar customs, mutual intelligibility of language, belief in a common or related identities, a common psychological makeup, and who inhabit an identifiable, predominately contiguous territory.

Art. 47 of the constitution provides that 'Nations, Nationalities and Peoples within the States enumerated in sub-article 1 of this article have the right to establish, at any time, their own states'. Regardless of this article, however, it is widely understood that the federal government, which is controlled by the TPLF, will not allow a state the 'unconditional right to self-determination, including the right to succession' (Gilkes 1999: 25 *passim*).

In Eritrea the EPLF rapidly formed the government, created and staffed key ministries and began the task of reconstructing a country torn by 30 years of civil war and drought. The EPLF adopted the 'Eritrean Nationality Proclamation' (no. 21 of 1992),[4] which established the basis on which Eritrean nationals – defined to include Eritreans in the diaspora and most (but not all) individuals residing within the territorial boundaries of the country – could register and vote in the forthcoming 1993 referendum. The only question on the ballot was: 'Do you want Eritrea to be an independent and sovereign country? Yes or No.' The referendum, which was observed by the UN, was held in the ten administrative districts of Eritrea, the Sudan, Ethiopia and other countries where the diaspora resided (Table 1.3).

The Referendum Commission organized the ballot and deployed 40 observers to monitor voting in Ethiopia and the Sudan. An independent state of Eritrea was supported by 99.8 per cent of registered voters. The UN Observer Mission certified that, 'on the whole, the referendum process in Eritrea can be considered to be free and fair at every stage' (Eritrea Department of External Affairs 1993: 3). On 28 May 1994 Eritrea was formally declared an independent nation.

The EPLF immediately declared a four-year transitional period during which the country would be governed by individuals appointed to a Consultative Council, a National Assembly and to the judiciary (Rake 2002). Independence in 1994 witnessed the formal transformation of the EPLF from a guerrilla movement into a political party, the PFDJ. The party confirmed its support for the creation of a plural political system and a new national constitution was drafted and submitted for public consultation (within Eritrea and the diaspora). Consultation led to a draft of the constitution that was approved by a Constituent Assembly in 1997,

Table 1.3 Results of the 1993 referendum on Eritrean independence

Area	Total vote	No	Invalid	Yes Number (%)
Eritrea	730,261	1,131	172	728,960 (99.8)
Fighters	77,579	21	46	77,512 (99.9)
Sudan	154,058	352	0	153,706 (99.7)
Ethiopia	57,706	204	36	57,466 (99.6)
Other countries	82,806	135	74	82,597 (99.7)
Total	1,102,410	1,822	328	1,100,260 (99.81)

which limited the term of office of an elected president (who appointed key officials) and which allowed 'conditional' political pluralism but barred religious and ethnically based political parties. In 1998, before the constitution could be adopted, war with Ethiopia intervened and the PFDJ postponed a referendum on the constitution and national elections. Shortly after the war ended in 2000 the PFDJ suspended elections, refused to adopt the constitution and introduced military rule.

In the early 1990s Eritrea and Ethiopia put into place a number of bilateral agreements including the 'Asmara Pact' (signed in September 1993), which foreshadowed all the politico-economic issues which contributed to war in 1998. The Pact contained 25 protocols and was understood, wrongly it appears, to reflect the shared political view of both parties (Tekeste Negash and Tronvoll 2000: Chap. 5). Most of the documents in the Pact have not been released but, judging from the minutes of various meetings, the Pact appears to have encompassed an agreement to harmonize trade and economic policy and expand cooperation in defence, tourism, education and 'public affairs' generally. Kidane Mengisteab and Okbazghi Yohannes (2005: 229–30) have argued that the agreement focused on: (a) preserving the free flow of goods and services, capital and people between the two countries; (b) maintaining Ethiopia's access to Eritrean ports; (c) 'cooperation in monetary policy and continued use of the birr in both countries until Eritrea issued its own currency'; (d) harmonization of customs; and (e) cooperation and consultation on foreign policy. However, until all the documents are released it is not clear what understandings were envisaged or reached.

Between 1991 and 1997 the two countries did operate a '*de facto* currency union' based on the Ethiopian birr, which meant that decisions about the value of the birr and economic policy generally were largely in the hands of the National Bank of Ethiopia (Gilkes and Plaut 1999: 13–15). This policy provided Eritrea with a stable reserve currency and 'risk-free trade' with Ethiopia (which was Eritrea's largest market and supplier) while Ethiopia benefited from the expansion of cross-border trade (Kidane Mengisteab and Okbazghi Yohannes 2005: 254, Table 1).

Though the EPLF announced in 1992 that it would introduce its own currency, the nakfa, there appears to have been no communication with Ethiopia on this matter until early 1997, when Eritrean officials announced that the currency would be introduced at the end of the year (Tekeste Negash and Tronvoll 2000: 34–7; Writenet 1998). In October 1997, in an apparent snub, Ethiopia announced that trade with Eritrea would be governed by a 'normal, arms-length trade regime', as between sovereign countries, and would be regulated by hard currency and letters of credit (see Tekie Fessehazion undated). Following the introduction of the nakfa in December 1997 Ethiopia issued new bank notes, apparently to avoid any 'leakage' of the old currency held in Eritrea. By this time, however, Eritrean banks held large deposits of birr and had run up significant debts to the Commercial Bank of Ethiopia (estimated at Birr 1.2 billion). Eritrea was also heavily dependent for foreign exchange on Ethiopia's payment of port dues for handling Ethiopian-bound cargo (Abbink 1998: 559). By the outbreak of hostilities in May 1998 Eritrea's principal exports to Ethiopia had been increasingly disrupted and her major source of foreign exchange (port dues by Ethiopia) had declined because Ethiopia was importing fewer goods.

Despite the benefits of peace and expanded trade it appears that Eritrea's pursuit of free trade was increasingly at odds with TPLF ambitions: very early on Tigrayan officials introduced taxes and duties and import-substitution industries ('owned' by party officials) which frustrated Eritrean trade (Alemseged Tesfai undated: Pt. I; Schroeder 2006). In particular a government parastatal, 'The Endowment Fund for the Rehabilitation of Tigray' (EFFORT) vastly expanded TPLF commercial and trading operations at the expense of private enterprise at a time when the province was benefiting from federal investment (Young 1997: 83–7; Tekeste Negash and Tronvoll 2000: Chap. 5; Alemseged Tesfai undated: Pt. II).

A further unresolved issue was the legal status of 'dual national' Eritreans in Ethiopia. While the issue was discussed it was subordinated to the bigger issue of Eritrean independence. The EPRDF facilitated the Eritrea referendum and it issued special ID to resident 'Eritreans'. One of the bilateral agreements signed in 1993 was between the Ministries of Internal Affairs[5] that set out their understanding about the status of 'Eritreans' in Ethiopia and which:

> confirmed an earlier agreement to exempt citizens of the other country from entry visa requirements. This provision was intended 'to promote and further consolidate the historical and cultural relationships long cherished by the peoples of the two countries, further strengthen the affinity and bonds of friendship between them.' Article 2.3 of the same agreement declared that 'until such time that the citizens of one of the sides residing in the other's territory are fully identified and until the issue of citizenship is settled in both countries, the traditional right of citizens of one side to live in the other's territory shall be respected.
>
> (Cited in Human Rights Watch 2003a: Sec. 3)

This understanding prevailed until 1996 when:

> the Ethiopian and Eritrean government agreed to settle the question by asking those involved to choose their nationality. The two sides agreed that 'on the question of Nationality . . . Eritrean's who have so far been enjoying Ethiopian citizenship should be made to choose and abide by their choice'. It was clear that participation in the Referendum alone could not and was not construed as their having done so.
>
> (Human Rights Watch 2003a: 15–16; Negash and Tronvoll 2000: Chap. 5)

However, the understanding was *not* implemented by either government.

Their failure to demarcate the border added a further issue that would prove decisive. Italy had expanded the boundary of colonial Eritrea by force and/or by negotiating treaties with Ethiopia but, critically, their mutual border was not demarcated on the ground. Nevertheless, as Abbink (1998: 555) has argued, 'the line of this border was well known and was generally respected except for limited areas where Italy continued to encroach' prior to 1935. A further complicating factor was that throughout this period many people from Eritrea and Tigray settled the area without regard to political boundaries.

During their struggle against the *Derg* the EPLF and TPLF postponed discussion about the border (Gilkes 1999; Abbink 1998). However, their shared border became a political problem in the early 1990s when the TPLF, following the 1991 expulsion of Ethiopians from Eritrea, began to expel Eritrean peasants living on the border. It appears that the TPLF leadership in Tigray may have been pursuing an agenda that was at odds with that of the government in Addis Ababa.[6] Thus in the Badme area the TPLF implemented 'Project Rectification' which allegedly seized land from Eritrean peasants and reallocated it to demobilized TPLF fighters (Tekie Fessehazion undated; Tekeste Negash and Tronvoll 2000: 26–9). Subsequently, the TPLF's ambitions appear to have expanded as it sought to redraw the boundary between Tigray and Eritrea by pushing Eritrean peasants out of a much wider area on the border (Alemseged Tesfai undated: Pt. III; Kidane Mengisteab and Okbazghi Yohannes 2005: 244). The expulsions appear to reflect a perception of Tigray as a bounded cultural community linked by a shared language and culture to a defined territory within which only nationals of Tigray should live.

By the mid-1990s incidents involving land erupted in communities along the Ethiopia–Eritrea border. Whereas in the past traditional forms of dispute resolution would have dealt with local disputes, these disputes were taken out of the hands of local communities by regional officials who escalated the conflict. In 1997 TPLF officials in Tigray complicated political relations by printing a new map of Tigray for use in its schools: the map incorporated areas along its northern border claimed by Eritrea. Political relations were further compounded when, in December 1997, Ethiopia printed new currency notes which incorporated the TPLF's contested map[7] of Tigray. Ethiopian actions were seen by Eritrea as proof that the TPLF was seeking to realize its dream of 'Greater Tigray' by incorporating Tigrinya-speaking areas of Eritrea.

In mid-1997 Ethiopian troops entered the area of Bada (claimed by Eritrea), prompting President Issais to write to Prime Minister Meles to complain about the incursion. Issais is said to have proposed the creation of a Joint Border Commission to resolve border disputes (Plaut 2005: 15–16). The Commission met briefly in November 1997 but did not meet again until 8 May 1998 (the start of the war) and it failed to agree mechanisms that might address the issue (Gilkes and Plaut 1999: 18–19; Tekeste Negash and Tronvoll 2000: 26–9).

By early 1997 a growing number of problems – conflicts over land, taxes on trade, monetary policy, currency regulation etc. – had emerged between Eritrea and Ethiopia, in part because the two ruling parties relied on the informal political relationship between the two heads of state[8] (rather than establish an interstate/institutional framework or organization with the authority to demarcate their shared border and agree common policies).

Events rapidly escalated. In July 1997 Ethiopian troops entered the area of Bada-Adi Murug in Eritrea and set up administrative offices (Eritrea 2005 ¶1.17 ff.). In early May 1998 Ethiopian troops entered the area of Badme, where they allegedly harassed local Eritreans. Eritrean troops were told not to intervene because the president was dealing with the issue. Shortly afterwards, and a little further to the north, Eritrean soldiers on patrol were confronted by 25 Ethiopian soldiers who fanned out around them and opened fire, wounding three Eritreans. The remainder of the Eritrean platoon came running to the scene and found their wounded colleagues but as it was dark, decided to camp. I paraphrase an official Eritrean account of what followed (ibid.: ¶1.25 f.):

> The group spent the night sleeping in the open and in the early morning while it was still mostly dark they heard unfamiliar voices. The strangers were speaking fluent *Tigrinya* [the language of Eritrea and of ethnic Tigrayans] . . . and so the group felt reassured. The strangers identified themselves as Ethiopian soldiers and asked for a chance to talk about the previous day's events. The commander and five other soldiers stepped forward and the Ethiopians shot them. The remainder of the squad ran for cover while the Ethiopians continued their attack.

Ethiopia's only response to this account was to deny the location of the incident.

This incident rapidly transformed socio-political relations in the region from a situation of growing tension to open hostility and violent conflict. In effect it reopened old memories of 'rivalry and long felt chains of collective resentment' between the two nations (Triluzi undated: 2). And the incident gave the political leadership in both countries justification for inflammatory comments that contributed to further violence and which directed public attention to the presence of enemy 'aliens' living in the country.

Following the incident Eritrea mobilized troops and demanded that Ethiopia withdraw from its territory. As Abbink (1998: 558–9) noted at the time:

> by forcefully bringing up the border issue, the Eritrean government has put pressure on the Ethiopian-leadership and tried to force it to return to a more Eritrea-favourable position by way of inducing the pro-Eritrea factions in the ruling EPRDF to assert themselves.

If this was the perception in Eritrea it may have been misconceived given the extent to which relations with Ethiopia had dramatically changed since the 1980s when Eritrean national identity was defined in opposition to 'the Ethiopians' (Tronvoll 1998, 1999).

In Ethiopia, public attitudes towards Eritrea[9] were strongly affected by EPRDF statements which were reported by the independent press and used to create a 'war of words', a 'massive propaganda effort' (Triulzi undated, p. 5). Ethiopian media used 'insulting epithets and debasing accusations' which linked 'Eritrean aggression to Italian [colonial] ambitions in the region and to the legacy of racist arrogance they had left behind' (ibid.). The media created and sustained widespread anti-Eritrean resentment, which played on tropes and images of the EPLF/Eritrean government as racists and fascists *and* it identified 'Eritreans' as the 'enemy within' allegedly because they were exploiting their dual citizenship to accumulate power and wealth. Triulzi argues that the effect of government propaganda, nationalist media coverage and rising tension was to create massive support for the government's pursuit of the war against Eritrea and 'Eritreans'.

Independent press reports on the confiscation of 'Eritrean' property (see Figures 1.1 and 1.2) can be read in different ways. First, by listing individuals whose property was to be taken, the public was being warned not to buy property which may later be confiscated by the government. However, because 'Eritreans' needed to sell some of their property quickly, prior knowledge enabled Ethiopians to acquire their property at prices far below what the market would ordinarily bear.

The 1998 war was a product of an elite political culture and of political institutions which do not hold officials accountable for their actions. Had the PFDJ and the EPRDF created institutional mechanisms to resolve inter-state issues then it is just possible that other pressures and forms of accountability might have emerged to restrain them from going to war. Instead, political leaders rapidly turned a minor border skirmish into a full-scale military conflict. Once they started the war officials in both states conducted a propaganda battle and prevented international mediation until a clear military outcome was reached in May 2000.

The 'enemy within': War and the expulsion of 'Eritreans'

The war and its impact on the people of the region has been extensively documented.[10] Though the international community saw the war as a border dispute, the principal issue was the survival of two autocratic regimes. This is why the war continued until May 2000, when Ethiopia was able to launch a successful assault against Eritrean positions allowing it to occupy the disputed border area (Ethiopia might well have rolled into Asmara).

An estimated 70–100,000 people were killed during the war, with an untold number injured. At its height approximately 1.3 million people were displaced by the conflict. The cost of pursuing war cost the region dearly, with military expenditure reaching 39 per cent of Eritrea's gross domestic product (GDP) (to mobilize and support 215,000 troops) and at least 10 per cent of Ethiopia's GDP (in mobilizing 310,000 troops). Unsurprisingly the war set development back by a decade or more (Kidane Mengisteab and Okbazghi Yohannes 2005: 262 f.).

Diplomatic initiatives began as early as 15 May 1998 with the US–Rwanda proposal. Efforts to mediate between the parties occurred throughout the conflict but were rebuffed. Furthermore neither the UN arms embargo of May 2000 nor US shuttle diplomacy in June 2000 succeeded in bringing the two countries to the negotiating table.

(a)

Figure 1.1 (a) Front page of an Addis Ababa newspaper and (b) a translation announcing the expropriation of 742 'Eritrean' businesses.

We Have Brought You A List Of 742 Names With Their Organizations.

ETH'OP   SPECIAL ISSUE

ETH'OP'   4th Year Number 153   13 Nehassie 1990 [19 August 1998] Price 1.00

"Young men! We are also invaded economically! Invaded!"

A court issued an order freez ing 742 Eritrean merchants' money and establishments including, Shewa Bakery, Belay Teklu Pastry, and Yakona Engineering.

We present you with a list of 742 names and their Companies.

The Appellate Court issued an order freezing 742 Eritrean's movable and immovable properties, including Yakona Engineering , Shewa Bakery, Belay Teklu Pastry. A special office has been established in the Mexico Square, Philips Building to deal with the Eritrean issue. It has been found out from the copy of the decision, that, in response to the written request of Addis Ababa Municipal Administration Finance Bureau, number C/A/49/1/4 Nehassie 1990 [10 August 1998], the court ordered that 742 Eritrean organizations be frozen. According to the copy of the decision, the request for an injunction made by region 14 is in order to collect the tax debt of those 742 people who were ordered to leave the country.

(b)

In early June 1998 Ethiopia began to arrest and detain 'Eritreans' and on 12 June the first group was expelled. On that day Ethiopia declared[11] that the position of '550,000 Eritreans in Ethiopia remains unchanged: they can continue to live and work peacefully in Ethiopia'. However, three classes of individuals were immediately subject to removal/'enforced leave': (a) Eritreans in 'senior positions of responsibility' within the Ethiopian government or government-owned companies; (b) EPLF officials; and (c) officials attached to the 'Eritrean Community Organization' in Addis Ababa. Ethiopia immediately arrested and expelled 800 Eritrean officials and an undisclosed number of 'Eritrean' businessmen.

By the end of June – a mere six weeks after the border skirmish – Ethiopia had expelled an estimated 1,045 persons into Eritrea (Amnesty International 1999: 14–15). In July Ethiopia expelled a further 1,000 persons due to 'national security'. Ethiopia also pressured the UN, the Organization of African Unity (OAU) and international aid agencies to dismiss 'Eritrean' staff from their jobs (they were expelled).

On 9 July the Ethiopian prime minister spoke on Radio Ethiopia stating that, 'We have unlimited right to expel Eritreans.' He said:

> Eritreans live in Ethiopia because of the good will of the Ethiopian government. It is the right of the Ethiopian government to expel Eritreans living in Ethiopia at any time . . . If we say, 'Go, because we do not like the colour of your eyes', they have to leave . . . For this reason we will do what we have done before, identify the members of *Shaebia's* fifth column one by one and take action against them.[12]

At roughly the same time the independent Ethiopian press were publishing anti-Eritrean propaganda and listing the names of 'Eritreans' in public and private employment, thereby increasing their vulnerability.

In Ethiopia considerable public resentment focused on the presence of 'Eritreans' in the country. Their presence and ambiguous legal status became an issue due in part to the dominance of the TPLF – whose leadership was perceived to be Tigrayan/Eritrean – in Ethiopian politics and because of statements in the media.

I draw on testimony from interviews with 'Eritreans' who were expelled at this time to indicate their shock at being arrested and to show the banality and cruelty of officials who saw themselves as merely doing their duty in destroying 'Eritrean' families and livelihoods.[13] Cases 1 to 4 show that among the first to be expelled were wealthy businessmen. Indeed a pattern quickly emerges: all those initially arrested were adult males (the deportation of family bread-earners meant that women and children left behind became destitute) who had lived many decades in Ethiopia, had married Ethiopians, had children born in Ethiopia and who possessed Ethiopian nationality. As Case 1 makes clear, some individuals were well-known members of their communities.

(a)

Figure 1.2   (a) Front page of an Addis Ababa newspaper, (b) the continuation of the article
and (c) a translation with a story of the seizure of 'Eritrean business'.

4   ልዩ ዘገባ

የኤርትራውያኑ የንግድ ድርጅቶች ዕጣ ምን ይሆናል?

እፍቃሪ ሻዕቢያ የሆኑ ኤርትራውያን ወደ አገራቸው እየተሸኙ ነው፡፡ ከአነዚሁ ውስጥ ባለሃብትና ባለንብረት የሆኑ ይገኙበታል፡፡ የሰብአዊ መብት ጥያቄ ያስነሱትም እነዚሁ ባለንብረቶች መሆናቸው እየተነገረ ነው፡፡

በ   በኩል ደግሞ ለንብረቶቻቸው ወኪል አቋሙው ወደ አገራቸው ስተተባረሩ ኤርትራውያን ንብረት ጉዳይ አንዳንድ ጥያቄዎ እየተነሱ ነው፡፡ ባለንብረቶቹ ተባረው ንብረታቸው በውክልና ይቀጥል ማለት ምን ማለት ነው? ደግሞስ እስከመቼ? ባለቤትነታቸው እስከነካቴው ተቋርጦ ጣጣቸው ጨርሶ እዚያው አገራቸው ተሰብስበው አርፈው የሚቀመጡትስ እንዴትና መቼ ነው? እየተባለም ነው፡፡

መንግሥት የሰውን ንብረት አላግባብ የማይቀማ መሆኑንም በአንድ ወገን እያገለፀ ነው፡፡ ባለንብረቶቹ በውክልናም ሆነ በሽያጭ ንብረቶቻቸውን ለወዴዱትና እንደወደዱት እንዲያደርጉ ሁኔታዎችን እያመቻቸ መሆኑንም እያሳየ ነው፡፡ ኤርትራውያን ባለሃብቶችም ይህን ቃል አምነውና ተቀብለው ንብረቶቻቸውን መልሶ እያስያዙ ወይም ጥቅሙንና ለውጡን እየያዙ ወደ አገራቸው እየሄዱና ለመሄድ በጓግጅት ላይ መሆናቸው እየታየ ነው፡፡

ለመሆኑ እነዚህ በቁጥር ቀላል የማይባሉ ኤርትራውያን አገሪቱን ለቀው ሲወጡ ደዛዋቸው የቆሩት የንግድና የቢዝነስ ተቋማት በአገሪቱ ኢኮኖሚ እንቅስቃሴ ላይ ምን ተፅዕኖ ያስከትሉ ይሆን? የሚል ጥያቄም አለጣቄም፡፡ በተለይ ይህ ኤርትራውያኑ ከእንግዲህ ኢትዮጵያ አበላሃት፤ ዓይኒ ይታወራል፤ ቀኝ እጄ ይሽባሸባል፤ ሥልጣኔ ይርቃታል እያስ በድፍረት ከመናገራቸው ጋራ ተደይዞ የመናጌ ጥያቄ ሆኗል፡፡ እውነት እነማን ሂደው እነማን ተዘጉተው ነው የተባለው ሁሉ የሚደርስብን?

በዚህ ዘገባ እነዚህን ጥያቄዎች ሊመልሱ ይችላሉ ያልናቸውን ይዘን ቀርበናል፡፡

የተዘጉ ወይም ባለቤቶቻቸው ተባረው በውክልና ያሉ የኤርትራውያን የንግድ ድርጅቶች ለናሙና ያህል የቀረበ

(መርካቶ አካባቢ ዞን አንድ ውስጥ የተዘጉ 62 የንግድ ድርጅቶች እዚህ ውስጥ ሰስተካተቱም፡፡)

1/ ሆርን ባንክ	14/ የኔሸርሳል ትሬዲንግ
2/ ትራንስ ሆርን	15/ ኢንተርናሽናል ሹራብ ቤት
3/ ግሬተር ሆርን ትሬዲንገዳ	16/ ጄጥሮስ ቡና ቤት
4/ ሬማትክ	17/ ሪታ ዐገር ቤት
5/ ቤልትራንስ	18/ ኤልሳ ሽቶ
6/ ነምበር ናይን ትራብ ኤጀንሲ	19/ ተክኤ ገ/ስሳሴ አሸዋ ቤት
7/ አንበሳ ሳውንድሪ	20/ ኤልያስ ሆቴል
8/ ፎቶ ፈሊ	21/ ስላሚኖ
9/ ፎቶ ቀልቢ	22/ ስካንያ
10/ ገ/ተንሳይ ኬክ ቤት	23/ ጽዮን ሆቴል
11/ ትግራይ ሆቴል	24/ ቢጎብብ
12/ ሜርን ሹራብ ቤት	25/ ጀሜትራ አንቶኔዋ
13/ ሆርን ኢንተርናሽናል	26/ ወልዱ ቡና ቤት

ረፖርተር ሐምሴ 1990

(b)

WHAT WILL BE THE FATE OF THE BUSINESSES OF THOSE ERITREAN?

Eritrean lovers of Shabia [PFDJ] are being deported to their country. Among them are many well-off. People say that it is they who raise the "human rights" issue.

On the other hand, certain questions are being raised regarding the Eritreans who were expelled after giving a power of attorney for their property. What does it mean to let property be held by a person with a power of attorney, after the owner is expelled? And until when? How and when will their ownership be terminated when they stay in their country for good? These are among the questions.

[The Ethiopian] Government is saying that it will not confiscate private property without due process. It is also setting the ground for the owners to give a power of attorney or to sell it to anyone whom they wish. The Eritreans, accepting and believing the [government's] word, are going to or getting ready to go to their country after appropriating their property or holding the value or exchange value of it.

Some ask, now that a large number of Eritreans left the country, what would be the effect of the business organizations they owned on this country's economy. Especially, the Eritreans daringly say "Alas Ethiopia, its eyes are blind, its right hand is crippled, civilization will abandon it." In truth, are the aforementioned evils going to befall us?

In this report, we try to answer these questions.

Sample Business Organizations Which are Attached Or Whose Owners were Expelled and Are Under Power of Attorney (62 business organizations in Mercato Area of the Zone One are not included)

27/ አርሲ ቡና ቤት መጠጥ አከፋፋይ
28/ ተስፋዬ ስብሃት ለአብ ብረት መሸጫ
29/ አብርሃም ሼል
30/ ሲና ቢዝነስ ግሩፕ
31/ መስፍን ኪኪ ቤት
32/ ፈጣን (ሞገጆልድ)
33/ ትሪያ (ልደታ ቤተክርስቲያን ፊት ለፊት)
34/ የሴና ቦርሳ ስፌር ፓርት
35/ አሳ ሆቴል
36/ በእብን እምነት መደብርና ሆቴል
37/ ዐጋዬ መሃ ጋራዥ
38/ ኢንተርናሽናል ፋርማሲ
39/ ተከስሃይማኖት አጄፕ
40/ አፍሪካ መጠጥ ግሮሰሪ
41/ አድዋ ጉዳና ሼል
42/ ደጉ ተዋበ አበባ ቤት
43/ ደህብ ሆቴል
44/ ዐጋዬ ጋይም ቡና ቤት
45/ ዓለም ተወልደ ብረታ ብረት
46/ ካዛዬ ገ/ጊዮርጊስ ብረታ ብረት
47/ ሀብቴ ጋራዥ
48/ ዕቁባይ አብረሃ ሕንፃ መሣሪያ መደብር
49/ ዐጋዬ ተ/ማርያም ሆቴል
50/ ኢትዮጵያ ትኑር ቡና ቤት
51/ መርሃበኝ
52/ ታሪቀኝ ማናዬ ፎቶ ቤት
53/ የሀንስ ምራጭ ጋራዥ
54/ ዘውዴ ገ/መስቀል ፋርማሲ
55/ ግርማ ባራኺ ቡቲክ
56/ ክፍላይ ኪዳኔ ጋራዥ
57/ ተ/ጊዮርጊስ ኪዳኔ ጋራዥ
58/ ዐጋዬ ተ/ማርያም መለዋወጫ
59/ የማነ ተክስተ ጋራዥ
60/ ስምኦን ጋራዥ
61/ የማነ ጋራዥ
62/ ተስፋማርያም ጋራዥ
63/ ተስፋ ስላሴ ፖምፕስታና ጋራዥ
64/ ቴድሮስ ፎጊድ ጋራዥ
65/ ክፍሌ ቴፍሩና መለዋወጫ
66/ አስመላሽ ተ/ሀይማኖት ጋራዥ
67/ ብርሃኔ መለዋወጫ
68/ ኢዮብ ጋራዥ
69/ መኩንን ጋራዥ
70/ ታቦቱ ተ/ልደት ሽቀጣ ሽቀጥ
71/ ኢንተርናሽናል ሹራብ ፋብሪካ
72/ ....

ሪፖርተር ሐምሴ 1990

(c)

Case 1

'Daniel' was born in 1962 in Asmara to Eritrean parents. He and his family moved to Addis Ababa in 1972 where he attended primary school, high school and university. He owned a company in Addis Ababa. Though he voted in the 1993 Eritrean referendum, he had also served as an official monitor of Ethiopian elections. He possessed an Ethiopian passport, an Ethiopian driving licence and other Ethiopian identity documents. He married an Ethiopian woman in 1989 and raised four children in Addis Ababa.

'Daniel' was aware that Eritreans were being arrested in June 1998 but felt that because of his strong 'Ethiopian connections' that he would be safe (even so he put his elderly mother on 'the last flight to Asmara' in May). In July 1998 at 5 a.m. four armed police entered his home and arrested him. The police lieutenant apologized saying, 'there is nothing I can do'. Within a few hours he was taken from the police station to a community hall where he was imprisoned with other Eritreans. At 4 p.m. his wife was allowed to give him food.

On day 2, and without explanation, everyone was lined up and photographed. He asked a guard, 'What is the problem? Why are you arresting us?' The guard replied, 'because you are Eritrean you have to go'. I said 'I am not Eritrean. I was born in Ethiopia. I've never been to Eritrea. If you want I can show you my passport.' On day three some of his neighbours came to speak on his behalf but with no effect; friends ensured that he was able to transfer power of attorney to his wife who, despite being Ethiopian, was told that she must sell their property and 'be prepared to go' (she quickly sold shop merchandise at heavily discounted prices; their houses were confiscated).

On 28 July 'Daniel' was placed in a bus and – without food, water or possessions – was driven north to the town of Dessie (where they were fed by a local Eritrean businessman who slaughtered two cows to feed them), then to Alamata where they slept in a disused food-aid store (and were fed bread and water). The next day they were driven to Mekelle where they were 'feasted' by the local Tigrayan community before being driven to the border. That night they were forced to walk across the border at Dekamhare where they were met by Eritrean soldiers. He was interviewed by officials and given a document stating the he was a 'deported Ethiopian'. Fearing conscription, his family secured him a forged Eritrean passport and in January 1999 he flew to Nairobi, where he bribed an immigration official and was allowed to board a plane to Frankfurt, from where he transited to London and claimed asylum.

Case 2

'Binyam's' parents were born in Eritrea but migrated to Ethiopia many years before his birth in Addis Ababa in 1987. In the mid-1990s his parents divorced and remarried. His father was a successful woodworker who owned his own business and rented the family home from the *kebele*. He attended primary and secondary school in Addis Ababa. In June 1998 police came to the family home in the middle of the night and arrested his father, who was detained with other Eritreans in the community hall. He was held for several days before being bussed to the border and expelled into Eritrea. His step-mother and siblings were told that they could stay in Ethiopia, but they agreed that 'the family must stay together' so they quickly sold all their assets and begged the government to be taken to Eritrea. Four months later they were taken by bus to a point near Assab and forced to walk across the border carrying their possessions.

Case 3

'Yohannes' was born in 1986; he was the youngest of seven children born in Addis Ababa to Eritrean parents who migrated to Ethiopia in the 1960s. His father was a truck driver and his mother a housewife. The family owned their own home in the Cherkos area of Addis Ababa and the children all attended local schools. In July 1998 police came to their home in the middle of the night and took his father. They said, 'You are an Eritrean, we need you.' His father was taken to a detention camp and within two days was bussed to the Eritrea border and expelled. In January 1999 the police returned to the family home and arrested and detained him, his mother and three brothers in a detention camp at 'Sarbeit' (Addis Ababa). Shortly afterwards they were bussed to the border near Assab and forced to walk across into Eritrea, where they were interviewed by officials who issued them an identity document stating that they were 'deported Eritreans'.[14]

Case 4

'Kiflom' was born in Addis Ababa in 1980 to Eritrean parents who migrated to Ethiopia many decades before the war. His seven siblings were all born in Addis Ababa. His father was a successful businessman who owned a multi-storey building and a beer distribution centre; the family owned their own home in Gotera, a suburb of Addis Ababa. He attended primary and secondary school in Addis and recalled that prior to the war, 'life was good', 'we were rich' and 'it was very nice in Addis Ababa'. In August 1998 armed security officers came to their street in the middle of the night and arrested and detained the adult males in three 'Eritrean' homes, including his father. The men were detained in the *kebele* 'prison' and bussed to the border two days later.

His step-mother and the rest of the family pleaded with the authorities to be allowed to join his father in Eritrea. While they waited for transport they sold all their possessions to raise money and closed the family business (the business premises was confiscated by the authorities and sold). In September they were put on a bus and taken to the border near Assab where they were forced to walk across the war zone carrying their possessions. Most, but not all, of their identity documents were seized by Ethiopian officials. The eldest daughter was allowed to remain behind in the family home because she was married to an Ethiopian.

Table 1.4 summarizes information about the property confiscated from individuals who were expelled into Eritrea between June and July 1998, i.e. in the first 'round'. These individuals were relatively wealthy compared to the majority of those expelled later and the assets they lost are by no means representative of the wealth of 'Eritreans'. It is also the case that subsequent to this initial expulsion and confiscation of property, additional businesses, homes and assets were confiscated and individual bank accounts were frozen.

What 'Eritreans' did not know at the time was that Ethiopia put into effect special 'measures' aimed at stripping 'Eritreans' of their wealth. Thus (a) measures were introduced which prohibited 'Eritreans', as 'aliens', from owning property; (b) limitations were introduced requiring the mandatory sale of expellee's property within 30 days; (c) discriminatory and confiscatory taxation on 'Eritrean' property was brought into force; and (d) a '100 per cent location tax' was applied to the proceeds of some of the expellee's real estate (Eritrea 2007: ¶2.42 f. and EECC 2009: ¶316 and ¶320).

In addition, banks were directed to collect loans held by Eritreans. But of course the banks – which only loaned money to nationals – did not have records identifying their clients as 'Eritrean'[15] so the government sent lists of the names of

Table 1.4 Property and cash confiscated from 'Eritreans' expelled by Ethiopia, June–July 1998

Persons	Value of property	Value of cash
1,402	US$212 million	US$944,939

Source: Eritrean Relief and Refugee Commission 1998.

expelled 'Eritreans' to the banks, who were required to match a name to their files. This task was 'difficult and tiresome' but was dutifully completed in part by providing the government with information on its clients and by seizing the property in question and auctioning it. Bank officials did not baulk at the order to confiscate 'Eritrean' property, nor do they appear to have put into place independent checks to ensure that the property they seized really belonged to 'Eritreans'. The Commercial Bank of Ethiopia confiscated homes, businesses, buildings, vehicles, goods etc. from 393 'debtors'. Other banks took similar measures. Once taxes and special deductions were taken from the sale proceeds the remaining balance was placed in special 'blocked' bank accounts in the person's name; their savings accounts were similarly 'protected' (Eritrea 2007: ¶2.44 f.; EECC 2009: ¶338 f.).[16] The case of one 'Eritrean' who was allowed to remain is documented who was given power of attorney over the family home before his parents were deported though he eventually lost his home because the authorities levied taxes against it.[17] If there was one case, there were others.

In its evidence to the EECC at The Hague, Eritrea entered a claim for Ethiopian Birr 10.1 billion (US$1.34 billion) – of which 5.1 billion was for real property, 3.9 billion for movable property and 760 million for financial assets – to reimburse an estimated 22,374 'Eritrean' expellees for the property confiscated from them (Eritrea 2007: ¶2.120–2.122; see Chapter 2).

As the cases below show, after the initial round of expulsions the authorities turned their attention to the families of deportees and to 'ordinary' 'Eritreans', many of whom were identified by co-workers, neighbours and informants (Human Rights Watch 2003a: 19). The case studies show that officials treated 'Eritreans' callously and brutally (many were arrested, released and rearrested and/or detained for varying periods of time and some were tortured etc.). Members of the public also behaved in a highly prejudicial and violent manner towards 'Eritreans'.

Case 5

'Medhin' was born in Ethiopia in June 1971 to parents who had migrated from Eritrea. She met, married and had a child with an Eritrean-born man who grew up in Ethiopia. Her husband was a trader who may have been involved in Eritrean opposition politics. As someone with limited education she saw herself as a mother and housewife. She was estranged from her family and her in-laws because they disapproved of her mixed marriage: she was Muslim and her husband was Christian. She did not vote in the Eritrean referendum and had never been issued Eritrean identity documents.

In early 1999, while she was out of town, 'Medhin' heard that her husband had been arrested and on returning to Addis was told that he had been deported and that the authorities were looking for her. She also discovered that her husband's family were about to be deported and, without consulting her, were taking her son with them. She decided that she could not go to Eritrea. She said, 'I did not participate [in the referendum on Eritrean independence] because I did not feel Eritrean, having lived all my life in Addis Ababa.' At the time '[L]ots of my friends and neighbours were deported. The situation was very bad; people were having their houses robbed when they were due to be deported. Ordinary Ethiopian people attacked Eritrean people, in some areas and looted property.' Fortunately friends of her husband paid an agent to take her to Kenya, from where she travelled to the UK and applied for asylum.

Case 6

'Solomon' was born in Addis Ababa in 1979 to an Ethiopian father (who died in 1992) and an Eritrean mother. Officials arrested his mother in July 1999 and detained him. He was interrogated about his mother's activities – he was later to learn that she was accused of raising money for Eritrea via a small-scale savings society run in her bar – and was accused of involvement with the EPLF and 'tortured' (beaten, punched, pushed, whipped and slapped). After a month he was released to find that his mother had been deported and her business confiscated. 'Solomon' did not report to the police as required but, with help from an uncle, went into hiding until an agent took him out of the country.

Case 7

'Tigist' was born in Addis Ababa in 1982 to an Eritrean father and a Tigrayan mother (who was born in Eritrea); her parents migrated to Ethiopia decades earlier. She grew up in the Teklehaimainot area of the city, where she attended primary school and high school. Her father owned a taxi; her mother was a housewife. The family rented a government-owned house. In February 1999 police came to the house while she was out and arrested, detained and expelled her parents and three siblings. For the next 11 months she worked at various cafés without registering as an 'alien' Eritrean. In early August 1999 she was arrested at work and taken to 'prison', where she was held for three days before being bussed to the border near Assab and expelled into Eritrea.

Case 8

An only child, 'Meriam' was born in Addis Ababa in 1968; her father (who died in 1991) was an Eritrean who had migrated to Ethiopia and her mother was Ethiopian. She considered herself to be an Ethiopian. After her mother's death in 1996 a Tigrayan security official sought to marry her but she rebuffed him. After the war began 'Meriam' refused to register as an alien Eritrean. The Tigrayan official had her arrested in April 2000 and she was briefly detained at her *kebele* and then, for four months, at a military barracks where she was interrogated about sending money to the Eritrean government.

The official collected her from the barracks and offered her a choice: return to prison or live with him. She told him that he had 'already ruined' her life and that she would stay. But she was driven to his home and imprisoned for a year, during which time she performed domestic work – 'I look like a servant' – and was sexually abused and raped. She became pregnant and he became increasingly violent towards her. His subordinates took her to a hospital for the pregnancy but she had a miscarriage. By befriending a nurse, 'Meriam' managed to slip past guards and was helped to escape to Sudan and fly to the UK where she claimed asylum.

The above cases reinforce the observation by Human Rights Watch (HRW) that 'Denied employment and business licenses, many were left without any means of support' and that due to hostility 'towards people of Eritrean origin . . . it was also dangerous even for their friends and neighbours to be seen to be assisting expellees or their families' (2003a: 21). Having been left behind and deprived of their livelihood many individuals were compelled to apply to the government for permission to be repatriated to Eritrea to join loved ones (e.g. Case 4), though they often waited for months to be allowed to leave.[18] After the war ended in 2001 the government pressured the remaining ethnic 'Eritrean' population to leave 'voluntarily' via the International Committee of the Red Cross (ICRC) (HRW 2003a: 20; see Chapter 2). Ethiopia claimed that 21,905 'Eritreans' left 'voluntarily' during the war (Eritrea 2007: ¶1.27 ff.).

In August 1999 the government ordered all 'Eritreans' in the country who were aged 18 years or older, and who had voted in the 1993 referendum, to register and obtain an 'alien residence permit'. Individuals who failed to register could not access hospitals, schools etc. and they faced arrest. The information obtained via the registration exercise made it easier for officials to monitor and control the 'Eritreans' who remained.

The arrests and expulsions were particularly hard on families which had been split up. The following two cases are 'uncles' of 'Tigist' (Case 7), and while they were not expelled they, and many others, were detained and subjected to severe ethnic discrimination.

Case 9

'Samuel' was born in Eritrea and migrated to Addis Ababa in the 1970s to work. In May 1998 he was working at a brewery. Officials came to his home and arrested and detained him for a month before releasing him. On release he faced continued harassment and discrimination as an Eritrean. He was dismissed from his job and sought to establish his own businesses but faced continued harassment. Due to his mother's Tigrayan 'roots' he obtained a *kebele* identity card (which was not taken from him) and eventually an Ethiopian passport. In 2000 'Samuel' obtained a visa to travel to the USA for business but shortly after arriving there he applied for asylum.

Case 10

Born in Addis Ababa 'Michael' had travelled to Eritrea but returned to Ethiopia shortly before the war began. He was arrested and detained for a month before being released. However, he was unable to find work due to the stigma of being 'Eritrean'. At this point the family of his fiancée in Eritrea announced that their daughter would not be allowed to marry an Ethiopian *amiche* (see Chapter 4), which completely demoralized him. 'Michael' started drinking and using drugs. Later he met and married an Ethiopian woman working for the UN and was able to obtain a 'green card', which allowed him to immigrate to the USA.

After the first round of expulsions in June–July 1998, and as the case studies indicate, Ethiopia rapidly widened the rationale for arresting and expelling 'Eritreans'.[19] The categories of person were stretched to include individuals who: (a) voted in the 1993 referendum on Eritrean independence; (b) were alleged to have supported organizations based in Eritrea; (c) were born in Eritrea (but who grew up in Ethiopia); (d) were born in Ethiopia but who had one parent/grandparent born in Eritrea; (e) were alleged to have visited Eritrea; or (f) were alleged to have undertaken national service in Eritrea. In reality the arrest and deportation of individuals was highly arbitrary.

In November 1998 the Ministry of Foreign Affairs issued a statement entitled, 'The Legal Aspect of Ethiopia's Deportation of Undesirable Eritreans' (Zakir 1998).[20] The statement argued that only 'foreign nationals' with no right in law to reside in Ethiopia were being deported. It stated that immigration decisions could not be appealed against, that individuals were informed of the reasons for their deportation and that 'persons of Eritrean origin may be deported from Ethiopia if only they have lost Ethiopian nationality, following circumstances surrounding the Eritrean separation from Ethiopia in 1991'. The argument is wrong with respect to Ethiopian and international law because specific guarantees must be in place to ensure that the revocation of nationality is fair. Nor does the statement describe the actual process used to identify, arrest and expel 'Eritreans'.[21]

In reality 'Eritreans' were processed for expulsion in one of three ways (Amnesty International 1999; Eritrea 2002 ¶2.106 f., 2.124 f. and 2.146 f.). While nearly everyone was photographed and had their name taken – at least in urban areas – an unknown number of individuals were interrogated, harassed and forced to sign documents indicating their support for the Eritrean government. Second, the vast majority of 'Eritreans' were never told why they were arrested, nor were they able to challenge the legality of their arrest. In fact such was the speed with which officials identified and expelled 'Eritreans' that the authorities also expelled 15,000 Ethiopian nationals (Eritrea 2007 ¶3.32 f.; EECC 2009 ¶303–8).[22] Finally, low-level *kebele* and *woreda* committees expelled 20–28,000 'Eritreans' living in rural areas with, at best, a cursory look at the individuals (EECC 2009 ¶298–302). In this manner entire communities of 'Eritreans' living in rural Tigray were forced across the border (while their livestock, land and crops were confiscated) (Eritrea 2002 ¶2.74 f.). These indiscriminate actions contravened Ethiopian and international law.

Ethiopian officials also expelled hundreds of 'Eritreans' at Moyale (on the Kenyan border) and at the border with Djibouti (Amnesty International 1999: 15) and they removed the passports and identity documents from thousands of 'Eritreans' fleeing the country via Addis Ababa airport (HRW 2003a; Eritrea 2007 ¶1.46).

Worse still, and as Case 11 shows, officials not only failed to protect resident 'Eritreans' they abused their authority to exploit vulnerable individuals.

Case 11

'Tigisti' was born in Asmara in 1990 to Ethiopian parents but for unknown reasons was placed in a state orphanage. Shortly afterwards Ethiopian officials moved her to an orphanage in Ethiopia, where she remained until she was 17. On being discharged in 1997 'Tigisti' attached herself to an Eritrean family in Addis Ababa who 'adopted' her. Shortly after the war began soldiers came to the family house and arrested everyone. An Ethiopian official running the detention camp told the family that they could not take 'Tigisti' to Eritrea because there were no legal documents proving that she was a member of the family. After a bitter argument her 'father' signed over responsibility for her to the official, following which the family was deported.

The official took her to his home and for a brief period treated her well. However, he tried to make her his 'girlfriend' and demanded that she go to bed with him. She refused his advances and he became increasingly violent towards her. One night he came home drunk and raped her. The next day he threatened her by saying that he would prevent her from joining her 'family' in Eritrea if she reported the incident. 'Tigisti' felt desperate and remained in the house hoping to be sent to Eritrea, but this never happened. After a few months she ran from the house but, because she had not registered as an alien in 1999, she earned a living as a prostitute. In 2004 she attempted to register with the authorities but, on going to the registration office she encountered the same official who had raped her and fled from the office. 'Tigisti' has given up all hope of being registered and survives by working as a prostitute.

Individual testimony demonstrates the brutal way that 'Eritreans' were treated and makes it clear that from July 1998 onwards individuals *were* singled out on the basis of their *presumed* 'Eritrean' ethnicity (UNDP 1998; Klein 1998: 10–12).

Following their arrest 'Eritreans' were held in temporary prisons run by local *kebele* (sometimes a prison but often an empty house or a lockable store), in temporary detention centres and even in metal shipping containers. Detainees were not provided with food or water (which was brought to them by family and friends; see Klein 1998: 3; HRW 2003a: 22 *passim*). Officials routinely removed or destroyed detainees' identity documents and personal papers (e.g. passports, school records, birth certificates, driving licenses) to ensure that expellees would not be able to prove their identity/entitlement to Ethiopian citizenship (Global IDP Project 2003: 6; Klein 1998: 8; Amnesty International 1999:19; Byrne 2002: 13; HRW 2003a: 21). Such actions violated Ethiopian and international law.[23]

While in detention 'Eritreans' were told to sign blank pieces of paper to transfer the power of attorney to Ethiopian officials who would keep their property safe (HRW 2003a: 22 f.; Eritrea 2002 ¶2.185 f.). Most detainees refused to sign such papers and/or they sought the right to assign power of attorney to a relative (as in Case 1). Whether or not they signed such papers all the property they were unable to sell prior to their expulsion was confiscated.

Transport to the Eritrean border by bus took from three to five days. Individuals were packed into buses like cattle and little if any food or water was provided. By late 1998 or early 1999 the number of persons expelled rose to 1,500 per week. The major limitation facing Ethiopia's policy of expulsions was logistical: given the continuing war with Eritrea there was a shortage of vehicles available to transport 'Eritreans' to the border (HRW 2003a: 26). Once they reached the border individuals were issued with a piece of paper marked 'expelled, never to return' and forced to walk across the border/war zone at night.

Ethiopia stopped expelling 'Eritreans' in March 2002 – nearly two years after the ceasefire came into effect – by which time an estimated 75,000 people had been expelled and denationalized (Global IDP Project 2003). As Byrne observed, the term 'deportation' – used by Ethiopia *and* Eritrea to legitimize their actions – 'connotes a legal process by which a person is required to leave a country' whereas the overwhelming evidence 'points to the absence of due process' (2002: iv). As the US Department of State (2002: 9) noted about the situation in Ethiopia at the time:

> The Government's actions raised serious issues of due process since there were no preliminary hearings to determine the merits of the deportations, no right to counsel was provided to detainees, and detainees only had a very circumscribed opportunity to register protests. In addition, the issue of the nationality of Eritrean-origin Ethiopians has not been settled.

Beginning in 1999 all 'Eritreans' who remained in Ethiopia were stripped of their nationality by decree and required to register with the immigration authority to obtain an 'alien residence permit'.[24] Registration identified all remaining 'Eritreans' and denationalized them. The process involved the following steps: (a) individuals were ordered to surrender their Ethiopian documents; (b) when their documents were turned in they were stamped 'Eritrean'; (c) individuals were then instructed to obtain a residence card, which carried a mandatory fee of 100 birr; (d) if the individual stated that they were born in Ethiopia their card nevertheless was marked to indicate birth in Eritrea (Eritrea 2002: ¶2,103 f). The process of applying for a card could take many months or a few days, and it could involve interrogation (Refugees International 2009). The identity card had to be renewed every six months.

'Eritreans' were issued a special 'yellow card' with their personal details on it. However:

> Those who were not registered were required to demonstrate that they were unable to do so at the registration time and to provide evidence of their whereabouts during that time to obtain an identity card and a residence permit. Those individuals without registration cards did not have access to hospitals or other public services.

> (US Department of State 2002: 16)

In 2002 Ethiopia admitted to having registered only 24,018 'Eritreans' (EECC 2009: ¶256). This figure appears to be a deliberate miscalculation for it is far below all previous estimates of the size of this ethnic group and, as will be shown later, it does not include all resident 'Eritreans' (see Chapter 4).

Conclusion

Historical and political factors help explain the deep ideological divisions between the TPLF and the EPLF, who have relied upon 'revolutionary' violence to survive and to seize and exercise power. Indeed both fronts have drawn from Marxism–Leninism and to a much lesser extent neo-liberal economic notions to define their political vision, instil discipline and project a public image that, in government, they are merely implementing their electoral mandate. However, the extent to which both states rely on violence to coerce, intimidate and/or secure compliance with policy decisions underlines the fact that, in the Horn, law serves the interests of those who hold political power.

The lack of trust between the two ruling parties, and between each party and those they govern, is reflected in the speed with which the political relationship between the two heads of state collapsed and war escalated in 1998. Rather than establish accountable institutions to address the politico-economic issues between their countries, the political leadership allowed events to escalate and they quickly used government-controlled media to give vent to old concerns and grievances about each other's conduct and the threat from the 'enemy within', i.e. dual national 'Eritreans' (in Ethiopia) and Ethiopians (in Eritrea).

In an immediate response to Eritrean aggression – which its own forces were responsible for provoking – Ethiopia escalated the conflict and arrested, detained and expelled an estimated 75,000 of its 'Eritrean' citizens. The decision to expel its nationals was well organized and occurred by targeting individuals on the basis of their presumed Eritrean ethnicity. The policy violated national and international law, and the individuals who were expelled were unable to exercise their constitutional rights as citizens. In a not too dissimilar fashion, Eritrea removed its protection from resident Ethiopians, which led to a massive flight from the country before a proper mechanism for repatriation was established.

2 Politics, law and the limitations of international arbitration at The Hague

The peace process arrived haltingly in the Horn. In August 1999 Ethiopia and Eritrea accepted the 'Framework Agreement' proposed by the OAU and the African Union, but because Ethiopia rejected the technical arrangements for its implementation the war continued (International Crisis Group 2003). In May 2000 Ethiopia launched a massive offensive which secured a great deal of the disputed territory on the border and forced Eritrea to sue for peace. The following month a ceasefire was agreed (the Algiers Agreement).

In July 2000 UN Security Council Resolution 1298 established the UN Mission in Ethiopia and Eritrea (UNMEE)[1] – the so-called 'blue hat'/peacekeeping force – which was dispatched to the region to establish a demilitarized 'Temporary Security Zone' (TMZ) located on the disputed border in Eritrean territory. UNMEE's mandate was to observe compliance with the Algiers Agreement and to monitor and verify Ethiopian and Eritrean troop movements. In December 2000 Ethiopia and Eritrea signed the Algiers Agreement under the auspices of the OAU, the UN, the European Union (EU) and the USA. The agreement required both states to terminate hostilities and, amongst other things, make submissions to two different commissions at The Hague regarding (a) claims over the border and (b) war reparations.

Accordingly, the first section of this chapter sets out the Algiers Agreement and examines the assumptions underpinning international law and of binding arbitration at The Hague. The second section examines the EEBC's arbitration of the international border between Ethiopia and Eritrea, a process that began in January 2001 and concluded in April 2002. The final section examines submissions and counter submissions to the EECC on the issues of mass expulsion, denationalization, the confiscation of private property and forcible family separation. I also look at the EECC's decisions on these issues. This process began in 2001 and ended in 2009. The chapter concludes by explaining why The Hague failed to resolve the dispute between Ethiopia and Eritrea.

The Algiers Agreement

Despite immense international pressure to mediate their dispute and suspend hostilities both states refused to do so until Ethiopia successfully broke through

Eritrean lines in late 2000 and occupied most of the disputed territory. At this point – when Ethiopia had in effect won the war militarily – Eritrea sued for peace and the international community imposed the Algiers Agreement, which was intended to break the earlier stalemate between the parties by arbitrating between their opposed positions.

The Agreement[2] contains six articles:

Art. 1(1) The parties shall permanently terminate military hostilities . . . [and] refrain from the threat or use of force against the other. (2) The parties shall respect and fully implement the provisions of the Agreement on Cessation of Hostilities.

Art. 2(1) In fulfilling their obligations under humanitarian law . . . and in cooperation with the International Committee of the Red Cross the parties shall without delay release and repatriate all prisoners of war . . . and (2) shall without delay, release and repatriate or return to their last place of residence all other persons detained as a result of the armed conflict.

Art 3(1) In order to determine the origins of the conflict, an investigation will be carried out on the incidents of 1 May 1998 and on any other incident prior to that date which could have contributed to a misunderstanding between the parties regarding their common border. . . . (2) The investigation will be carried out by an independent, impartial body appointed by the Secretary General of the OAU, in consultation with the Secretary General of the UN and the two parties. (4) The parties shall cooperate fully with the independent body.

Art 4(1) [T]he parties reaffirm the principle of respect for borders existing at independence as stated in resolution AHG/Resolution 16(1) . . . and in this regard, that they shall be determined on the basis of pertinent colonial treaties and applicable international law. (2) The parties agree that a neutral Boundary Commission . . . shall be established with a mandate to delimit and demarcate the colonial treaty border . . . (3) The Commission shall be located in The Hague. (11) The Commission shall adopt its own rules of procedure. . . . (15) The parties agree that the delimitation and demarcation determinations of the Commission shall be final and binding.

Art. 5(1) Consistent with the Framework Agreement, in which the parties commit themselves to addressing the negative socio-economic impact of the crisis on the civilian population, including the impact on the persons who have been deported, a neutral Claims Commission shall be established . . . to decide through binding arbitration all claims for loss, damage or injury by one Government against another, and by nationals (including both natural and juridical persons) of one party against the government of another party or entities owned or controlled by the other party. . . . (5) The Commission shall be lodged at The Hague. (7) The Commission shall adopt its own rules of procedure. . . . (8) Claims shall be submitted to the Commission by each of the parties on its own behalf and on behalf of its nationals . . . the Commission shall be the sole forum for adjudicating claims. . . . (9) In appropriate cases, each party may file claims on behalf of persons of Ethiopian or Eritrean origin who may not be its nationals. . . . (17) Decisions and awards of the [C]ommission shall be final and binding. The parties agree to honour all decisions and to pay any monetary awards rendered against them promptly.

Art. 6(1) This agreement shall come into force on the date of signature [12 December 2000].

Before examining how the claims were argued and decided it is important to understand why imposing a legal settlement on Ethiopia and Eritrea was always going to be problematic and how binding international arbitration works.

As the historian Christopher Clapham has astutely observed, there was a severe 'mismatch between the values and expectations with which the combatants on the one hand, and the would-be adjudicators on the other, approached the task' of deciding the boundary (and, I would add, deciding liability for reparations; 2009: 168).

The mismatch is based on differing understandings about territoriality and 'law'. The Western legal approach to territory is based on *uti possidetis*,[3] i.e. the parties to a treaty retain possession of what they had acquired at the time of independence. In this tradition claims to territory are buttressed by maps, treaties and documents (no matter what the quality or provenance of the documents may be). Eritrea, a former Italian colony, asserted its claims before the EEBC via the submission of such documents. Ethiopia, on the other hand, established its claims largely by dint of historic occupation, i.e. effective sovereign control. She had little need for maps or documents because of Italian chicanery but also because her traditional state practices differed fundamentally from modern European statecraft traditions. To the extent that Western legal traditions are based on the analysis of texts, international law may have been biased towards the better documented claim of Eritrea.

Second, and equally important, international law – which derives from the 'natural law' tradition – represents an attempt to impose a solution on a state in accord with Western notions of a 'civilized' standard of inter-state behaviour. The expectation is that states will submit their disputes for adjudication/arbitration and that they will accept the decision as binding. In Africa, and specifically in the Horn, state practice reflects the 'positive law' tradition, i.e. law serves the interests of those who hold political power. Not only is there little trust in international law, there is no expectation that other states will abide by it. As Clapham (2009: 165) has noted:

> It would . . . be difficult to find two neighbouring and conflicting states, anywhere in the world, to which the idea of subjecting their affairs to the neutral arbitration of international law would be more inherently repugnant, or which would be inclined to accord less legitimacy to the claims of international law itself. It is hard to regard their adherence to the Algiers Agreement . . . as resulting from anything more than an entirely instrumental calculation of their utility, coupled with heavy international pressure on Ethiopia, which as the militarily victorious state had the most to lose from legal adjudication.

However, the two states did not pursue their dispute via adjudication in the International Court of Justice (ICJ); they were required to submit to a legally binding arbitration process convened at The Hague. The anthropologist Laura Nader notes that this form of mediation, based on alternative dispute resolution (ADR) as this developed in the USA, reflects the distribution of international power which came to dominate international politics in the late 1970s in an effort to prevent developing countries from successfully litigating in the ICJ against the West (2002: 152). She argued (p. 153) that:

> Under the stimulus of ADR, the United States turned instead towards international negotiation' using 'teams drawn from a new professional class of negotiators and mediators . . . [who] had in common a distaste for confrontational adversarial process, for courts as a way to handle the problems of the masses.

This trend saw disputes removed from courts and put into a forum of government-to-government negotiation which favours the more powerful state. Subsequently the procedure was taken up by The Hague,[4] which adopted procedural rules requiring parties to submit to binding arbitration from which there is no appeal.

Chapter III of The EEBC's decision on the delimitation of the border sets out the procedural rules it used to decide the claims. First, treaties 'are to be interpreted in good faith'. Second, it can apply *estoppels* or *preclusion* to identify unreasonable conduct by a party in relation to actions undertaken subsequent to a treaty (i.e. in an attempt to exercise 'sovereignty on the ground'). This rule allows it to arrive at a stricter interpretation than might otherwise be agreed by treaty. Finally, the EEBC relies on various precedents which allow it to employ customary international law (not merely national law or law relating to the interpretation of treaties) to assess the material submitted to it.

The Hague's procedural rules are based on the 1992 Permanent Court of Arbitration Rules for Arbitrating Disputes Between Two States (see Chap. I, 1.2 (11).[5] The rules offer few choices to the parties on key matters and make it clear that the 'tribunal may conduct the arbitration in such a manner as it considers appropriate, provided that the parties are treated with equality and that at any stage of the proceedings each party is given a full opportunity of presenting its case' (Art. 15).

Specifically, while each party is free to submit its statement of claim and defence, they cannot amend or supplement their claim or defence without permission from the tribunal. The Hague also has the power to rule on claims by the parties that it lacks jurisdiction. In addition while each party can determine what evidence it wishes to put before the tribunal, 'each party will have the burden of proving the facts relied upon to support its claim or defence' (Art. 24) though the tribunal determines 'the admissibility, relevance, materiality and weight of the evidence offered' (Art. 25 [6]).[6] In short, The Hague possesses the authority to arrive at a decision irrespective of the submissions of the parties.

As I will argue, to the extent that binding arbitration at The Hague relies on informal, legal, reputational or political pressure on the disputing states to ensure compliance with its decisions (Gent and Shannon 2010), there is scope for state parties to refuse to comply with its decisions. The procedural rules redefine the core issue of political inequality between the disputing states into differing 'perceptions' or 'interests', which are submitted for binding resolution to an 'independent' party that imposes a decision.[7] If Nader's analysis is correct, we would expect binding arbitration between parties of relatively equal standing/status to be effective, whereas arbitration between unequal parties might be expected to reflect or *reproduce* existing political inequality without addressing the core political issues at the heart of the dispute.

The Hague's arbitration of the Ethiopia–Eritrea border dispute

The Hague quickly established the EEBC[8] and by October 2001 both parties had filed their 'memorials' and 'counter-memorials' (i.e. submissions), and had engaged in an 'exchange of replies' to the other party's submissions. Hearings convened in December 2001.

The EEBC made it clear that, despite the massive number of documents etc. submitted, it was able to establish that, '*None of the boundaries thus agreed was demarcated. Indeed, as will be seen, each of these boundaries was, to varying degrees, not fully delimited*' (my emphasis; EEBC 2002: Chap. II; ¶2.7, p. 11). The only issue agreed to by both parties was the termini of their borders with Sudan and Djibouti (ibid. Chaps IV–VII). Much of the wrangling took the form of disputes over differences in the language incorporated into treaty texts, the precise line/course of rivers named in treaties, the accuracy of maps and whether treaty maps could be compared with satellite photography etc.

The EEBC interpreted the evidence submitted by each state as sufficient to establish a geographically-defined line between the two states. The commission only varied that line slightly to reflect: (a) a preponderance of 'evidence' of effective administration – reflecting documentary evidence of referenda, local records, the structure of administration, educational facilities etc. – in a specific area[9] and (b) to render the boundary 'manageable and rational' on the ground (ibid. Chap. V; 90). In short, current and historic sensibilities and understandings, including the wishes of the population living on the border, were excluded from consideration.

Having unanimously decided the line of the boundary on a map the commission transposed the reference points to more precise geographic locations by using SPOT-satellite imagery (see Figure 2.1; ibid. Chap. VIII), which allowed it to announce its decision in April 2002. The final report, which is difficult to read, contains maps of the evidence submitted to it and maps which record its final decision. For reasons which are not clear none of the maps indicate the town of Badme, which was the flashpoint of the war (Figure 2.2).[10] In arriving at its decision the commission examined the evidence put forward by Ethiopia regarding Badme and concluded that:

These references represent the bulk of the items adduced by Ethiopia in support of its claim to have exercised administrative authority west of the Eritrean claim line. The Commission does not find in them evidence of administration of the area sufficiently clear in location, substantial in scope or extensive in time to displace the title of Eritrea that had crystallized as of 1935.

(EEBC 2002: ¶5.95, p. 84)

The commission's task was finished. All that remained was for the parties to allow UNMEE's field offices in the TMZ to implement the agreement by physically placing boundary markers.

However, a representative of the OAU who was attending the hearings mistakenly sent a message to the Ethiopian foreign minister in Addis Ababa that the EEBC had awarded Badme to Ethiopia. The minister immediately announced to the press that, 'The rule of law has prevailed over the rule of the jungle. This decision has rejected any attempt by Eritrea to get reward for its aggression . . . Badme and its surroundings belong to Ethiopia.'[11]

In May 2002, after it had become clear that it was not going to be awarded Badme, Ethiopia submitted a 'Request for Interpretation, Correction and Consultation' to the EEBC regarding the areas that Ethiopia had administered and/or occupied but which the commission had placed in Eritrea (i.e. Badme but also parts of the district of Irob; International Crisis Group 2003: 6). Ethiopia's letter questioned every aspect of the delimitation decision. In June 2002 the EEBC replied

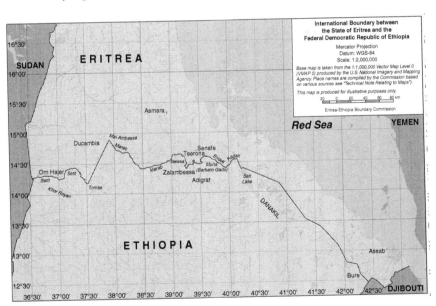

Figure 2.1 International border between Eritrea and Ethiopia as demarcated by the EEBC. Source: Map No. 13 from the list of maps 1–13 in 'The delimitation of the border between Eritrea and Ethiopia', The Eritrea–Ethiopia Boundary Commission, The Hague, 2002.

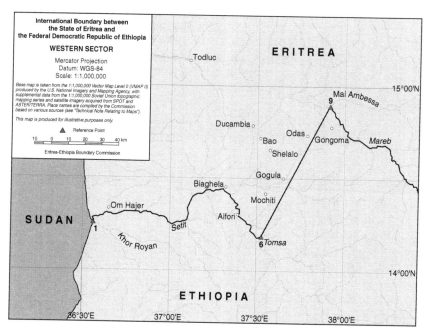

Figure 2.2   Western sector of the boundary between Eritrea and Ethiopia as demarcated by the EEBC. Source: Map No. 10 from the list of maps 1–13 in 'The delimitation of the border between Eritrea and Ethiopia', The Eritrea–Ethiopia Boundary Commission, The Hague, 2002.

to Ethiopia that its 'request appears to founder on a misapprehension regarding the scope and effect of Articles 28 and 29' of the rules of procedure, which allows requests for 'interpretation' *only* with regard to statements that require 'clarification in order that the Decision should be properly applied' (p. 3). In short, Ethiopia could not appeal or reopen 'matters clearly settled by decision'; her request was inadmissible.

At this point Ethiopia suspended cooperation with the EEBC. The Ethiopian prime minister complained that it was 'unimaginable for the Ethiopian people to accept such a blatant miscarriage of justice' and he appealed to the UN Security Council on the grounds that the decision was unfair. Furthermore he asked the Security Council to set up 'an alternative mechanism to demarcate the contested parts of the boundary in a just and legal manner' (Healy and Plaut 2007: 4). Both requests were denied.

In November 2002 the Commission issued a statement reiterating its jurisdiction and powers as set out in the Algiers Accord and noted that both parties were now required to implement its decision. It also noted that Ethiopia had failed to 'remove from Eritrean territory persons of Ethiopian origin who have moved into that territory subsequent to the date of the Delimitation Decision' (p. 2). In an attempt to break the stalemate a special representative was sent to the region but Eritrea refused to speak to him. Ethiopia met the special representative but refused to implement the Commission's decision. Instead, Ethiopian officials unsuccessfully sought diplomatic support for its position.

There matters stood until November 2006, when the EEBC reported the failure of both parties to cooperate with its decision to allow permanent boundary pillars to be affixed to the ground. As a way round this problem the commission served high-quality maps to both states on which the delimited boundary was indicated. They were given 12 months to allow the UN to demarcate the border or they would have to undertake it themselves. Failure to implement the commission's decision would, it said, result in the establishment of a 'virtual' border. In July 2008 the UN Peacekeeping Force withdrew from the TMZ having failed in its mission at a cost of $US1.32 billion.[12] To date, no physical demarcation of the border has occurred.

Arbitration of war reparation claims before the EECC

The EECC[13] met informally in mid-2001 prior to issuing key 'Decisions' in August 2001 which: defined (a) its temporal mandate/jurisdiction (i.e. only events between 12 May 1998 and 20 December 2000 would be considered); (b) the nature of claims to be filed; (c) an agreement that compensation would take monetary form; (d) a statement that the EECC is bound by rules of international law; and (e) established the procedure for making multiple/mass claims.[14] The EECC also adopted its standard rules of procedure.

An analysis of how the EECC arrived at its decisions is difficult for several reasons. First, procedural rules provided the Commission with considerable scope for defining its approach to legal and evidential submissions which, in light of the absence of a public record of the proceedings, makes it difficult to understand how it arrived at a specific decision. For instance, even though it was expressly barred[15] from interpreting the Algiers Agreement, the EECC nevertheless made findings of fact and law that Eritrea had caused the war (Box 2.1).

The term *jus a d bellum* refers to 'the branch of law that defines the legitimate reasons a state may engage in war and focuses on certain criteria that render a war just'.[16] In effect the commission decided that because Eritrea had sent troops

---

Box 2.1 The Eritrea–Ethiopia Claim Commission's 2005 *jus ad bellum* finding

'[T]he Commission holds that Eritrea violated Article 2, paragraph 4, of the Charter of the United Nations by resorting to armed force to attack and occupy Badme, then under peaceful administration by Ethiopia, as well as other territory in the Tahtay Adiabo and Laelay Adiabo weredas of Ethiopia, in an attack that began on May 12, 1998, and is liable to compensate Ethiopia, for the damages caused by that violation of international law.'

Source: EECC 2005: ¶16

into the town of Badme she was responsible for starting the war. This decision presented serious problems for Eritrea, which had wanted the events leading up to 12 May to be investigated (as had been promised by Art. 3 [1] of the Algiers Agreement). Eritrea strenuously objected to the way the Commission had arbitrarily defined its jurisdiction and to certain of its findings.

The EECC also excluded certain war-related claims from consideration on the basis that the claim was filed too late or because the submissions concerned events that occurred before or after its temporal jurisdiction.[17] A further problem concerns the standard of proof that the commission used in reaching its decisions. The procedural rules allowed the EECC to vary the standard depending upon the matter before it, which meant that the actual standard used varied and was 'somewhere between the standard of probability common in civil court proceedings in the US and the standard of "beyond a reasonable doubt" common in US criminal proceedings' (Won Kidane 2007: 72). Critically, the EECC reiterated that it 'required proof of liability by clear and convincing evidence. Thus conflicting, yet credible, evidence has perhaps resulted in fewer findings of unlawful acts than either party might expect' (EECC 2004b: ¶35).

It is worth noting that the EECC limited itself to attributing liability to one or other state and that it did not seek to determine the responsibility of individuals for illegal acts or omissions (EECC 2004a: ¶90). As already noted, because there is no record of the proceedings it is not possible to clarify the legal arguments made to the court nor is it possible to arrive at an independent assessment of the evidence submitted to the Commission.

Furthermore, and apart from the agreement of the parties to limit claims relating to mass expulsion[18] and that all compensation was to be paid to a state, it is not clear whether the parties disagreed with the commission's conduct of the enquiry or with its decisions. Nor is it clear, except with regard to some of Eritrea's submissions, which were released to me by her co-agent, precisely what legal arguments and evidence were relied upon by the parties. It is with the above reservations that I analyse the decision of the EECC in relation *only* to breaches of international law which are central to this study, namely: (a) mass expulsions; (b) denationalization; (c) forcible family separation; and (d) deprivation of property.

Both parties filed their claims and evidence in December 2001 and their counter-claims/memorials in February 2002. In the meantime, and following discussions with the parties, the Commission set out a schedule for filings and initial hearings on each claim: Eritrea's claims 'covering expellees, civilian detainees and "persons of Eritrean extraction living in Ethiopia"' (claims 15, 16, 23 and 27–32) was heard in March 2004. The Commission issued a 'partial decision' on liability on these issues in December 2004 (EECC 2004a). Ethiopia's civilian claims (claim 5) were heard in March 2004 and a 'partial decision' was issued in December 2004 (EECC 2004b).

From the outset the EECC (2004a: ¶32) observed:

> deep and wide-ranging conflicts in the evidence. The hundreds of sworn declarations submitted by the two Parties contained disagreements on many

key facts. There are sharp conflicts regarding matters as fundamental as the numbers of persons who left Ethiopia (Eritrea's evidence indicating at least twice the numbers indicated by Ethiopia's); the treatment of expellees' family members; the role of the International Committee of the Red Cross ('ICRC'); the treatment of expellees' property; and other basic issues. These massive conflicts in the evidence again show the difficulty of determining the truth in the aftermath of a bitter armed conflict. In such circumstances . . . there can indeed be 'nationalization' of the truth.

The EECC applied the fourth Geneva Convention (which provides fundamental guarantees of a minimum standard of human rights protection to all parties in a conflict[19]) and customary international humanitarian law in its assessment of the evidence.

Eritrea contended that following the outbreak of war in May 1998 'Ethiopia wrongfully denationalized, expelled, mistreated and deprived of property tens of thousands of Ethiopian citizens of Eritrean origin in violation of multiple legal obligations' (EECC 2004a: ¶10). Specifically, Eritrea argued that Ethiopia pursued 'ethnic cleansing' by 'rendering an area ethnically homogeneous by using force or intimidation to remove persons of given groups from the area' on the basis of their ethnic identity (Eritrea 2002: ¶2.03).[20]

Eritrea cited the 'precautionary measures' announced by Ethiopia in June 1998 and the subsequent official statement that 'deportation was to be a measure of last resort, judiciously employed against a carefully select group of dangerous aliens' (¶2.25). Eritrea then cited a 1998 Amnesty International report that the 'campaign swiftly degenerated from selective targeting to indiscriminate deportations', which it buttressed with evidence from a contemporaneous database compiled by the Eritrea Relief and Refugee Commission (ERREC) that 'contained the names of 32,000 expelled heads of household, accounting for a total population in excess of 71,000' people (¶2.27).[21] Such mass expulsions were, Eritrea contended, in violation of international and Ethiopian law.[22]

A key issue was whether Ethiopia instituted some form of due process to assess the individuals who were expelled, or whether individuals were arbitrarily arrested and expelled. Extensive evidence – in the form of human rights reports and witness statements – was submitted to substantiate the claim that Ethiopia had not put into place due process procedures and that 'Eritreans' were ill-treated, detained and wrongfully expelled. Citing the Ethiopian prime minister's 1998 statement justifying the expulsion of aliens by 'the colour of their eyes', Eritrea argued that the rationalization for Ethiopia's conduct was 'entirely dependent on a newly coined, and legally misconceived, re-characterization of its entire Eritrean minority community as aliens . . . [of which] by far the largest portion were legally Ethiopian nationals' (¶2.79).

For its part Ethiopia acknowledged the expulsion of a much smaller number of people but contended that all such persons had acquired Eritrean nationality by voting in the Eritrean referendum and that as aliens they were expelled legally (EECC 2004a: ¶11). Against this argument Eritrea contended that until the war began, Ethiopia did not challenge the nationality of this class of 'Eritreans'; in fact Ethiopia had continued to renew the passports of 'Eritreans'. Furthermore Eritrea did not apply mandatory national service regulations to Ethiopians of Eritrean ethnicity nor did it expect them to possess Eritrean passports (Eritrea 2002: ¶2.86). Citing a number of legal precedents Eritrea argued that deprivation of nationality 'as a form of punishment' violated international law. Finally, Eritrea argued that the individuals expelled 'were required to relinquish their Ethiopian passports upon their departure',[23] that nationals in third countries were not allowed to return to Ethiopia (and were in effect denationalized), and that currently at least 200,000 'Eritreans' resident in Ethiopia were denationalized, forced to register as aliens and deliberately impoverished (¶2.100 f.).

In support of this argument Eritrea submitted a survey of the individuals deported between June and July 1998 by an Eritrean organization called Citizens for Peace, which revealed that '80 per cent [of 'Eritrean' deportees arriving at the border] carried Ethiopian ID cards, 70 per cent of which identified the bearer as Ethiopian citizens', and that 20 per cent held Ethiopian passports (Eritrea 2002: ¶2.108).

Two important questions required an answer. First, were the individuals who were expelled dual nationals of Ethiopia and Eritrea? Second, and in light of conflicting accounts, how many people had been expelled and how many had been repatriated or had left 'voluntarily'? With respect to the first question, Ethiopia argued that by registering and voting in the 1993 referendum on Eritrean independence, individuals had acquired Eritrean nationality even though at the time Eritrea was not an independent state (EECC 2004a: ¶39 f.). Regardless of the fact that neither state had informed 'Eritreans' that voting in the referendum would have implications for their Ethiopian nationality, the commission (¶51) found that:

> those who qualified to participate in the Referendum in fact acquired dual nationality. They became citizens of the new state of Eritrea pursuant to Eritrea's Proclamation no. 21/1992, but at the same time, Ethiopia continued to regard them as its own nationals.

As Won Kidane observed of the Commission's decision, it was 'a creative resolution commensurate with its arbitral role' in dealing with unprecedented issues (2007: 53). Even so, the decision relied upon one legal theory of dual nationality.[24]

In examining whether deprivation of citizenship was arbitrary the EECC noted Ethiopia's claim that, in accord with Sec. 10 (a) of the Ethiopian Nationality Law of 1930, nationality is lost when 'an Ethiopian acquires another nationality'. However:

> Given . . . that Ethiopia did not implement that law until sometime in 1998 with respect to its nationals who had acquired Eritrean nationality between 1993 and 1998 the possibility could not be excluded that some persons who had acquired Eritrean nationality had subsequently lost it and thus were made stateless.

(EECC 2004a; ¶62)

Individuals whose cases were assessed by the immigration authority (SIRRA), were deemed to have been properly assessed and legally expelled (¶70). However, there was evidence that many 'Eritreans' had not been assessed by 'an objective decision maker' (¶71). In such cases this indicated the absence of due process and of reasonable human rights safeguards. The commission identified three classes of individuals who had been arbitrarily denationalized.

First, a large but unknown number of 'dual nationals remaining in Ethiopia' were 'deprived of their nationality and, in August 1999, [were] required . . . to present themselves and register as aliens and obtain a residence permit' (¶74). These individuals were issued with 'yellow alien identity cards.' The two parties disputed the exact number of 'yellow-card' persons: Eritrea claimed that 50,000 persons were affected; Ethiopia claimed that it had only issued 24,000 cards. Because '[t]here was no process to identify individuals warranting special consideration and no apparent possibility of review or appeal . . . [t]he Commission finds that this wide-scale deprivation of Ethiopian nationality . . . was, under the circumstances, arbitrary and contrary to international law' (¶75).

Second, the Commission found that Ethiopia arbitrarily denationalized dual nationals in third countries and those who left Ethiopia to go to third countries because, as with the 'yellow-card' people (¶76), there was no evidence that these people could reasonably be presumed to be a security threat. Nor were such persons assessed via an individualized assessment process.

Third, the Commission found that 'an unknown, but considerable number of dual nationals living in smaller towns and agricultural areas near the [Eritrean] border were also unlawfully deprived of their nationality'. This is because they were expelled without having been subject to due process; indeed most of them 'were rounded up by local authorities and forced into Eritrea for reasons that cannot be established . . . [t]he termination of the Ethiopian nationality of all such persons was arbitrary and unlawful' (¶78).

In its assessment of the evidence the EECC observed (¶80):

> Ethiopia maintained that 15,475 persons with Eritrean nationality were individually identified through its security process and then deprived of Ethiopian nationality and expelled. This is a large group, but it is less than 25% of the more than 66,000 persons in Ethiopia who qualified to vote for the Referendum. It is 3% of the more than 500,000 persons in Ethiopia both parties cited as having Eritrean antecedents . . . even if the total were much higher, the record indicates an expulsion process involving deliberation and selection, not indiscriminate round-ups and expulsions based on ethnicity. Eritrea's claim that Ethiopia engaged in indiscriminate mass expulsions based on ethnicity or in ethnic cleansing is rejected for lack of proof.

One especially contentious issue between the parties was whether Ethiopia and Eritrea had expelled each other's nationals or whether individuals 'voluntarily' left by their own means or via repatriation programmes overseen by the ICRC. In as much as 150,000 persons were estimated to have been expelled/repatriated during the war, a finding of liability could have had major implications at the compensation stage of the proceedings. This fact was not lost on either party, who had every incentive to inflate claims against each other while simultaneously minimizing their own responsibility by, for instance, withholding evidence. In short, because the EECC was not able to compel the parties to submit evidence, the very process of arbitration created a situation which ensured that the 'truth' about events during the war would be 'nationalized' by each party. It was left to the commission to arbitrate between competing 'truths'.

In fact the ICRC possessed the only complete record of the individuals who were repatriated but it forbade both states from submitting its documents to the commission because it feared that, in the future, its ability to repatriate people fleeing war and its access to prisoners of war etc. would be jeopardized (EECC 2003: ¶51 f.). The parties attempted to fill in the huge lacunae in the evidence by submitting the reports of human rights organizations[25] and their own records. Thus Ethiopia submitted files held by its Disaster Preparedness and Prevention Commission (DPPC) recording arrivals into Ethiopia from Eritrea via Tigray (which represented one part of the border through which returning Ethiopians entered the country). Eritrea submitted data from ERREC's comprehensive database. Even so, independent data regarding how individuals were returned during the war was incomplete. Both parties also sought to undermine the veracity of their opponent's submissions by deploying quite imaginative if dubious arguments and/or by undertaking a careful analysis of their opponent's evidence.

Ethiopia admitted only to lawfully expelling 15,755 'Eritreans' via an individualized assessment, and that a further 21,905 family members had left the country voluntarily (on the same buses that took expellees to the border; Eritrea 2007: ¶1.27). In short, it argued that its actions were completely legal. Against this position Eritrea (2007: ¶1.28–1.30 and *passim*) contended that Ethiopia submitted a very small number of security reports/assessments of the 'Eritreans' expelled legally (indeed Ethiopia failed to produce a list of these persons). Eritrea also argued that if Ethiopia permitted family members on to the buses then a record of their expulsion was required by law (but no such evidence was submitted). Furthermore it appeared that Ethiopia introduced special procedures which required departing 'Eritreans' to list their property and identify the dependents they were leaving behind. Finally, of course, there was a major discrepancy between the *total* number of persons Ethiopia reported as having left the country and the number of individuals on Eritrea's database. In short, Eritrea argued that because Ethiopia systematically understated the number of persons arrested and expelled its evidence constituted a denial of responsibility for its actions (¶1.40).

Faced with a mass of conflicting claims and evidence the Commission (EECC 2004a: ¶93–7) found that:

> the evidence did not permit judgements as to the nationality of the children and spouses of those said to have left 'voluntarily' (and thus whether they were illegally expelled) nor was it able to come to a judgment about 'the frequency or extent of varying types of departures.

In short, it found that Ethiopia was not liable for compelling 'Eritreans' to depart the country (voluntarily or otherwise).

Regarding the conditions under which Ethiopians departed/fled from Eritrea, Ethiopia argued that many departures were the result of 'indirect' or 'constructive' expulsions resulting from unlawful Eritrean government actions and policies' (EECC 2004: ¶91). Citing testimony by a DPPC official and various DPPC files listing the arrival of individuals in Tigray, Ethiopia argued that the physical conditions of departure were unnecessarily harsh and dangerous. It entered a claim on behalf of 33,000 persons which it said had been expelled (Eritrea 2008: ¶2.3.61).

Eritrea countered this argument by, in part, extensively analysing Ethiopia's evidence. She argued that Ethiopian evidence and legal submissions clearly indicated: (a) 'the pervasiveness of ICRC oversight of convoys carrying Ethiopian returnees to the border' (¶2.3.70); (b) that official testimony, the DPPC data and Ethiopian witness statements supported its contention of ICRC oversight (¶2.3.71 f.); (c) that during the early months of the war Ethiopians 'repatriated spontaneously', only turning to the ICRC from July 1998 onwards (¶2.3.75); (d) that DPPC data shows that thousands of Ethiopians left on commercial airlines (¶2.3.94); and finally (e) that thousands crossed the border on foot (¶2.3.97). Eritrea also sought to argue that 'in the vast majority of cases' documented by Ethiopia that the trip was not 'unduly harsh' or that the same conditions applied for ICRC repatriations and that Eritrea should not be held liable (¶2.3.109 f.).

Faced yet again with conflicting arguments and evidence, the EECC found that 'departures of Ethiopians before May 2000 in very large measure resulted from economic or other causes . . . for which the Government of Eritrea was not legally responsible' (EECC 2004b: 95). However, in relation to conditions after May 2000, when Ethiopian troops displaced 750,000 Eritrean civilians, it found 'that a very high proportion of the thousands of Ethiopians who were held in Eritrean detention camps, jails and prisons were expelled by Eritrea directly from their places of detention' (¶121). The Commission found that the expulsion of these individuals was legal and that generally, with three exceptions (see p. 67), individuals were transported by the ICRC, or under its supervision, to the border and that expellees were not exposed to harsh and hazardous conditions (¶130). Yet again, the absence of independent information from the ICRC about repatriation prevented the Commission from accurately assessing the evidence and determining liability.

Eritrea contended that Ethiopian policy constituted a deliberate and unlawful separation of 'Eritrean' families which 'resulted in suffering to large numbers of families and the children of those families'. Specifically Eritrea argued that:

> Families have been split up, the male head usually deported first, and his wife, parents and children weeks or months later. The many Ethiopians married to Eritreans are forbidden to leave and forced to watch helplessly while their spouse[s] and children are deported.
>
> (Eritrea 2002:¶2.194)

An August 1998 report by the UN Children's Fund (UNICEF) was cited indicating that '64 per cent of the expellees interviewed had left children behind; their pleas to bring their children had been ignored' (¶2.195 f.). A September 1999 report by ERREC (Figures 2.3 and 2.4) identified 1,128 children under the age of 18 who were left behind (of whom 15 per cent were completely abandoned) as a result of their parents' expulsion. The children were left in the care of a wide variety of persons, including one parent, a sibling, a relative, a maid and neighbours. Witness statements underlined the frantic efforts made to keep families together and the grief of leaving children behind, which occurred because 'men were routinely separated from their wives and families'. Indeed '[M]any of the abandoned children were subsequently expelled and had to make the trip unaccompanied'. Some families, Eritrea argued, have never been reunited.

Ethiopia contended that over 20,000 individuals left 'voluntarily' to join Eritrean expellees, to which Eritrea argued that the number was far larger and that many were compelled to leave by 'hostile conditions'. In short, 'Ethiopia left them no practical choice but to follow' their families (EECC 2004a:¶ 90).

The Commission stated that 'the evidence was not clear regarding the nationality of many family members, and the matter was not clarified during the proceedings' and further that 'the evidence does not permit judgments as to the frequency or extent of varying types of departures' (¶94). Generally speaking, Ethiopia was found not liable for the majority of 'voluntary' departures. However, there was evidence that 'some ['Eritrean'] family members were forcibly expelled' and that 'family members who did not hold Eritrean nationality were expelled' (¶97). Even so, the commission rejected the Eritrean argument that Ethiopia had pursued a policy of splitting up families.

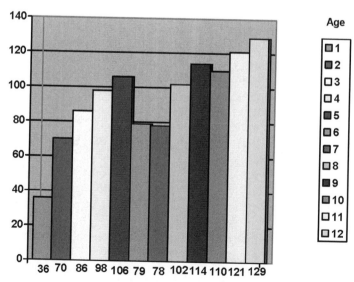

Figure 2.3 'Eritrean' children left in Ethiopia without parents, September 1999. Source: Eritrea 2002: 2.102, Chart B.

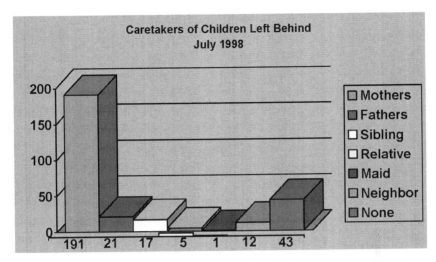

Figure 2.4   Caretakers of 'Eritrean' children left behind in Ethiopia, July 1998. Source: Eritrea 2002: 2.102, Chart C.

Regarding the claim that Ethiopia had unlawfully confiscated the private property of 'Eritreans', Eritrea:

> alleged that Ethiopia implemented a widespread program aimed at unlawfully seizing Eritrean private assets, including assets of expellees and of other persons outside of Ethiopia, and of transferring those assets to Ethiopian governmental or private interests. Ethiopia denied that it took any such actions. It contended that any losses resulted from the lawful enforcement of private parties' contract rights, or the non-discriminatory application of legitimate Ethiopian tax or other laws and regulations.
>
> (EECC 2004a: ¶123)

Citing international and Ethiopian law, Eritrea (2002: ¶2.168) argued that:

> In practice, it quickly became apparent that the goal was not merely ethnic cleansing, but 'economic cleansing', as the two primary selection criteria that emerged were Eritrean extraction and affluence. Ethiopia took quick and decisive advantage of the absence of property's owners by auctioning off or simply converting to its own use the property left behind. The BBC reported that '[o]ne aid official believes it was the wealthier Eritreans who were the first targets for deportation. Eritreans formed a substantial part of Addis Ababa's business community.'

Eritrea contended (2002: ¶2.174) that the expropriation of 'Eritrean' property took several forms, including:

arbitrary revocation of business licenses possessed by members of Ethiopia's Eritrean minority (resulting in abrupt closure of businesses, typically accompanied by expulsion of the owners); forced sale of property at a fraction of its actual market value; and direct government seizure of private property, which was then usually auctioned off at fire-sale prices, frequently to relatives or supporters of the Ethiopian government. Savings accounts, often containing substantial sums, were frozen, and once expelled the owners lost the opportunity to present their passbooks to reclaim deposits. In addition, members of Ethiopia's Eritrean minority community were often arbitrarily and illegally fired from their jobs, entailing not only loss of salary but also loss of other job-related benefits, such as accumulated pension and credit union funds.

The revocation of business licences ranged from large institutions such as the Horn Bank (with a substantial asset and savings account base) to small family-run firms. Using ERREC's database Eritrea argued that of the 28,860 heads of household expelled there were 2,182 merchants, 245 health care professionals, 114 technicians and 626 'financial intermediaries' (Eritrea 2007: ¶2.11–13). In short, 'Eritrean' expellees were well educated and relatively affluent.

The evidence regarding the forced/compulsory sale of assets and the public auction (and/or private appropriation) of houses, businesses, real estate, cars etc. was examined in Chapter 1. Many fixed assets, like blocks of flats and houses, were also 'sealed' and confiscated (including the contents of the buildings; Eritrea 2007: ¶2.184; see Case 18). A notable feature of the expropriation was the attempt by officials to convince deportees to sign power of attorney over to them, an action which is illegal in Ethiopian law (¶2.185 f.). Also, hundreds of individuals were dismissed from their jobs and expelled (e.g. from Ethiopian Airlines etc.), and the pensions of retired professionals and civil servants were terminated. The net effect of these actions was to reduce individuals and their families to penury.

Eritrea entered a claim against Ethiopia for Birr 10.1 billion (US$47 million) – of which Birr 5.1 billion was for real property, Birr 3.9 billion for movable property and Birr 760 million was for financial assets – to reimburse 22,374 'Eritrean' expellees for their losses (Eritrea 2007: ¶2.120–2.122).

Ethiopia did not deny the measures. Instead, it refuted the number of valid claims, objected to Eritrea's claim forms, objected that the types of property loss identified on the forms did not correspond to the commission's liability findings, disputed Eritrea's calculations of the value of property and argued that the proceeds from forced sales etc. had been placed in special 'blocked' accounts in the Commercial Bank of Ethiopia on behalf of affected individuals (EECC 2009: ¶326–30).

At the end of the hearing the EECC (2004b: ¶38) found Ethiopia liable for:

1.   Limiting to one month the period available for the compulsory sale of Eritrean expellees' real property;

2. The discriminatory imposition of a 100 per cent 'location tax' on proceeds from the forced sales on some expellees' real estate;
3. Maintaining a system for collecting taxes from expellees that did not meet the required minimum standards of fair and reasonable treatment; and
4. Creating and facilitating a cumulative network of economic measures, some lawful and others not, that collectively resulted in the loss of all or most of the assets in Ethiopia of Eritrean expellees, contrary to Ethiopia's duty to ensure the protection of aliens' assets.

It remained, however, for the Commission to assess the extent of Ethiopia's liability, which it calculated (EECC 2009: ¶331–54) by readjusting elements of Eritrea's claim in light of its previous findings. Thus the number of 'Eritreans' who were deprived of their Ethiopian nationality was adjusted downwards from 70,000 individuals (as contended by Eritrea) to approximately 30,000 (¶318). Because the expellees were 'less affluent' than Eritrea contended, the Commission substantially lowered the value of the assets which Ethiopia confiscated. It also expressed reservations about the value of the claims filed through Eritrea's claims process and it rejected Eritrea's claims regarding the bank accounts set up by Ethiopia for lack of evidence about their number and assets held in them – even though expellees did not have access to these accounts. However, it upheld claims regarding lack of access to personal bank accounts which Ethiopia had a duty to return to the individuals after the war. In short, because it found difficulties with the evidence submitted by both parties it arrived at its own conclusions regarding the number and value of claims which Ethiopia was held liable for.

It is worth noting that six individual 'Eritrean' claims were also decided by the EECC (EECC 2009). All six individuals alleged that Ethiopia had unlawfully deprived them of their Ethiopian nationality, but the commission found that they had been expelled lawfully or that the absence of evidence precluded a finding. However, their claims regarding Ethiopia's refusal to allow them access to their bank accounts, for the seizure of personal property and for compensation for lost investments were upheld. Under an agreement between the parties, however, any compensation on individual claims was to be paid to the Eritrean government (see 'Conclusion').

I turn now to Ethiopia's contention that Eritrea unlawfully abused its nationals. Ethiopia argued that there were seven categories of claim (EECC 2004b: ¶38): (a) physical and mental abuse out of detention; (b) other unlawful treatment out of detention; (c) confiscation and discriminatory levies; (d) unlawful arrest, detention and internment; (e) physical and mental abuse in detention; (f) unlawful conditions of detention; and (g) expulsion under inhumane conditions.

On this issue too the Commission found 'frequent glaring conflicts in the evidence and of the disputes about its accuracy and credibility'[26] (¶34) as well as a disagreement about whether and when humanitarian law ceased to apply (¶23). The Commission found it necessary to distinguish between claims relating to events before *and* after 12 December 2000, when the Algiers Agreement was signed: before this date the Geneva Convention applied but after that date international humanitarian law applied.

The Commission considered and dismissed a number of Ethiopia's claims for lack of proof or because Eritrea was not responsible for the alleged actions or omissions. The claims dismissed included (2004b: ¶46 f.):

1. Implementation of an identity card system that 'constituted a form of prohibited collective punishment or of reprisal' against Ethiopians;
2. Discriminatory dismissal of Ethiopians from jobs, publicly owned housing and revocation of business licenses (up to May 2000);
3. Harassment and the forced withdrawal of Ethiopian children from school;
4. Confiscation and discriminatory levies, i.e. exorbitant fees for identity cards and exit visas;
5. Arrests and detentions for identity card violations;
6. The rape[27] of Ethiopian women by soldiers during the conflict; and
7. 'Indirect' or 'constructive' expulsion under inhumane conditions (prior to May 2000).

With respect to the remaining allegations about incidents prior to May 2000, Ethiopia successfully argued that Eritrea failed to allow Ethiopians access to medical care because of their nationality and that Ethiopians were incarcerated in detention facilities/prisons without being charged or tried (i.e. at Hawshaite in western Eritrea in 1999). Conditions in jails, prisons and police stations were judged by the Commission to be unduly harsh and inhumane.

In relation to events after May 2000, when Ethiopian troops had launched a successful attack that displaced 750,000 Eritrean civilians, Ethiopia alleged, and the Commission upheld, that Eritrea was responsible for the physical and mental abuse – i.e. harassment, threats and acts of violence by Eritrean civilians – of Ethiopians. Ethiopia also contended that Eritrea had arrested and interred thousands of its nationals. Eritrea, for its part, maintained that it took these actions for security reasons. While evidence suggested that such actions occurred predominately in Massawa and outlying areas, the Commission found that Eritrea's actions did not indicate a 'generalized rounding up of the entire Ethiopian population'. Nevertheless, it decided that Eritrea had failed to show that the 'mass detention' of Ethiopians was 'absolutely necessary' for its security, i.e. that it satisfied Art. 42 of the fourth Geneva Convention. In detaining individuals in hurriedly prepared camps which lacked rudimentary shelter and basic facilities etc. the Commission found that Eritrea did not ensure that detainees received humane treatment. Events at Wia detention camp were the subject of further Ethiopian allegations. Specifically there was evidence, which Eritrea confirmed, regarding widespread physical violence and other forms of abuse – including torture – against Ethiopian detainees and clear and compelling evidence of an incident at which 15 Ethiopians were killed and a further 16 wounded by a camp official. Eritrea was found responsible for these actions.

There were sharply conflicting arguments about the conditions that prevailed after June 2000 when Ethiopians were leaving the country. Ethiopia argued that conditions at the time amounted to the indirect and constructive expulsion of its nationals and that it was illegal. Eritrea completely denied this argument. The commission found a way through the conflicting evidence by establishing that (EECC 2004b: ¶121–7):

(i) 'The evidence indicates that a very high proportion of the thousands of Ethiopians who were held in Eritrean detention camps, jails and prisons were expelled by Eritrea directly from their places of detention. The personal consequences of these enforced departures from Eritrea may have been harsh in many cases. Nevertheless, Eritrea acted consistently with its rights . . . '

(ii) The 'expellees were entitled to adequate opportunity to protect any property or economic interests they had in Eritrea.'

(iii) 'The evidence does not establish that other Ethiopians who left Eritrea between June and December 2000 were expelled pursuant to actions or policies of the Government of Eritrea'.

(iv) 'The record did not include any decrees, directives or other documentary evidence indicating an Eritrean Government policy of forcing the departure of other Ethiopians who were properly registered with the immigration authorities. Likewise, the evidence did not show an unwritten policy of deliberate expulsion.'

(v) 'Further, a substantial population of Ethiopians remained in Eritrea following the departures in 2000 covered by these claims . . . [thus] Ethiopia's claim that large numbers of persons who were not in detention were wrongly expelled by direct State action by Eritrea after hostilities ended must fail for lack of proof.'

Ethiopia also argued that the physical conditions under which its nationals were repatriated violated Art. 36 of the Fourth Geneva Convention. The evidence was that most Ethiopian prisoners/detainees were repatriated by the ICRC. However, in several instances individuals had been directly expelled – notably 2,700 individuals in August 2000[28] – and where this occurred Eritrea was liable for failing to ensure safe and humane conditions for such departures. Finally, it was also contended that Eritrea was responsible for the property lost by Ethiopian nationals. Once again the commission differentiated between the situation facing individuals who left voluntarily and those who were expelled: the former were judged to have had sufficient opportunity to collect personal property and make arrangements for their affairs though the latter group was denied this opportunity.

At the end of the proceedings in 2009 the EECC awarded Eritrea damages for Ethiopia's violation of international law (Box 2.2). The Commission also awarded Ethiopia damages for Eritrea's violation of international law (Box 2.3).

With respect to the four breaches of international law examined in this chapter, the commission awarded approximately US$161 million to the Government

Box 2.2 Damages awarded to Eritrea by the EECC

- $US50,000 in respect of a small number of dual nationals who were arbitrarily deprived of their nationality while present in a third country.
- $US15 million in respect of the wrongful expulsion of an unknown but considerable number of dual nationals by local Ethiopian authorities.
- $US2 million for the failure to provide human and safe treatment for persons being expelled from Ethiopia.
- $US46 million for expellee's loss of property on account of Ethiopia's wrongful actions.

Source: Compiled from EECC 2004a, 2004b, 2005 and 2009.

Box 2.3 Damages awarded to Ethiopia by the EECC

- $US11 million for death, physical injury, disappearance, forced labour and conscription of Ethiopian civilians.
- $US2 million for failure to prevent rape of known and unknown victims in Irob, Dalul and Elidar *woredas*.
- $US7.5 million for mistreatment of Ethiopian prisoners of war.
- $US2 million for failure to protect Ethiopian civilians in Eritrea from threats and violence.
- $US1.5 million for failure to ensure that Ethiopian civilians in Eritrea had access to employment.
- $US50,000 for failure to ensure that Ethiopian civilians in Eritrea were able to receive medical care to the same extent as Eritreans.
- $US2 million for wrongful detention and abusive treatment of Ethiopian civilians in Eritrean custody.
- $US1.5 million for harsh treatment of Ethiopian civilians at the Hawshaite detention camp.
- $US10 million for detaining significant numbers of Ethiopian civilians under harsh conditions during and after May 2000.
- $US500,000 for deaths and injuries suffered at Wi'a Camp.
- $US2 million for failure to protect the property of Ethiopian detainees expelled from Eritrea.
- $US1 million for failure to protect the property of other departing Ethiopians.
- $US10 million for detaining significant numbers of Ethiopian civilians under harsh conditions after May 2000.

Source: Compiled from EECC 2004a, 2004b, 2005 and 2009.

of Eritrea (including $2 million to individual Eritreans named in its claim) and approximately $174 million to the Government of Ethiopia. In each case the amount awarded was far below the sums claimed by the parties and reflected a pragmatic and cautious deliberation by the commission faced with the conflicting nature of the evidence submitted to it. However, both states have refused to pay compensation.

Conclusion

Somewhat paradoxically, and seemingly oblivious to the violence on the battlefield and towards 'the enemy within', the international community imposed the terms of peace. While the fighting ended when both states signed the Algiers Agreement, the terms of the agreement and the stipulation that both states submit to binding arbitration at The Hague was bound to fail. The idea that the Security Council could impose a solution on Ethiopia and Eritrea in accord with Western notions of a 'civilized' standard of inter-state behaviour was quickly proved wrong.

The reason why The Hague proved to be an inappropriate forum is due to The Hague's procedural rules, which give it the power to decide the evidence and impose a binding decision. The rules redefine and transform the core political issues underlying the conflict into a matter of differing 'perceptions' or 'interests' which are subject to binding resolution. However, The Hague's decisions did not bind the parties. There are two possible explanations for the failure of The Hague. First, Ethiopia and Eritrea are firm adherents of the tradition of 'positive law' – i.e. that law serves the interests of those who hold power. In short, neither party trusted The Hague to find a solution which supported its position. Second, and equally important, binding arbitration might have had some purchase on the two states early in the conflict but, following Ethiopia's seizure of the disputed territory in mid-2000, arbitration could only be achieved at the expense of Ethiopia's costly victory over Eritrea on the battlefield.

In effect, by submitting the dispute to arbitration the political issues between the two states were left to The Hague to deal with or ignore at its own peril. It chose to ignore them. By failing to consider regional politics and the initial cause of the war, namely a military clash over the town of Badme, The Hague's decision was guaranteed to rebound against it. The situation was further compounded by the decisions of the EEBC which, among other things, made a *jus ad bellum* finding that Eritrea caused the war.

The problems did not end there. Procedural rules required that both parties establish 'clear and convincing evidence' about violations which occurred in a 'frequent or pervasive manner'. Because this did not happen the EECC made relatively few 'findings of unlawful acts'. The problem arose from its role as the arbiter of truth: in the face of 'deep and wide ranging conflicts in the evidence', the absence of proof, and the failure of both parties to assist it to find the truth it was left to the EECC to define a 'truth'. In short, the arbitration process created a situation in which both parties had every reason to 'nationalize the truth' to prevent the commission from making findings of fact and deciding liability against them for breaching international law.

By 2002, Eritrea and Ethiopia had both refused to be bound by the findings of the EEBC. Well before the EECC issued its final decision in 2009, events in the Horn had completely undermined the Algiers Agreement and cost the UN dearly in prestige and money. Today the border remains un-demarcated, no compensation has been paid and Eritrean and Ethiopian troops once again face each other across a disputed border.

3 Flight from the Horn

Transiting Africa to find refuge

In contrast to the international community, 'Eritreans' did not look to The Hague to remedy their difficulties. Those who were expelled from Ethiopia quickly moved on in search of refuge and in an attempt to find family members. 'Eritreans' in Ethiopia, however, confronted a very different set of choices: they could (initially) repatriate to Eritrea; they might remain as aliens in Ethiopia (in the face of ethnic discrimination) or they could leave the Horn. This chapter situates the flight of 'Eritreans' within a larger exodus of people leaving the Horn. The first section, 'Politics, repatriation and the haemorrhage of population from the Horn', examines the ICRC's post-war repatriation of individuals from Ethiopia and Eritrea and a second, unregulated, movement of people out of Eritrea as refugees. The second section, 'Transit routes out of the Horn and the experience of flight', examines the movement of 'Eritreans' (and others) out of the Horn as they merge with a much larger, heterogeneous flow of individuals fleeing political persecution and/or seeking economic betterment. All of these individuals are moving outwards along one of four 'transit' routes, each of which contains its own difficulties and dangers. The different routes are examined in some detail. I conclude by noting that there are tens of thousands of 'Eritreans' in Ethiopia who are likely to leave and thousands stuck in transit across Africa who are looking for refuge; however, a relatively small number of individuals make it to the West.

Politics, repatriation and the haemorrhage of population from the Horn

After the peace agreement of December 2000 the border between Eritrea and Ethiopia was to have been demarcated and political relations normalized. The Algiers Agreement called for prisoners of war and all other individuals who wished to return to 'their last place of residence' to be repatriated under the auspices of the ICRC and, by 2008, approximately 30,000 people had been repatriated (Table 3.1).

The repatriation programme gradually became hostage to the unresolved political problems between Eritrea and Ethiopia and, in 2009, Eritrea suspended cooperation with the ICRC, citing Ethiopia's 'unilateral cancellation of two repatriation operations in late 2008 and early 2009'.[1] Eritrea's decision followed her refusal to cooperate with The Hague and growing international isolation. While there has

Table 3.1 International Committee of the Red Cross (ICRC) repatriations, 2001–2009

Year	Repatriations to Eritrea	Repatriations to Ethiopia
2001	n/a	21,255
2002	1,373	703
2003	A total of 1,041 persons from both states	
2004	174	798
2005	44	848
2006	40	934
2007	72	2,360
2008	52	1,766
2009	Eritrea suspended cooperation with the ICRC	
Total	1,755	28,664

Source: ICRC annual reports for Eritrea and Ethiopia.

been some irregular, informal return of individuals from Eritrea via the Sudan to Ethiopia, repatriation under the auspices of the ICRC stopped in 2009, leaving an unknown number of individuals stranded in both countries.

Shortly after the Algiers Agreement was signed a trickle of young people began to leave Eritrea to escape conscription by illegally crossing into the Sudan and Ethiopia. That trickle developed into a haemorrhage as growing numbers of people of all ages and both genders have continued to leave (Table 3.2). Once across the border into Ethiopia, individuals are picked up by soldiers and taken to an office of the National Intelligence and Security Services, Administration of Refugee and Retournee Affairs (ARRA), where they are interviewed. Officials and senior military officers are separated and taken away to help ARRA with its work (many are not registered with UNHCR). Everyone else is taken to UNHCR, which registers them as a refugee and places them in a refugee camp in northern Ethiopia.

In the spring of 2010 the situation in the camps was said to be poor: there were few facilities and the quality of shelter was very poor. Eritrean opposition political

Table 3.2 Eritrean refugees in Ethiopia, by year

Year	Number
2002	1,066
2003	1,580
2004	2,187
2005	2,966
2006	13,078
2007	14,218
2008	16,674
2009	19,174
2010	44,790
2011	51,298
2012 (January)	59,090
2013 (January)	92,900

Source: *UNHCR Statistical Yearbook* 2005, p. 329, Table C; *UNHCR Country Operations Plan 2008 (Ethiopia)*; *UNHCR Statistical Yearbook* 2010, p. 79, Table 5; *UNHCR Country Operations Profile 2012 – Ethiopia*, p. 2; *UNHCR Ethiopia Monthly Refugee Update* February 2012, p.2.

parties hosted by Ethiopia were given access to the camps to recruit new members and, inevitably, there were concerns about resettlement. A relatively small number of individuals were issued 'urban refugee' permits, which allowed them to leave the camp to reside in a designated town; however, individuals often walked out of the camps and made their way to Addis Ababa, Sudan, Egypt and Israel (see Chapter 4).

Accurate statistics on the number of Eritreans who fled to the Sudan are not available (in any event many will have transited to another country without registering with UNHCR, see Table 3.4) but it is possible that an equally large number have taken this route out. Those fleeing Eritrea[2] include nationals of Eritrea *and* a large number of 'Eritreans' who had previously been expelled into Eritrea. The exodus of population is directly related to deteriorating socio-political conditions in Eritrea in the wake of the internal coup in 2001, permanent military conscription and deteriorating human rights (Gaim Kibreab 2009; HRW 2009).

Clearly the political and economic conditions that would allow 'Eritreans' and others affected by the war to re-establish their lives were not established, a fact which has led thousands of individuals to leave. In fleeing the region 'Eritreans' merge and become indistinguishable from others fleeing previous conflicts, including individuals: (a) from ethnic groups fleeing political 'persecution' as supporters of banned political parties (e.g. Oromo supporters of the Oromo Liberation Front [OLF]); (b) from liberation fronts/political parties involved in the Eritrean revolution (e.g. supporters of the ELF and associated splinter parties in the Sudan, and former members of the EPLF); (c) from political groups who supported autonomy in the Ogaden (e.g. the Ogaden National Liberation Front backed by Somalia); and finally (d) tens of thousands of Somalis displaced by war.

Tables 3.3 and 3.4 summarize UNHCR data on the number of Ethiopian and Eritrean refugees for the period from 1992 to 2010. The tables indicate that the volume of refugees fleeing the Horn – 148,900 Ethiopians per annum in the 1990s declining to 52,300 per annum between 2000 and 2010, and 371,800 Eritrean refugees per annum in the 1990s declining to 172,600 per annum between 2000 and 2010 – totalled 6.26 million persons. Ethiopia, Eritrea and other states in the region have used refugees to further national interests in a process that has internationalized conflict and exacerbated the scale of population displacement and exodus (Assefa Bariagaber 1999). Long before the 1998 war, repatriation exercises have been held hostage by regional politics.

In recent years the scale and recurring nature of refugee flows in the Horn, which produced 61 per cent of Africa's refugee population in 2010 (UNHCR 2011c: Table 1), has contributed to the West's growing reluctance to fund UNHCR. The most recent evidence of 'donor fatigue' became apparent in 2010 when donors pledged just US$477.5 million towards the UN refugee agency's appeal for US$3 billion.[3] The West's unwillingness to fund UNHCR means that many internally displaced persons (IDPs) are unable to return to their homes for fear of violence, that states which have hosted refugees in the past now refuse refugees the possibility of integration/settlement and that 'Eritreans' and others currently transiting Africa confront high levels of extortion and violence.

Table 3.3 Ethiopian refugees by main countries of asylum, 1992–2010

	1992	1993	1994	1995	1996	1997	1998	1999	2000	2001
Kenya	68.6	26.5	10.5	8.5	7.1	8.6	8.1	8.2	4.1	13.5
Djibouti	8.0	16.4	12.8	6.0	2.0	2.0	1.9	1.6	1.5	1.4
Sudan	200.9	173.2	160.6	48.1	51.5	44.3	35.6	35.4	34.1	16.1
Yemen	—	—	—	—	—	2.5	—	—	—	—
Canada	—	—	—	—	3.8	2.5	1.7	1.4	1.6	2.0
UK	3.5	5.0	7.8	5.7	5.0	5.0	4.8	4.4	4.9	0.7
USA	15.6	16.7	5.0	5.0	10.2	7.8	5.6	7.8	9.8	5.1
Sweden	8.6	8.5	16.7	13.3	7.6	6.4	5.0	3.3	2.1	11.5
Other	—	—	8.5	8.2	23.7	21.1	19.7	18.2	16.8	15.7
Total	305.2	246.3	221.9	94.8	96.2	84.4	70.6	71.0	66.4	59.0

	2002	2003	2004	2005	2006	2007	2008	2009	2010
Kenya	11,200	11.1	12.6	14.8	16.4	18.1	22.6	17.1	21.2
Djibouti	1,400	1.6	—	—	—	—	—	—	—
Sudan	14,600	15.3	14.8	14.6	11.0	1.4	8.6	9.1	9.1
Canada	2,200	2.9	3.5	4.0	—	—	—	—	—
UK	3,100	2.2	—	—	—	—	—	—	—
USA	12,500	12.8	12.9	13.8	24.8	—	12.5	12.2	13.5
Sweden	400	0.4	—	—	—	—	—	—	—
Germany	8.1	8.0	6.6	5.1	—	—	—	—	—
Other	12.6	12.6	12.5	13.0	—	—	—	—	—
Total	61.2	62.6	63.1	65.4	52.2	19.5	43.7	38.4	43.8

Source: *UNHCR Statistical Yearbook* (various years).

Table 3.4 Eritrean refugees by main countries of asylum, 1992–2010

	1992	1993	1994	1995	1996	1997	1998	1999	2000	2001	2002	2003	2004	2005	2006	2007	2008	2009	2010
Sudan	502.6	424.5	419.3	282.8	328.3	315.0	342.3	342.1	37.7	324.5	305.3	108.3	110.9	116.7	157.2	108.8	124.7	113.5	103.8
Ethiopia	—	—	—	—	—	—	—	—	3.2	4.2	5.1	6.7	8.7	10.7	13.1	20.7	21.0	36.1	44.8
Israel	—	—	—	—	—	—	—	—	—	—	—	—	—	—	—	—	—	11.8	17.0
Italy	—	—	—	—	—	—	—	—	—	40	94	177	785	2.7	5.0	—	9.0	10.3	11.0
Switzerland	—	—	—	—	—	—	—	—	—	—	—	—	—	—	—	—	—	—	7.0
UK	—	—	—	—	—	—	—	—	—	—	975	1.7	2.4	3.6	—	—	7.7	8.8	9.4
Germany	—	—	—	—	—	—	—	—	—	—	2.5	2.7	2.9	2.7	—	—	—	—	—
Other	—	—	—	—	3.9	4.0	4.4	5.0	5.8	4.4	4.1	4.4	5.3	7.5	—	—	—	—	—
Total	502.6	424.5	410.3	282.8	332.2	319.1	346.8	347.1	376.8	333.2	318.1	124.1	131.1	144.1	175.0	129.5	162.4	190.5	192.6

Source: *UNHCR Statistical Yearbook* (various years).

In addition to refugees there are an unknown number of displaced/dispossessed people who are also on the move. Attempts to conceptualize and explain this phenomenon became mired in a sterile debate: do such people leave their countries voluntarily or are they forced out? Are they voluntary migrants, forced migrants or refugees fleeing persecution? Turton (2003) has argued that research on this issue has tended to focus on the 'motives' of migrants rather than on the way a nation governs its nationals and 'ethnic' minorities.

For this reason the dichotomy – voluntary/forced – and a focus on the 'intention' of individuals is too simplistic to grasp the complex factors behind large-scale population displacement and movement. Reflecting this concern Papadopolou has argued (2005: 4) that:

> the intention [of the migrant] is not always clear at the beginning of the journey, but is usually affected by the structural context of the first country of reception and by the nature, operation and inter-relations of an individual's social network.

A number of factors contribute to large-scale population movement, including 'push' factors, geography and state policies. For instance, individuals leave their country of origin in response to poverty, the absence of employment, poor/inadequate services, discrimination and/or persecution as well as a desire for family reunification. The geographic location of a country may also be a factor. Thus countries located near to, or the route to, a more desirable state tend to attract sojourners. Finally, state policies directed at 'foreigners' also affect population movement – for example, the impact of existing laws or administrative procedures regarding migration and asylum is often critical, as is the effect of policing, border controls and venal officials etc., all of which can bottle up or propel individuals along transit routes (Papadopoulou 2005). In short, sojourners often do not settle in the first country they arrive in and they may become bottled up somewhere along a route for varying periods of time. It is also important to note that (ibid.: 5):

> most transit countries have increasingly become themselves countries of destination, either because their own economic situation and administrative systems are improving, or because the migrants' temporary waiting periods have been transformed to *de facto* formalized or semi-official extended residence.

Transit routes out of the Horn and the experience of flight

In the 19th century the initial impetus driving people out of the Horn was to escape drought in the mountainous highland areas. Displacement tended to be into the Sudan (Gaim Kibreab 1996: 135), east/north-east into Somalia or Djibouti (Ingrams and Pankhurst 2006) or southward into the lowlands. More recently a fourth route has been established via commercial air travel to Europe and North America (some smuggling on seaborne vessels also occurs). Each route has expanded and changed over time as individuals and smugglers encounter new obstacles, 'costs' and difficulties along a route.

Some early sojourners settled along the land routes and, in subsequent years, came to play an important role in sheltering, feeding and assisting those who followed. Population movement from the late 19th century onwards was characterized by rapid, episodic movements of large numbers of people seeking temporary refuge from famine, drought and war, followed by their subsequent return. However, since the late 1960s growing numbers of people have embarked on a transcontinental journey out of the Horn with little intention of returning.

In terms of the volume of human traffic, the *principal route* out has been west into the Sudan (Figure 3.1). Thus in early 1967 about 60,000 'Ethiopians' – at this time Eritrea was a province of Ethiopia – resided in Sudan due to civil war. By mid-1967 conflict displaced a further 26,000 refugees into Sudan. Successive waves of refugees were to follow the 1974 coup against Haile Selassie (Smock 1982).

During the 1983–4 famine 190,000 people were displaced from Tigray (northern Ethiopia) into the Sudan, though most returned (Assefa Bariagaber 1999: 610). However, thousands more soon arrived following their escape from resettlement schemes in southern Ethiopia, where the government had forcibly moved 600,000 people from the northern highlands (Clay and Holcomb 1985; Yintinso Gebre 2002). In 1980 there were 390,000 Eritreans and Ethiopians in Sudan; by 1994 the number reached 850,000. Between 1984 and 1991 only 33,195 of these refugees

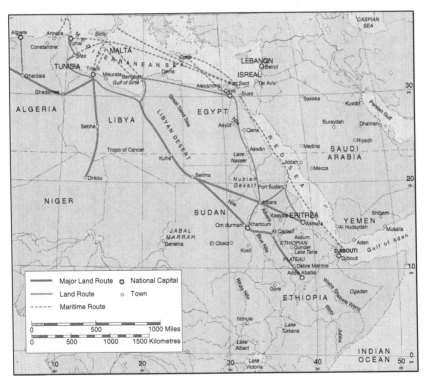

Figure 3.1 Transit route from Ethiopia/Eritrea to Libya and Egypt via Khartoum. Source: Horwood 2009: 45.

had been resettled in the USA and only 11,060 were resettled in Canada (Tekle Woldemikael 1998; Matsuoka and Sorenson 2001: 60).

Individuals living in Sudanese refugee camps received limited humanitarian assistance, which led many to move to small regional towns and to Khartoum, where they worked and lived illegally (and/or relied on remittances from relatives; Kuhlman 1994: Chap. 8; Smock 1982; Weaver 1985; Gaim Kibreab 1996). In 1994 an estimated 40,000 refugees were living illegally in Khartoum; by 2001 the number had increased to 237,000 (UNHCR 2001). The authorities made life difficult for refugees by refusing to countenance self-settlement and by imposing restrictions on their movement, on employment and on access to services. Indeed, throughout the 1980s and 1990s the authorities *refouled* Ethiopian/Eritrean refugees.

With the success of the EPLF in the late 1980s it became possible for Eritreans to return home from camps in Sudan. Following independence in 1993 about 130,000 returned voluntarily. However, as late as 2005 an estimated 116,000 remained in Sudan where, as supporters of banned political parties, they applied for refugee status (Bascom 2005: 167; Rake 2007: 437). There are many reasons why individuals have been unwilling to return. Some believe that their land and homes had been occupied by strangers, but many are also integrated into Sudanese society. Furthermore, conditions in Eritrea during the mid-1990s were poor; severe drought undermined agricultural production (70 per cent of the population depended on food aid[4]) and the Eritrean government instituted compulsory military conscription.

In 1992 UNHCR invoked the cessation clause for Eritrean refugees and in 1999 it invoked the cessation clause for Ethiopian refugees. This meant that from 1992 and 1999, respectively, Eritreans and Ethiopians 'no longer had a well-founded fear of persecution' and could lawfully be returned to their country of origin.[5] Those who refused to return faced a stark choice: they could stay illegally – in which case they might be arrested and forcibly returned[6] – or they could move elsewhere (see Cases 8 and 12).[7]

Case 12

In November 2009 a young man named 'Million' walked across the USA–Mexico border and claimed asylum. He had been born in Addis Ababa but moved to Eritrea in 1994, where he attended school and became a Pentecostal Christian. In 1999 his family in Ethiopia were arrested and deported to Eritrea. On completion of his education in 2002 he was conscripted into the Eritrean military. After he reported an official for corruption he was imprisoned and tortured but managed to escape to Sudan in December 2008 (where he hid from the authorities for seven months). He then travelled by plane to Dubai, from where he flew to Moscow, to Havana and on to Quito, Ecuador. He travelled by car to Colombia, by boat to Nicaragua, by truck to Mexico (where he stayed for one month to recover from an injury) before entering the USA. He was granted asylum in April 2012.

The political situation in Sudan led some refuges to move north to Cairo while others moved north-west into Libya. 'Ethiopians' arrived in Cairo in four 'waves': in 1978–9 (to escape the 'red terror'); in 1984–8 (to escape conscription); in the early 1990s (when the *Derg* fell); and following the 1998–2000 border war (Cooper 1992: Table 1.6, p. 13; Zohry and Harrel-Bond 2003: 57–8).

The experience of Taddele (1991) illustrates how individuals moved along this route. In 1982, Taddele, a minor government official, was accused of belonging to a banned political party. To escape prison he walked for 13 days to reach the Sudanese border. It took another three days to reach a town (where he was jailed). On release he made his way to the town of Gedaref, where he registered as a refugee and worked for several months. He then travelled to Khartoum and worked. He met an Ethiopian who had been deported from Egypt and decided to go to Cairo. On the train to the Egyptian border he joined a small group of Eritreans but the party got lost in the desert. They stumbled into fishermen on the Nile who fed, sheltered and helped them to reach Aswan, from where they boarded a train to Cairo.

The 'Ethiopian' population in Cairo is in constant flux because individuals whose asylum claims are not recognized by UNHCR, and most are not, move on (Cooper 1992: 17). 'Ethiopians' live in small apartments dispersed across the city, often with others of the same ethnicity. Cooper describes them as forming 'mini-communities' whose day-to-day lives consist of going to the UNHCR office and attending Protestant churches or non-governmental organizations (NGOs) in search of support (1992: 25; Brown, Riordan and Sharpe 2004). In the early 1990s the 'community' was composed of single men in their mid-twenties who came from towns and had middle-class backgrounds (Cooper 1992:17). While 19 per cent arrived on a direct flight, over half had spent two or more years in Sudan, Djibouti, Somalia or Saudi Arabia before reaching Cairo. They are in every sense long-term sojourners who are constantly on the move.

In Cairo, as in Khartoum and elsewhere, they face discrimination and racism and must live and work illegally. Even with valid ID they are frequently harassed and arrested by the authorities or blackmailed by ordinary Egyptians. An unknown number are detained before being deported (to the Sudanese border or just dumped in the desert). Some of those who are deported find their way back. In 1992 there were perhaps 1,000 Ethiopians in Cairo; by 2002 the number had risen to 5,000.

In 2002 the community included some single women, some families, Eritrean nationals and an unknown number of stateless persons who had been deported and/or stripped of their nationality by Ethiopia during the war (Thomas 2006). Once their asylum claim is refused by UNHCR these individuals live in poverty and, without access to medical or social services, they are dependent on the support provided by a small number of Protestant churches. Neither the Eritrean nor Ethiopian embassy will assist 'mixed nationals', i.e. 'Eritreans' because officials say as 'the son of a snake' they 'have no place' back home (p. 19).[8] It is not surprising that 'Ethiopians' move on fairly quickly.

In December 2005 a demonstration by Sudanese refugees outside the UNHCR office in Cairo was crushed by the police.[9] Refugees reacted to this event by crossing the Sinai and entering Israel. The arrival of Eritreans in Israel prompted the Eritrean ambassador to demand that they be deported as military deserters.[10] Today, more than 60,000 Africans – of whom 58 per cent are Eritrean nationals and an estimated 350 are stateless 'Eritreans' – are seeking asylum in Israel. Here too they are discriminated against and refused the right to work and access to basic services; their asylum claims are not registered and they face arrest and expulsion as economic migrants/'infiltrators' (Campbell *et al.*, forthcoming).

Case 13

'Shewit' was born in Ethiopia in 1988 to an Ethiopian father and, as she subsequently learned, an Eritrean mother. She grew up in Ethiopia without experiencing any difficulties but in 2009 she was contacted by two Eritrean half-brothers who had fled Eritrea to the Sudan. She immediately left for Sudan to join them. They travelled to Libya but were unable to cross the Mediterranean to Italy (where another brother lived) so they returned to Sudan (where one brother remained) before travelling to Egypt and on to Israel, where they arrived in 2010. The brother who travelled with her was recognized by the authorities as an Eritrean national and given temporary status but she was arrested and detained. Without assessing her asylum claim the authorities decided that she was an Ethiopian national and began proceedings to deport her. 'Shewit' provided documentation attesting to her Eritrean nationality, including a letter from the Eritrean embassy in Tel Aviv, but this evidence was set aside and in early 2012 she was deported to Ethiopia.

In the early 1990s a second stream of sojourners paid smugglers to take them from Khartoum north-west across the Sahara to Libya, which has been an important destination for hundreds of thousands of Africans. The journey to Kufra, an oasis just inside Libya, takes six days by truck[11]but many do not survive the trip (Fortress Europe 2007). Sojourners pay to be taken to Tripoli but nearly all are forced out at Kufra, where they were detained by the authorities in an attempt to extort money from them (Hamood 2006: 31, footnote 23).

In 1992, following the imposition of a UN air and arms embargo, Libya encouraged labour migration from West Africa and the Horn (Hamood 2006, 2008; Bakewell and de Hass 2007). However, changes in the Libyan economy and growing resentment against foreigners resulted in an anti-immigrant backlash and the adoption of repressive measures against foreigners. As early as 1994 1,000 Eritreans/Ethiopians were detained and repatriated. By May 2007 approximately 60,000 Africans were held in detention centres and prisons across Libya. Reports suggest that up to 600 Eritreans (including women and children) were detained in 2006 (Amnesty International 2005, 2006; Fortress Europe 2007: 6). Between 2003 and early 2007 – a period of political rapprochement with Europe – Libya deported 258,000 'irregular immigrants'. Detainees were routinely subjected to beatings and abuse. Once in detention they had four options: (a) bribe their way out; (b) those unable to pay were taken to a detention centre in the south where, on threat of expulsion, they paid to be released; failing which (c) they were kept hostage (and their family overseas must pay a ransom to release them); finally (d) they were deported (either by plane or they were dumped in the desert; Fortress Europe 2007: 5). Between 1998 and 2003 approximately 14,000 people were dumped in the desert, where many must have died (p. 4).

In 2004 two chartered planes were used to deport 'irregular immigrants'. Most of the one-hundred Eritreans on the first flight to Asmara were detained, beaten, interrogated and imprisoned on arrival in Asmara.[12] The second flight, containing 60 persons, was hijacked over Sudan and forced to land in Khartoum, where many were granted asylum.[13]

To date, Libya does not have an immigration policy or asylum procedures (Baldwin-Edwards 2006: 10) nor is it a signatory to the 1951 Geneva Convention. In 2007 Libya entered into bilateral agreements with Italy and the EU to accept individuals intercepted on the Mediterranean; Libya then deported these individuals to their country of origin without assessing their asylum claims. Despite the lack of protection for refugees and migrants in Libya, the EU established 'external border controls' there aimed at preventing the illegal entry of Africans into Europe (Boswell 2003). EU cooperation continued despite Libya's treatment of migrants and smuggling operations worth an estimated €100 million per annum (Fortress Europe 2007: 7).

Case 14

'Lemlem' was born in Ethiopia in 1985 to an Ethiopian father and an Eritrean mother. In 1998, while living in Addis Ababa, her mother was arrested and told that she would be deported to Eritrea. She was released to prepare herself and her daughter to be bussed to the Eritrean border. To avoid expulsion her mother decided to take her daughter to Sudan. In 2006 'Lemlem' left on her own for Libya. In 2008 she travelled to Cairo and entered Israel by crossing the Sinai. In mid-2012 the Israeli authorities decided that she was 'Ethiopian' and, using an unpublished 'return agreement' with Ethiopia, they attempted to deport her without assessing her asylum claim. Following legal intervention the authorities agreed to undertake a new assessment of her claim which was summarily refused. 'Lemlem' is now appealing against that refusal.

Today Libya remains a principal staging post for sojourners attempting to enter southern Europe.[14] It is from Libya that many Africans secure a boat to cross the

Mediterranean only to arrive at Lampedusa (Italy) or Malta. Though the number of individuals arriving in Italy via Libya was down by one-fifth in early 2007 (to 12,753), nevertheless 21,400 sojourners landed in Sicily in 2006, including 2,500 Eritreans (Fortress Europe 2007: 8). In 2008 an estimated 59,000 individuals landed in Italy followed by a four-year decline due to Italian naval interceptions (Table 3.5) and political turmoil in north Africa. Approximately 54,000 individuals crossed the Mediterranean to Italy in 2011. The number of sojourners who died crossing the Mediterranean between 1998 and July 2012 is estimated at 13,500 (HRW 2012).

Between 1998 and 2004 Italy intercepted boats containing 170,198 refugee-sojourners, the vast majority of whom were prevented from landing in Italy/the EU and were instead illegally returned to Libya without attempting to assess individual refugee claims (Table 3.5).[15] Despite the high cost of policing the Mediterranean, Italy continues to pursue this policy even though it drives up the number of deaths among those seeking to enter Europe and violates the international legal principle of *non-refoulement* (Albahari 2006).

Between 2004 and late 2006 a further 2,800 migrants were returned to Libya via a 'readmission' agreement where they once again confronted a cycle of detention and extortion (HRW 2006; Amnesty International 2005).[16] As a result of the demand to cross the Mediterranean the size and sea-worthiness of boats has decreased sharply, which has increased the risk of drowning for subsequent travellers. Depressingly, both the Maltese and Italian authorities have refused to rescue migrants from sinking boats.[17]

In 2002, sojourners who left from Libya arrived in Malta, which subsequently decided to deport 223 Eritreans to Asmara where they were arrested, detained and held incommunicado on arrival (HRW 2003b).[18] In mid-2006 Malta refused to take any more migrants until EU member states accepted 'their share'. In July 2006 Malta refused to allow a boat of Eritreans to land until Spain (the country in which the boat that had rescued the migrants was registered) accepted them.[19] In the face of growing numbers of illegal migrants Malta has failed to provide adequate shelter or assistance and it too sought a 'readmission' agreement with Libya.

The *second most important route* out of the Horn is eastward. Following the 1977–78 war between Ethiopia and Somalia an estimated 700,000 Ethiopians sheltered in refugee camps in Somalia. While most eventually returned to Ethiopia, a new wave of refugees was created by the 1983–84 Ethiopian famine and by a policy of compulsory 'villagization' which pushed 30,000 Ethiopians into Somalia. By the late 1980s the UN estimated that 450–620,000 Ethiopians were residing in Somalia and in 2000 and 2003 the numbers were 121,096 and 22,276,

Table 3.5 Italian naval intercepts of refugees, 1998–2004

	1998	1999	2000	2001	2002	2003	2004
Total	38,159	49,999	26,817	20,143	23,719	14,331	13,635

Source: Adapted from Lutterbeck 2006: 76, Table 7.

respectively (after 2003 UNHCR no longer maintained refugee camps in Somalia due to conflict there).

The 1977–78 Ethiopia–Somalia war displaced a further 42,000 people northeast into Djibouti (Crisp 1984). However, Ethiopian pressure forced Djibouti to *refoule* a small number of individuals back; by 1983 approximately 7,000 Ethiopians had been repatriated. While the 1983–4 famine pushed 10,000 people into Djibouti, the number of Ethiopians dwindled to about 3,000 by 2005.[20]

Sometime in the 1990s Ethiopians joined with Somalis to cross the Gulf of Aden into Yemen. In late 2006 the International Organization for Migration (IOM) interviewed a small number of an estimated 5,000 Ethiopians bottled up at the port of Bosaso (Yitna 2006). These individuals came from poor farming families in north-eastern Ethiopia and sought work in Saudi Arabia. They financed their trip – which cost US$115–800 per person – from savings, the sale of property and loans. Nearly all travelled with the support of their families. Their journey was punctuated with numerous stops and at each stage they paid a 'broker' to move forward. IOM found that the smuggling networks were well organized and that there was little evidence of human trafficking.

Though the route is well established,[21] individuals are subjected to considerable violence and the Somali government has, on occasion, *refouled* Ethiopians.[22] Individuals rely on smugglers to ferry them from Bosaso to Aden at a cost of US$50–70 per head.[23] Thousands have died on this route at the hands of 'pirates' who murder, rob and/or force people into the sea (leading to thousands of drownings) to avoid Yemeni coastal patrols. Between 2000 and 2005 an estimated 25,000 Somalis attempted the journey each year.[24]

In recent years, and in response to efforts by the authorities in Puntland to regulate smuggling, the route to Yemen has altered: the vast majority of people now transit via Hargeysa/Obock in Somaliland (which exposes travellers to robbery, violence and rape). The boat crossing is less lethal because the journey is shorter and the Yemeni coastguard, in an effort to end mass drowning, now allows smugglers to discharge their passengers close to the shore (Soucy 2011). In 2010 the Saudi authorities began to deport Ethiopians caught in its territory back to Yemen, where an estimated 3,000 Ethiopians were stranded without money, food or water. In 2011 over 50,000 Ethiopians transited to Yemen, where they pay smugglers to help them enter Saudi Arabia (a task which requires them to circumvent a wall built by the Saudi authorities on the Saudi–Yemen border; US Department of State 2003).[25]

An estimated 40,000 Ethiopians/Eritreans reside and work in Saudi Arabia illegally (unless they are attached to a recognized political party[26]) from where an unknown number transit to northern Syria and enter Turkey. Brewer and Yukseker report that 622 'Ethiopian' migrants were arrested by the Turkish authorities between 1995 and 2005 (2005/6: 71). Though they constitute a small proportion of the sojourners in Istanbul, their numbers – which include single women and some families – are increasing. Seventy-seven per cent of Ethiopians went to Turkey because friends were there, compared with 28 per cent of Eritreans. They share a derelict room with co-ethnics or co-religionists but are isolated from other migrants and Turkish society (p. 40, 77). Living conditions are poor: there is little support/charity available and most work in the informal sector (11 per cent of Ethiopians receive help from their families). Because Turkey retains a 'geographical limitation' to the Refugee Convention, only Europeans are able to claim asylum.[27] The best that non-European refugees can hope for is to be resettled in a third country. It is no doubt for this reason that Ethiopians/Eritreans there attempt to enter Europe through Greece.

A *third route* out of the Horn has been to move south (Figures 3.2 and 3.3). As Table 3.3 shows there was a large movement of people into Kenya in 1991 when the *Derg* collapsed. Though many of these individuals will have returned there has been a consistently high number of ethnic Oromo, political refugees, journalists, academics, professionals and economic migrants from Ethiopia in Kenya.

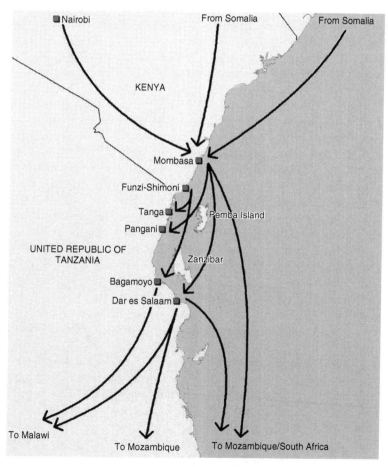

Figure 3.2 Transit routes from Kenya into Tanzania. Source: Horwood 2009: 47.

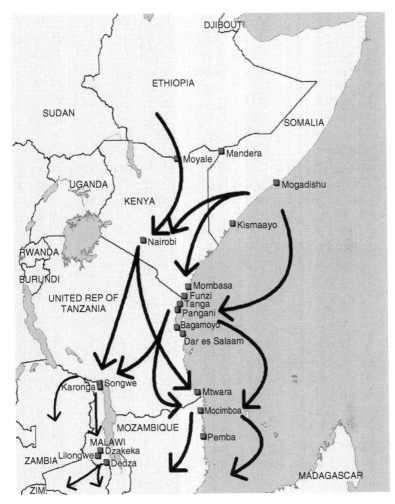

Figure 3.3   East African transit routes. Source: Horwood 2009: 45.

Growing numbers of Ethiopians, Somalis as well as some Eritreans[28] travel to Kenya, which does not have a comprehensive or effective migration legislation framework or migration management strategy. As the International Centre for Migration Policy Development (ICMPD) has noted, 'The existence of the Immigration Department would allow, at least in theory, for a unification and concentration of efforts, however the Department lacks human, financial and technical resources and co-ordination with other state actors to ensure efficiency of its action' (2008: 48–9). In addition to an extensive land border which is poorly policed, there is an extensive network of sea-based travel (including dhows) as well as air travel to Europe and North America. It is also well known that officials in the police, military, finance and immigration departments are corrupt.

As Cases 1 and 5 show, 'Eritreans' (and others) bribe officials to fly out of Nairobi.

The Kenyan government views refugees as a security problem and it has consistently failed to enact refugee legislation. During the 1990s the authorities turned a blind eye to Ethiopian agents abducting, harassing and killing resident Ethiopians and with regard to their own police, who harass and detain refugees to extort bribes (HRW 2002a). Refugees in UNHCR camps in northern Kenya have for many decades been subjected to extensive violence which has led thousands to flee to Kenyan towns (Crisp 2000), where they bribe Kenyan staff in the UNHCR office to process their refugee applications.[29]

The same factors which make it a country of destination also make it a country of transit, namely a relatively well-developed infrastructure, good air and land connections, large migrant communities and well-connected smuggling networks. Sometime in the late 1980s – in response to the changing economic situation in Kenya – the route began to extend south towards South Africa and west into Uganda. Movement along the route is largely in the hands of Nairobi-based smugglers. According to a study by ICMPD (2008: 64):

> Smuggling groups consist of loosely connected individuals and organised crime groups which use a very flexible range of *modi operandi* adapted to various types of facilitation. Taking full advantage of the high level of corruption in the country, the smuggling groups provide legitimate but illegally obtained passports, fake identity cards, false or falsified passports and visas fraudulently obtained. They also offer a full service package, which includes the guarantee for several attempts, infiltration of resettlement programmes etc.

The movement of Ethiopians along this route became noticeable in 1991 following the collapse of the *Derg* and accelerated with the collapse of apartheid in 1994. By 2009 an estimated 45–50,000 'Ethiopians' were living in South Africa with many more in transit or bottled up at various points between Nairobi and Johannesburg (Horwood 2009: 32). The majority of Ethiopians are young men aged 18 to 35 who left for economic reasons, though 39 per cent of individuals in the study cited war/insecurity as the main reason for leaving. Few if any Ethiopian women make the trip, apparently because the migration 'costs' are met by families/relatives who expect individuals to work and remit money back and because of the violence and uncertainty experienced on the route.

On average it takes eight weeks to travel from Kenya to South Africa (though some may take months while others fail to make it). The mode of travel varies (e.g. air, various types of ships/boats, by foot, various types of vehicles etc.), with individuals using several types of transport along the route, punctuated by varying periods of time hiding from the authorities (Box 3.1).

Box 3.1 The route from Kenya to Tanzania through Funzi-Shimoni

Shimoni village, situated in a small mangrove peninsula two hours south of Mombasa by car, is the southernmost Kenyan settlement before Lunga Lunga, the border town with Tanzania. Wasani is a low island between Shimoni and Pemba, one of the Zanzibar islands. A small tarmac jetty has a half-dozen boats moored to it. The boats are open dhows or small motorboats. Swallows dive through the air as boys dive into the water. The customs and immigration offices line the shore a couple of hundred metres away. It's a sleepy village. A smuggling village. Smuggling of slaves, spices and other contraband has defined Shimoni's history, resulting in its famous Slave Caves in the middle of the coastal village, offering the only source of tourist revenue to this otherwise poor village. Today, smuggling from Pemba Island to and from Kenya is active and consists mainly of trade in cowry and other shells, seafood, scrap metal, oil, cloves and cooking oil. Reportedly, smugglers do not trade in illegal goods but avoid customs duties or exceed quotas. A new, revived trade is the smuggling of persons, predominantly Ethiopians and Somalis, from Shimoni to Tanzania, some few hours' sailing away.

Perhaps only a dozen dhows are involved in human transportation, but they pack the migrants in and are one of the major nodes in the smuggling network that feeds Tanzania hundreds of transitory migrants per month. They come from Mombasa and Nairobi. They are brought on buses, trucks and taxis or guided on foot. They avoid the ferry at Likoni in Mombasa that connects the north and south coasts for fear of detection. Despite the throngs of pedestrians and cars on the Likoni ferry, a group of Ethiopians or Somalis would stand out.

They come at dusk through the '*panya* routes', evading any police or roadblocks. These 'rat' routes are the unregulated maze of tracks and unofficial routes connecting rural Kenya. They cover the last few miles from the main road to the waters at the edge of the mangrove swamps by foot in the dark. In groups of 20, 30 or more (all men), they stumble through the night past knowing villages to the sea in an area called Majorani. The smugglers previously used nearby Funzi Island, but now the police and immigration officials there bother them too much. The guides' torches and cell phones then call in the prepared dhows waiting along the coast, which take them to Tanga or Bagamoyo in Tanzania. For most migrants, this is the second international border crossed on their quest to reach South Africa or beyond. Sometimes while they are waiting or approaching the water through the trees, the migrants are ambushed by police or immigration officials. This occurs rarely, and normally only because an informant or a competing smuggler has tipped off the authorities. Sometimes people run into the night and the authorities catch only a few. Typically, according to smugglers and migrants interviewed, there are discussions between the authorities and the guides (smugglers) and payments are made. "There are few situations that money cannot smooth out in Shimoni," said one boat captain while talking about dealing with the authorities.

A seasoned dhow captain squats at the stern of his craft with six young men taking some food and waiting for nightfall. They seem to occupy about a third of the space in the dhow, which is about 12 metres long and 4 metres wide, but the captain says that when he picks up Ethiopians and Somalis he regularly crams 20 or 30 people inside. He claims to have once taken 47 people, but he admits it is dangerous to be overloaded on open seas. He is told, by phone, of new groups to be picked up by agents in Mombasa. He makes the trip about twice a week, and his boss – a boat owner in Pemba, Tanzania – receives 300,000 Kenyan shillings ($4,500) for every trip, irrespective of how many people come aboard. By Shimoni standards, this is big money and the risks are small. According to boat captains interviewed for this study, 20,000 Kenyan shillings ($300) is the standard payment to any police or immigration official in order to be allowed to continue on one's way. What happens when the passengers are delivered in the shallows near a forest in Tanzania is none of his business, the captain says.

Source: Horwood 2009: 48.

The 17–20,000 men who travel this route each year are said to be 'following their dreams' to South Africa, where the opportunity to earn money and transit to the West is reputedly much better (Horwood 2009). However, the 'cost' of this journey is seldom understood at the time of departure, when Ethiopians pay a fee equivalent to US$1,750–2,000, which is said to cover the cost of leaving Ethiopia (at Moyale) and arriving in South Africa (p. 115). Everyone travelling this route, which is normally done in groups of 15–20 persons, encounters 'unforeseen' problems including robbery, beatings, rape, long periods spent hiding in the bush without food or shelter, arrest (including multiple shakedowns by the authorities), deportation (accompanied by robbery or abuse) and increasingly death and long-term incarceration.

The reason why 'migrants' are encountering growing levels of danger and violence along the route arises from the massive amount of money which is made from smuggling – estimated at US$28–36 million per year – which many people along the route, including officials, want a share of.

In recent years regional governments have responded to the growing number of foreigners entering their country by clamping down on transit migration. For instance by early 2008 approximately 1,100 smuggled Ethiopian and Somali migrants had been arrested and detained in Tanzania (ibid. p. 45). In early 2011 a group of 100 Ethiopian and Somali migrants were arrested at Mtwara, on the Tanzania–Mozambique border, while waiting to be taken into Mozambique by a smuggler.[30] As the authorities clamp down, smugglers take greater risks in the way they move migrants: in June 2012, 42 out of an estimated 127 Ethiopian migrants died of asphyxiation in a container truck in central Tanzania.[31] At roughly the same time a boat carrying Ethiopian migrants capsized in Lake Malawi killing at least 47 persons.[32]

South Africa has begun to arrest and deport individuals illegally entering at the border post of Beitbridge (Box 3.2).[33] The vast majority of those who successfully entered South Africa prior to 2010 applied for asylum and were granted the right to stay and work. However, as of April 2010 the Home Affairs Department has refused to register new applicants in effort to prevent 'economic migrants' from entering the country.[34] Africans from outside the country are stigmatized and discriminated against (see Liqu Teshome Gebre, Maharaj and Pillay 2011). Resident Ethiopians live together in relative isolation from South Africans and earn a living in petty retailing. They aspire to leave for greener shores in the USA and indeed a growing number of individuals have used false papers to fly from South Africa to the West via a transit country (Horwood 2009: 34).

Box 3.2 Moving along the southern African corridor

In July 2003 a young 'Eritrean' woman applied for asylum in New Zealand. She had been born in Eritrea but lived in Ethiopia between 1983 and 2000. In mid 2000 her mother was arrested and deported to Eritrea. She sold the contents of her mother's shop and set off by bus for the Kenyan border, where she stayed for about a year before travelling to Nairobi (where she fell ill and, assisted by Pentecostal Christians, stayed for 10 months). With financial assistance from her family she travelled by air to Maputo (Mozambique) before crossing into South Africa. She stayed in Johannesburg long enough to obtain false papers from an 'agent' who arranged her flight to New Zealand.

Source: Refugee Status Appeals Authority, New Zealand. Refugee Appeal No. 75028, 13 May 2004.

The *fourth route* out of the Horn is to fly. This route too has undergone modifications in response to growing demand and constraints affecting travel out of the region and arrival at certain destinations. From the 1970s onwards tens of thousands of individuals flew on student visas to North America and Europe, where many overstayed (becoming an illegal immigrant) or claimed asylum (Terrazas 2007).

Indirect routes are increasingly used to enter the West. In recent years individuals coming from Eritrea have travelled overland to Sudan (because of official barriers to legal exit) and fly out of Khartoum whereas Ethiopians and Somalis fly from Addis Ababa and Nairobi (ICMPD 2008: Sec. 2.4.2). From the Horn individuals fly to Dubai, Turkey, Saudi Arabia or Syria, from where they pick up a flight to Europe; on arrival in Europe they transit between airports before disembarking at a final destination.

In a further modification of this route the Saudi authorities issue visas to young women (and others) to attend major Muslim festivals; thus in 2000 they issued 11,000 visas to Ethiopians to attend Hajj. However, young women stay and work as domestic labour. Emebet Kebede (undated: 4) reports that Ethiopia has done little to curb this route out of the country, which dates to the mid-1980s and involves officially sanctioned labour recruiting agencies and illegal recruiters/traffickers (*ibid.*: 3). One study has estimated that 14,000 Ethiopian women are currently employed as domestic workers in Beirut, another suggests that there may be as many as 130,000 Ethiopian women and children working in the Gulf States (Jureidini 2002; Fransen and Kuschminder 2009:19; see Case 15).

According to the US Department of State (2011: 2):

> Young women, most with only three to four years of primary education, from various parts of Ethiopia are subjected to domestic servitude throughout the Middle East, as well as in Sudan, and many transit through Djibouti, Egypt, Libya, Somalia, Sudan, or Yemen as they emigrate seeking work. Some women become stranded and exploited in these transit countries, unable to reach their intended destinations. Many Ethiopian women working in domestic service in the Middle East face severe abuses indicative of forced labour, including physical and sexual assault, denial of salary, sleep deprivation, and confinement. Many are driven to despair and mental illness, with some committing suicide.

The situation facing these women is well illustrated by the case of 'Lul' (Case 15) whose Saudi Arabian employer exploited her vulnerability by taking her to the Gulf, where for many years she was employed as an unpaid domestic and exploited until she was dumped in the UK when her contribution to the household was no longer valued. As is clear in 'Lul's' case, when these women are abandoned the host government where they are left attempts to compulsorily return them to their country of origin.

Case 15

'Lul' was born in a village in central Eritrea in 1950, when it was under British mandate. In 1978 her village was attacked by the Ethiopian military, at which time everyone fled. Her family were killed or dispersed by the attack, but together with others she reached the Sudan. She worked as a domestic for a Sudanese family until 1984, when she was employed by a Saudi Arabian family. Sometime in the early 1990s her employer took her to Saudi Arabia, where she earned a living as a domestic worker. In the mid-1990s her employer took her to the Eritrean embassy, which refused to issue her a passport because she could not provide three witnesses. Subsequently, her employers took her to the Ethiopian embassy and applied for a passport on her behalf; when the passport was issued her employer kept it (to ensure their control over her; also because 'Lul' is illiterate she did not know what she had signed). She travelled with her employer on a number of trips, on one of which she badly damaged her hip and leg. She eventually resumed work for the family but on a visit to the UK she was abandoned. She applied for asylum but the Home Office and the Tribunal refused her application and she was scheduled to be removed to Ethiopia, a country where she has no family (nor does she speak an Ethiopian language). The British community where she had been 'dispersed' to as an asylum seeker rallied round her to provide support and petitioned the Home Office and the local Member of Parliament asking that she be given status because she was destitute, in poor health and too old to be removed to Ethiopia. After a lengthy campaign and a further failed attempt to secure a fresh asylum application, the community protest on her behalf succeeded and 'Lul' was given status.

The 'cost' of leaving the Horn depends on the route taken and the mode(s) of transport used. Flying directly from the Horn to Europe is very costly (i.e. for a ticket, a passport, a visa and the services of a trafficker/agent) but it has the advantage of substantially reducing the time required to reach a destination and reducing the risk to the life of the person. Viewed from this perspective it is likely that the choice of air travel reflects concerns about the potential risk that a person is likely to face in comparison to travelling a land-based route and it is therefore not surprising that hundreds of unaccompanied minors (children) enter Europe every year via direct flights from the Horn. A very large percentage of the unaccompanied minors in the UK arrive by air at London's Heathrow Airport (Table 3.6). By contrast, the staged nature of travelling overland allows 'costs' to be paid over a longer period (some costs are met by the sojourner who works along the route) and the risks encountered on land routes may be seen as more manageable by men.

In any event the decision to transit out of the Horn is informed partly by financial costs (paid by family/relatives and by working in transit) and in part by how urgently a person needs to flee. Since about four per cent of migrants in OECD countries come from sub-Saharan Africa – and only 2.5 per cent of the population

Table 3.6 Unaccompanied children entering the UK at London Heathrow Airport from the Horn by year and by nationality

Year	Ethiopia	Eritrea
1992	19	—
1993	21	—
1994	16	6
1995	21	6
1996	12	10
1997	9	20
1998	66	91
1999	54	93
2000	62	85
2001	141	111
2002	140	220
2003	115	135
2004	105	160
2005	50	195
2006	25	320
2007	20	250
2008 (1st quarter)	5	85
Total	765	1687

Source: UK Home Office. 'Asylum statistics'. Available at: www.homeoffice.gov.uk/rds/pdfs2/hosb902.pdf; www.homeoffice.gov.uk/rds/pdfs2/hosb803.pdf; www.homeoffice.gov.uk/rds/pdfs04/hosb1104.pdf; www.homeoffice.gov.uk/rds/pdfs/hosb1498.pdf; www.homeoffice.gov.uk/rds/pdfs07/asylumq107.pdf; www.homeoffice.gov.uk/rds/pdfs07/asylumq207.pdf; www.homeoffice.gov.uk/rds/pdfs07/asylumq307.pdf; www.homeoffice.gov.uk/rds/pdfs07/asylumq407.pdf; www.homeoffice.gov.uk/rds/pdfs08/asylumq108.pdf.

of the OECD are refugees (World Bank 2011) – it necessarily follows that the vast majority of individuals travelling regional transit routes remain in Africa[35] and, despite media accounts, these individuals do not constitute an 'uncontrolled movement' of people to Europe. The changes to the modes and routes of transit which have occurred in the past two decides reflect changing regional politics and thus a new travel 'itinerary', even though it may have a strong similarity with pre-colonial and colonial trade routes (Collyer, Duvell and de Hass 2012).

Conclusion

The failure of the Algiers Agreement and continued political tension between Ethiopia and Eritrea brought the ICRC repatriation programme to an abrupt end at about the same time as political conditions in Eritrea saw a substantial outflow of refugees to Ethiopia and the Sudan. While fighting along the Ethiopia and Eritrea border ceased in 2000, neither country established the conditions that would enable 'Eritreans' and others affected by the war to re-establish their lives.

'Eritreans' have therefore fled the Horn and have joined thousands of other refugees and migrants moving along one of four transit corridors. Unfortunately, the individuals travelling these routes have encountered serious difficulties and/or death because of smugglers and because states on the transit routes have instituted policies to prevent foreigners from entering. Officials along the routes have subjected sojourners to arbitrary round-ups, arrest, extortion, torture, deportation and *refoulement*. Increasingly, regional states have adopted restrictive immigration/asylum policies aimed at preventing genuine refugees from registering and from being resettled in their territory.

Predictably, sojourners moving along these routes attempt to avoid officials by living dispersed in urban areas, by not applying for asylum and by constantly being on the move to avoid harassment, corrupt officials and racist abuse. In keeping a low profile to avoid officials they strengthen the power of smugglers over them. There are tens of thousands of 'Eritreans' still in the Horn who are likely to leave, and thousands who are already moving along these routes in an attempt to find refuge. Many of those transiting the continent will die and the vast majority will be indefinitely bottled up along the transit corridor. Chapter 4 looks at why 'Eritreans' who escape from Eritrea back into Ethiopia do not find refuge there, and Chapter 6 examines the fate of the small number of 'Eritreans' who reach the West and apply for asylum.

4 The illusion of citizenship and of return

Politics and persecution in the Horn

A political stalemate has prevailed between Eritrea and Ethiopia since 2001, when relations between the two countries took the form of 'Cold War' politics – when nations pursued war *indirectly* via policies intended to destabilize their enemies. Thus Ethiopia hosts Eritrean opposition political parties, provides arms to Eritrean opposition groups whose objective is to destabilize Eritrea and in March 2012 sent troops into the TMZ.[1] Likewise, Eritrea has hosted and armed Ethiopian political parties and is alleged to have supported the OLF and other armed groups via supply lines running through Mogadishu (Lyons 2009: 173).

The prevailing 'cold war' has had important implications for the 'Eritreans' deported to Eritrea and for those living in Ethiopia. The first section '*Amiche* in Eritrea: Bearers of a stigmatized identity', examines the experience of *amiche* – the 'Eritreans' expelled by Ethiopia – in Eritrea and traces their flight back to Ethiopia. The second section, 'Ethiopia's unsatisfactory regularization of its resident "Eritreans"', examines the halting and incomplete efforts of Ethiopia to regularize the legal status of 'Eritreans' residing in Ethiopia. The final section, 'Normalizing the "state of exception" for 'Eritreans', examines a 2009 Ethiopian policy entitled the 'Directive Enabling Deported Eritreans to Reclaim and Develop their Properties in Ethiopia' and assesses its implementation. I conclude that despite making belated efforts to regularize the status of resident 'Eritreans' the Ethiopian government has opted to enunciate new norms of citizenship which ignore its responsibility for deporting ethnic Eritrean nationals during the war and its failure to register the entire population of 'Eritreans' in the country, which has left thousands of individuals without rights as stateless persons.

Amiche in Eritrea: Bearers of a stigmatized identity

The 'Eritreans' who were expelled from Ethiopia came to be known as *amiche* – a term that takes it meaning from an Italian company based in Ethiopia (the Automotive Manufacturing Company of Ethiopia [AMCE]) which assembles imported car parts from Italy to make cars which are exported. As Riggan (2011: 140) notes:

Like AMCE vehicles, *amiches* had parts (parents) that came from one country (the Italian colony of Eritrea) and were assembled in another (Ethiopia). *Amiches* grew up in Ethiopia, were educated in Ethiopian schools, indoctrinated into Ethiopia discourses of nationalism, and [were] required to participate in Ethiopian nationalist projects . . . And yet, conversations with *amiches* suggest that being *amiche* was synonymous with being Eritrean. But being *amiches* also drew on an array of other identities that constituted a particular way of understanding their symbiotic attachment to both places.

While my understanding of *amiche*[2] suggests an attachment to Eritrea which is more nuanced and less compelling than Riggan suggests, nevertheless her description of these individuals as possessing a hybrid identity – part Ethiopian and part Eritrean – neatly captures the ambiguous and politically awkward position they found themselves in during and after the war.

As 'Eritreans' were expelled Ethiopian officials handed them a paper, or their documents, marked, 'Deported, never to return'. When these individuals crossed the border they were screened by Eritrean officials. The majority of the expellees were recognized as having a right to enter Eritrea and were given assistance (food, money, a temporary place to stay) until they could be collected by relatives or were able to establish themselves. Critically, however, from the moment of their arrival their problematic identity was reflected in the document issued to them by Eritrean officials, which said 'Ethiopian deportee' (or words to that effect).[3]

In one sense *amiche* experienced the same economic and political difficulties as nationals. For instance both were subjected to identity checks and police sweeps, and both were conscripted into the military and assigned either to the war front or to forced labour camps (Gaim Kibreab 2009). On the other hand *amiche* were relatively easy to identify on the basis of language (they spoke Amharic and/or limited Tigrinya) and their urban cultural orientation. Many Eritreans actively discriminated against *amiche* because of their supposed failure to identify with and support Eritrea during her struggle for independence from Ethiopia.

Riggan argues that following the outbreak of war in 1998 the Eritrean government – and the population at large – 'recalibrated the rules that determined national belonging' in an effort to control the process of identity formation, homogenize national identity 'and to purge the visible attributes of their (*amiche*) attachments to Ethiopia' (2011: 144). Not only were all Eritreans expected to support the state, the state also sought to 'clean up the identities of *amiches* to make them more Eritrean' (p. 146). Towards this end steps were taken to control public social space by preventing Amharic from being spoken and by banning Amharic music from being played. There was also a clear tendency to stereotype *amiche* as a negative influence, indeed in the eyes of many Eritreans *amiche* were responsible for social problems and were a corrupting influence (Reid 2005a: 477). When the first *amiche* arrived they were feted by street parades, but as their numbers grew the state conscripted them into the army in an effort to incorporate them directly into the 'national-military body, effectively to inscribe a more pure, holistic, homogeneous national identity on them' (Riggan 2011: 147).

Official attitudes toward them, and public views about them, quickly became apparent to *amiche* who chafed at their treatment. Thus in addition to the general suspicion which greeted them on arrival they encountered discrimination. The following interviews illustrate their experience and highlight the difficulties they faced, which led to a growing disenchantment with the country. For instance Case 16 reflects the view of 'Berhane', who travelled to Eritrea before the war and who remained there until 2007 when he fled to Ethiopia.

Case 16

'Berhane': 'So the main thing here is, for example, people they know me that I am from Addis because of my accent. Without knowing my name, they will rather to call me *amiche*. So, hearing this name from different people . . . you feel something sometimes, you know? Because while you have the right name, while people call you with your right [personal] name instead of calling you *amiche*, whenever you see people they say, "*amiche, amiche*". This is sometimes you feel, those who know you its ok. But those who don't know you, when they call you *amiche*, you feel something because this person doesn't know you.' Speaking about how Eritreans treated *amiche* during the war 'Berhane' observed that:

'When we went from here, those who lived in Asmara during the independence war, they considered us to be living [in Ethiopia] under very luxurious conditions. When you go to Asmara, some people they faced problems with their close relatives. A kind of isolation. That bad [feeling] is past for most of the *amiche* people. This is happening always. So [*amiche*] people try to keep aside [from] their relatives and prefer to join their folk. That's the main issue apart from the culture. This isolation comes from some distasteful reactions to us. Otherwise we do have a very good affinity, if you are educated with us and also with friends. Generally the cooperation between *amiche* is very high in all social events.'

Riggan's description of a wedding in Assab in 2004 between an Eritrean woman and an *amiche* illustrates how this 'cooperation' worked. At the last minute the groom was loaned money destined for another *amiche* to pay for his wedding (2011: 149). Furthermore, while the wedding music was in Tigrinya, as the couple departed the wedding party spontaneously sung an Amharic wedding song.

The rapport between *amiche* was, understandably, born of a shared experience of having been expelled from their homes and was not matched by their relationship with Eritreans. Indeed during the war tensions were extremely high, such that individuals who were perceived as not fully contributing to the war effort were viewed as a problem and treated harshly. The experience of 'Yohannes' (Case 17) illustrates this.

Case 17

Born in Addis Ababa of Eritrean heritage, 'Yohannes' married an 'Eritrean' he met in high school and they had two daughters (aged four and one) prior to the eruption of war in May 1998. On 22 September 1998 security officers arrested him at his house; he was detained for several days before being bussed to the Eritrean border, where he was forced to walk across the war zone to Dekamhare. On arrival 'Yohannes' was interviewed and registered as an 'Ethiopian national with Eritrean roots' and was given some cash and household utensils. He was sure that his wife (who was ill) and his elder daughter were about to be deported so he travelled to Asmara to find them. In December 1999 he was conscripted and taken to Sawa military camp for three months' training before being sent to the front. However, he deserted his unit to help his wife and child but, in March 2000, he was arrested, jailed for three months and returned to his unit.

In 2001, while he was at the front, his wife died and his elder daughter was taken by his wife's parents. In mid-2002 'Yohannes' was again sent to Sawa for training but jumped from the truck to find his daughter. He attempted to put her in an orphanage but his in-laws reported him to the police. He was soon caught and taken to Truckbi Prison (near Asmara) and then to Embadaro prison, where he was tried for desertion and found guilty. Shortly after being jailed he was able to escape but was once again caught. This time the authorities imprisoned him for nearly two years at Teserat Prison before returning him to his unit on the front. On 26 June 2004 'Yohannes' fled to Ethiopia to try to find his younger daughter, who had been left with a neighbour.

Understandably, conscription and life in the military – where a soldier night have to kill an Ethiopian – loomed large in the life of *amiche*. In Chapter 1, I set out the arrest and deportation of 'Binyam', a young man who was expelled to Eritrea in September 1998 with most of family. His treatment by the Eritrean authorities as an underage conscript and a university student sheds light on how Eritrea was governed and it illustrates how outspoken *amiche* came to be seen as a problem and how they were treated.

Case 2 (cont'd)

'Binyam's' family found a place to live in the town of Senafi, where he completed secondary school at the age of 17. Upon graduating he was conscripted and taken to Gelalo Training Camp, where he met 30 other 'underage' children who, like him, were unable to cope with military life. He was sent to Afinbo Government Plantation to undertake hard agricultural labour[4] but at the last minute he was offered a place to study at university and was sent to Asmara, where he registered at Asmara University in September 2000. Unfortunately he failed his first-year exams in May 2001.

At about this time the Student Union held a demonstration and demanded that university students should not be sent to undertake arduous summer work.[5] Following the demonstration students were summoned to the sports stadium, where they were arrested, put into buses and dumped in the desert near Wia (without food, water or shelter). The following day soldiers arrived and took them to a river but for three days no food was provided (students became sick and several died). The students were divided into two groups; 'Binyam's' group was sent to a military camp, where they stayed for 45 days. Near the end of this period General 'Wuchu', a well-known army officer, addressed the group and instructed them to sign a paper admitting their guilt. Students were humiliated, threatened and forced to sign the form. However, when several *amiche* refused to sign the document they were subjected to a mock execution.

In September the students were allowed to resume their studies, but because 'Binyam' had to wait nine months to resit his first year examinations he was sent to Belezar Military Camp to teach uneducated soldiers. After passing his resit examination he returned to university and completed a diploma in June 2004. However, because he had to wait a year before collecting his diploma he was allocated by the Ministry of Education to teach in a school as part of his national service. As he waited to be allocated a school, he and thousands of others were arrested in a *giffa* in Asmara and detained at Adibeto Prison for three days (following which the Ministry of Education secured his release).

The Ministry sent 'Binyam' to North Red Sea Province to teach. On arrival he found that students feared that if they passed their exams they would be conscripted, so the majority purposely failed their examinations in May 2005. The school administrator ordered teachers to make up the marks so that students would pass, but teachers, led by 'Binyam' and another *amiche*, refused. At this point officials from the Ministry arrived and warned teachers to do as they were told; specifically they told 'Binyam' that they knew he was an *amiche* and a trouble maker. At this point his school refused to give him a permit to go to Asmara to attend his university graduation so, having had enough of the system, he left for Ethiopia in June 2005.

As demonstrated in the cases presented in the chapter, during the war *amiche* found themselves in very awkward situations where their volubility and social visibility marked them out for attention by those in power. The continuation of Case 4 takes up the story of a young 18-year-old 'Eritrean' who was expelled with his family to Eritrea in September 1998.

Case 4 (cont'd)

On arrival in Eritrea, 'Kiflom' and his family were given a green card, 500 nafka and a blanket and were taken to Assab, where they boarded a ship to Massawa and then a bus to Asmara, where his father lived. 'Kiflom' registered to study at Asmara University but could not afford to study because his family needed him to earn money to support them. He travelled to Massawa, where he worked for three to four months before being picked up in a *giffa* and taken to Sawa camp for military training, following which he was assigned to a mortar brigade near Mendifera in early 2000. Shortly after arrival at the war front Ethiopian troops broke through Eritrean lines and in the ensuing fight 'Kiflom' was shot and hospitalized for four months. On release from hospital he returned to his unit. Following the Algiers Peace Accord in May 2000 he repeatedly asked his commanding officer (CO) to be released to attend university but the officer refused. His CO asked him why he did not want to serve his country and commented that, as an *amiche*, he 'had he no love for his country'.

In October 2005 heavy rain leaked through the roof of the brigade food store, which he and two other soldiers were responsible for. His CO accused him of deliberately ruining the supplies and imprisoned him for seven days in a metal shipping container, where he was given water but little food. When he was released all three soldiers were sent to the brigade 'farm' to undertake hard labour (breaking and carrying stone, farming, etc.). This was a punishment detail consisting of 14 to 15 soldiers. However, though the 'farm' was guarded, 'Kiflom' escaped and crossed into Ethiopia in March 2005, where he was interviewed before being placed in a refugee camp.

Female *amiche* were also subject to conscription and required ID cards. In the continuation of Case 7 I take up the story of the young woman who worked illegally in Addis Ababa for 11 months before being arrested and expelled into Eritrea in February 1999.

Case 7 (cont'd)

Once across the border Eritrean officials interviewed 'Tigist', issued her an identity document marked 'Eritrean living in Ethiopia' and gave her money and utensils. She was taken to Assab, put on a ship to Massawa and bussed to Asmara, where she stayed with her elderly grandmother before joining her family at Adikaye. Two of her brothers were conscripted on arrival in Eritrea (one died at the front) but her married sister was exempted from military service. 'Tigist' stayed with her family for six months but hid in the house to avoid conscription. Because her parents were not well she was sent to Asmara to work and care for her grandmother.

In Asmara she hid from the authorities and worked (but constantly changed jobs) for several years. Neither of her parents were well and they had no one to support them. Following her grandmother's death in 2009 she stopped working and, frustrated by her inability to support her family and the likelihood that she would be caught, she escaped to Ethiopia that October. The Ethiopians put her in Maini refugee camp and she was subsequently given a permit to go to Addis Ababa for four months.

As bearers of an increasingly stigmatized identity *amiche* found their situation in Eritrea increasingly difficult to accept. As the product of a very different and distinguishable political culture, *amiche* found themselves in conflict with Eritrean relatives, officials and army officers, as a result of which many illegally left Eritrea and entered the Sudan and Ethiopia.

In addition to 'amiche' an estimated 15,000 Ethiopian nationals were expelled into Eritrea (see Chapter 1, 'Seeing the present though the past'). Their situation in Eritrea also appears to be difficult (Box 4.1)

Ethiopia's unsatisfactory regularization of its resident 'Eritreans'

During and after the war Ethiopia directly and indirectly pressured 'Eritreans' to 'voluntarily' repatriate to Eritrea through the ICRC (see Chapter 1, 'Seeing the present though the past' and Chapter 2, 'Arbitration of war reparation claims before the EECC'). This policy was partially successful in as much as 21,000

Box 4.1 Stateless Ethiopians in Eritrea

In 2009 the Open Society for Justice observed that 15,000 stateless Ethiopians in Eritrea are being illegally discriminated against on the basis of their ethnicity, i.e. because they are of Ethiopian origin they are classified as aliens and are refused the right to acquire Eritrean nationality. Open Society argued that they are *de facto* stateless persons. The evidence about who these people are and about their current situation in Eritrea is confused.

The International Committee of the Red Cross (ICRC) reports the presence in Eritrea of a large but undisclosed number of individuals of 'Ethiopian origin' who are not allowed to work because they are registered as aliens. The ICRC has assisted many of these individuals who are destitute and unable to pay the required fee to register as an alien (ICRC annual reports for Eritrea). It is possible that the population in question are the Ethiopian nationals who were wrongly expelled from rural Tigray in to Eritrea during the war (EECC 2009: ¶303–306). In the evidence submitted to the Permanent Court of Arbitration Eritrea argued that it resettled 11,000 Ethiopian nationals in a specially created, planned and developed resettlement called 'Gerenfit' in Gash Barka region (Eritrea 2007: ¶3.32 f.). The group were said to be rural farmers and they were ostensibly assisted to establish farms. At the time Eritrea argued that these individuals did not wish to return to Ethiopia. It is possible that some of these 'Ethiopians' were repatriated to Ethiopia by the ICRC and it is possible that after Eritrea suspended its cooperation with the ICRC that some are now stranded in Eritrea. The situation of this group, and indeed their exact number, will probably never be known given the current state of politics in the region.

Source: Open Society Justice Initiative 2009a.

---

people chose repatriation over destitution. However, an estimated 75–200,000 'Eritreans' remained in Ethiopia. In 1999 this latter group was compelled, by an unpublished directive, to register as 'aliens' to receive a six-month residence permit allowing them to work and access educational and health facilities. Even though these individuals were Ethiopian nationals, the directive stripped them of their citizenship and transformed them into stateless persons with no political or civic rights.

However, given the circumstances in which the registration took place, namely during a war and the round-up and deportation of other 'Eritreans', an unknown number of 'Eritreans' failed to register out of fear (e.g. Case 11), which meant that they were illegally resident and could be arrested and deported at any time. Case 18 illustrates the situation that some 'Eritreans' found themselves in after 1999.

Case 18

Now in her mid-fifties, 'Maaza' has two daughters and a son, and cares for two grandchildren. She and her husband (who died in the early 1990s) were born in Eritrea but migrated to Ethiopia 'long ago'. Prior to his death her husband worked for a printing company in Addis Ababa and she raised their family.

In 1998 soldiers came to her house and asked her whether the children were Ethiopian or Eritrean. She told them, 'we are all Ethiopian'. They said that she and her husband were Eritreans because her husband had voted in the Eritrean referendum in 1993. 'I had no idea what they were talking about and I called one of my neighbours to read . . . the paper and explain what was happening. My neighbour told me that it was a form given to all government workers to choose whether they want to be sent to Eritrea (as an Eritrean) or to remain here in Ethiopia (as an Ethiopian) if the separation happened.' She had no idea that her husband had done this and asked the soldiers to give her time to discuss the issue with her children. The soldiers left the house telling her that they would be back the next day.

However, her children 'ran from the house' and she lost contact with them for several years. The soldiers returned the next day and took her to a detention camp at 'Sarais' (her neighbours hid her grandchildren). 'Maaza' was held in the camp for three weeks but was not ill-treated. Suddenly, and without explanation, she was released. On returning to her house she found that it had been 'sealed' with tape: 'I wasn't allowed to get in, even to take out my personal things. Some kind of seal was put across door of the house and I was barred from entering.'

Her neighbours tried to get the *kebele* to return her house and property to her but the *kebele* told her, 'you are an Eritrean' and that the property now belonged to the government. They also told her to bring papers to prove her claim. As she said, 'It's already bad enough that I can't read and know which paper is what, even though I had my neighbours who were willing to help me out with this. But none of us had access to the house, where the papers were.' Her house was sold to another family. 'Maaza' used her Ethiopian ID card to get her savings out of the bank but was unable to access her husband's bank account and pension.

Sometime in 1999 'Maaza' went to the *kebele* where she was living and handed in her old *kebele* ID card and was given a 'yellow card' that said she was 'Eritrean'. She never applied for citizenship because after the war two of her children got back in contact and began to send her money. 'Then I started a new life, rented a house and my grandchildren are going to school. I have enough food to feed us and life is OK, thank God.'

In 2001, immigration officials and the Ministry of Foreign Affairs considered the possibility of recognizing dual nationality but they decided that such an act would allow too many deported Eritreans and ethnic Somalis access to Ethiopian nationality.[6] So they opted instead for a national identity card for 'Individuals of Ethiopian Origin' which could also be given to foreign nationals to honour their contribution to the country.

Proclamation No. 270 was issued in February 2002 establishing a card for 'Individuals of Ethiopian Origin' (Box 4.2). By April 2010 an estimated 21,000 individuals had paid the US$500 application fee and been granted most of the benefits of nationality, with the exception of the right to vote and to participate in politics. Clearly the authorities saw no contradiction in creating this new legal status – which was granted to individuals who had fled Ethiopia as refugees – at a time when so many stateless 'Eritreans' still resided in the country.

Box 4.2 Ethiopia Proclamation No. 270/2002

A Proclamation to Provide Foreign Nationals of Ethiopian Origin with Certain Rights to Be Exercised in Their Country of Origin

Whereas, a significant number of foreign nationals of Ethiopian origin wish to strengthen their tie with their country of origin;

Whereas, it is believed that foreign nationals could contribute to the development and the prosperity of the peoples and country of their origin if the legal restrictions pertaining to the enjoyment of certain rights and privileges are lifted;

Now, Therefore, in accordance with Art. 55(1) of the Constitution of the Federal Democratic Republic, it is hereby proclaimed as follows:

2. Definitions

(1) A Foreign national of Ethiopian Origin means a foreign national, other than a person who has forfeited Ethiopian nationality and acquired Eritrean nationality, who had been Ethiopian national before acquiring a foreign nationality; or at least one of his parents or grandparents or great grant parents was an Ethiopian national.

3. Objectives of the Proclamation

(1) By identifying foreign nationals of Ethiopian origin who have acquired foreign nationality due to their life circumstances or other factors, entitle them to various rights and privileges by lifting the legal restrictions imposed on them when they lost their Ethiopian nationality;

(2) In order to create a legal framework whereby persons of Ethiopian origin fulfil their contribution to the development and prosperity of their country or origin.

Part Two – Rights and Responsibility of the holder of the Identification Card

5. Rights

(1) He shall not be required to have an entry visa or residence permit to live in Ethiopia;

(2) Without prejudice to Art. 6(2) of this proclamation, he shall have the right to be employed in Ethiopia without a work permit;

(5) He shall have the right to be considered as a domestic investor to invest in Ethiopia.

6. Exception

(1) He shall have no right to vote or be elected to any office at any level of Government;

(2) He shall have no right to be employed on a regular basis in the National Defence, Security, Foreign Affairs and other similar political establishments.

Part IV. Miscellaneous Provisions

(14) Conditions for the cancellation of the identification card:

(1) If the card was obtained by means of fraud;

(2) If the holder of the card has been convicted for a crime of terrorism or smuggling of narcotics or armaments;

(3) If the holder is a citizen of a country at war with Ethiopia or is found willingly helping such country;

(4) If the holder is proved to have served in the regular army or intelligence of another country.

Source: http://www.unhcr.org/refworld/pdfid/4c5844de2.pdf.

It was not until December 2003, however, that the government issued Proclamation No. 378,[7] which amended Ethiopian nationality law and established the basis for 'foreigners' – and by extension stateless 'Eritreans' – to acquire nationality. The proclamation set out the means by which a person could acquire nationality, namely by 'descent' ('where both or either parent is Ethiopian' Pt II, Sec. 3) and by application (Pt II, Sec. 5), providing that applicants met certain 'conditions'. The conditions were:

1. He/she had 'attained the age of majority';
2. He/she had established domicile in Ethiopia for at least four years prior to submitting an application;
3. He/she is able to communicate in 'one of the languages of the nations/nationalities of the Country';

4. He/she has a 'sufficient and lawful source of income to maintain himself and his family';
5. He/she is of good character;
6. He/she has 'no record of criminal conviction';
7. He/she is 'able to show that he has been released from his previous nationality or the possibility of obtaining such a release upon the acquisition of Ethiopian nationality; and
8. He/she is 'required to take an oath of allegiance'.

The proclamation also set out key exceptions which barred certain classes of individuals from making an application. Specifically Art. 20 stated that 'any Ethiopian who voluntarily acquires another nationality shall be deemed to have voluntarily renounced his Ethiopian citizenship.' Furthermore Art. 21 stated that 'An Ethiopian who acquires another nationality by virtue of being born to a parent having a foreign nationality or by being born abroad shall be deemed to have voluntarily renounced his Ethiopian citizenship unless he has declared to the Authority his option to retain it by renouncing his other nationality.' The two exceptions appear to be aimed at individuals who possess Eritrean nationality including 'Eritreans' who, on being expelled into Eritrea, were recognized as having a right to enter Eritrea.

In short, the proclamation established a framework for regularizing the status of resident 'Eritreans' who, in 1999, had registered as 'aliens'. Furthermore, Art. 22 of the proclamation left open the possibility that expelled 'Eritreans' and their children might be able to reacquire Ethiopian nationality providing that they returned to Ethiopia and lived there for a period of four years, renounced their foreign nationality and applied for 'readmission' to Ethiopian nationality. Applications for nationality were to be made to a 'nationality affairs committee'.

In January 2004 Ethiopia established a procedure for resident 'Eritreans' to regularize their status when it published the 'Directive Issued to Determine the Residence Status of Eritrean Nationals Residing in Ethiopia'.[8] The stated objective of this directive, which referred directly to Proclamation No. 378, was (Part I, Sec. 1):

> to provide the means to any person of Eritrean origin who was a resident in Ethiopia when Eritrea became an independent State and has continued maintaining permanent residence in Ethiopia up until this Directive was issued to confirm whether he or she has acquired Eritrean nationality, and to determine his or her status of residence in Ethiopia.

Under this directive 'a person holding an Eritrean passport and/or 'serving the Eritrean government' was deemed to possess Eritrean nationality (i.e. he/she was unable to acquire Ethiopian nationality; Pt II, 4.1). However, 'A person of Eritrean origin who has not opted for Eritrean nationality shall be deemed to have decided to maintain his or her Ethiopian nationality and his or her Ethiopian nationality shall be guaranteed' (Pt II, 4.2). Furthermore, 'An Eritrean registered in accordance with this Directive and who desires to regain his or her Ethiopian nationality may be readmitted to his or her Ethiopian nationality' (Pt II, 4.3). Those who qualified were directed to register in person with the Department for Immigration and Nationality Affairs in Addis Ababa or in the region where they resided.

Resident 'Eritreans' could apply for a 'permanent residence permit' giving them the right to own a house and immovable property (Pt III, 8.1); to use agricultural land (Pt III, 8.2); to engage in private employment (9.2); and to use educational and health services (Pt III, 10). However, if an 'Eritrean' qualified and was accepted by the authorities under this decree, registration did *not* confirm or grant citizenship to them. Registered individuals were only allowed to reside in Ethiopia as a 'foreigner' or dual national/'alien'. In effect the directive allowed resident 'Eritreans' the *possibility* of registering but it did not set out a procedure for them to reacquire Ethiopian nationality.

Ethiopia has refused to provide information about the implementation of the 2003 Proclamation or the 2004 Directive. Thus it is not known how many 'Eritreans' were registered as 'aliens' nor is it known how many individuals were able to acquire 'residence status' or reacquire Ethiopian nationality. In 2007 the government refused to speak to Refugees International about the legal status of ethnic Eritreans, but the organization learned that resident 'Eritreans' faced delays of at least three years in being registered and that some applicants faced lengthy interrogations as part of this process (Refugees International 2008, 2009). At the time, UNHCR confirmed that individuals who had been expelled or who had fled the country were not allowed to register (2007d). To date, the Government of Ethiopia has neither published/made available any information about registration nor has it provided the UN International Convention on the Elimination of All Forms of Racial Discrimination[9] with information about the legal status of several hundred Eritrean children whose parents had been expelled (UN Committee on the Elimination of Racial Discrimination 2008).

However, some information has recently come to light about the registration process as a result of an asylum claim in the UK.[10] In that case Gunter Schroeder reported that 'Eritreans' who registered with the authorities during the war were allowed to legalize their status under the 2004 Directive. It appears that the registration exercise occurred between March and June 2004 during a two-week period and that individuals who had not previously registered, but who sought to do so in 2004, were allowed to legalize their status. Those who registered were given a special residence permit which, unlike previous permits, did not need to be renewed. Schroeder's sources estimated that 100,000 Eritreans reacquired Ethiopian nationality though it took several years to process all the applications.

Given the extent of inter-ethnic marriage and the arbitrary nature of the expulsions during the war there would not seem to be any rational way that officials could differentiate between individuals who were allowed to register and individuals who were refused the right to register. Even so, officials decided that if an individual had voted in the 1993 referendum on Eritrean independence, or if they held an Eritrean identity card, they could not register. One has to presume that most, if not all, of this class of person had already been expelled. This being the case, there was considerable scope for government officials to define 'Eritrean-ness', i.e. who was or was not 'Eritrean' for the purpose of registering and acquiring rights. It appears that descent in the male line from a person born in Eritrea disqualified an applicant *and* that the 'actions' – perceived or real – of the 'Eritrean' parent of a child might prevent a child from being registered. In this way children of 'Eritrean' parents who were arrested and deported during the war, or who fled Ethiopia, were not registered. It is known that some of the individuals who registered did reacquire Ethiopian nationality. These individuals were issued passports which stated – in English on the first page – that they are 'Eritrean nationals'[11], a terminology which strongly suggests 'second class' citizenship and a vulnerability not shared by other nationals.

The definition of 'Eritrean-ness' which informed the registration exercise excluded the 'Eritreans' who had been expelled (and many 'Eritrean' children left behind) but also individuals who *may* have acquired Eritrean nationality when they were processed at the Eritrean border, those who fled the country without waiting to be arrested and all 'Eritreans' living in a third country during the war (estimated at 10–15,000 individuals). The number of those excluded from reacquiring Ethiopian nationality is clearly very large. Following the war Ethiopia has haltingly introduced policies which give the *appearance* of regularizing the status of stateless 'Eritreans', but the arbitrary implementation of policies has excluded large numbers of individuals. In effect, the various directives and proclamations have not remedied the problems confronting stateless 'Eritreans'. Rather, officials have enunciated new norms of citizenship which include former refugees as 'Individuals of Ethiopian Origin' but which continue to ignore their responsibility for illegally expelling 'Eritrean' nationals during the war and for thousands of resident 'Eritreans', including all those who were too young to register in 2004, from Ethiopian nationality.

In his evidence to the UK's Immigration and Asylum Tribunal, Gunter Schroeder argued that the 2004 Directive – which was developed partly in response to diplomatic pressure from states which had absorbed the deportees – was principally aimed at a foreign audience to show that Ethiopia was redressing the problem created by the mass deportations. His conclusion is amply supported by other evidence and the subsequent policies adopted by the Ethiopian government.

Normalizing the 'state of exception' for 'Eritreans': 'Bare life' in Ethiopia today

In April 2009 the Ethiopian Council of Ministers issued a directive purporting to allow deported Eritreans the right to reclaim their property – variously estimated[12] to be worth $US46–800 million dollars. Information about the directive was disseminated in the press and on Ethiopian television and was criticized as a 'move that could endanger national security' (Yonas Kibru 2009). Deportees viewed the directive with suspicion but were hopeful that they might be allowed to regain their assets (indeed many applications were filed by individuals in Eritrea, the UK and the USA).

On 16 June 2009 I interviewed the First Secretary of the Ethiopian Embassy in London about the 2009 directive and the current legal status of 'Eritreans' in Ethiopia. Because he was unable to provide specific information on either subject I wrote to the Ethiopian prime minister in November 2009 enquiring about the 2009 directive. However, my letter, which was sent via the London embassy, was intercepted and on 2 December I received a letter from H. E. Kebede Berhanu, the Ethiopian ambassador to the UK (see Appendix). The ambassador sent me a copy of the directive in Amharic and an 'unofficial' translation in English (Box 4.3). According to Ambassador Berhanu the reasoning behind the 2009 directive was:

> 'Ethiopia deported: Eritreans who were being deemed a threat to national security during the 1998–2000 Ethio-Eritrean war, the war that was launched by the Eritrean government.
>
> When Eritreans were deported, Ethiopia made sure as much as possible, that every deportee delegated an agent who can administer his/her property in Ethiopia.
>
> In the absence of such agent/representative in Ethiopia, deported Eritreans have been administering their own properties in Ethiopia by delegating somebody of their choice who is in Ethiopia. This process requires the individual to provide power of attorney at the Ethiopian embassy or consulate abroad.
>
> After a decade, when it is felt that the threat of most of these people to Ethiopia's national security is felt to be minimum or manageable, the Government of Ethiopia issued directives that will allow deportees to claim properties which were under the custody of their agents in Ethiopia, under the administration of government organs (where the deportee has not had agent at all and the government organs have been looking after the property), and in blocked accounts (as banks kept their money in safe place, i.e. blocked accounts).
>
> *Ethiopia did not deport its own nationals, nor was there any property of Ethiopians confiscated* [my emphasis]. If we have some Eritreans who were deported and still they claim to be Ethiopians, then we will be forced to consider them as Eritreans as dual citizenship is not permissible under the current nationality laws.

The directive appeared to provide a procedure through which deported Eritreans could reclaim fixed assets like houses and obtain their assets in the 'blocked' bank accounts created by the government (see Chapter 2, 'Arbitration of war reparation claims before the EECC'). There were, however, several provisos in the directive (see Box 4.3), namely that individuals could 'carry on commercial activities upon presentation of the necessary proof, if the property or business has not been sold or wound up and it is being managed by their agents' (Sec. 3) and that they had not worked 'in collaboration with Eritrean commercial and security entities located in Eritrea or other countries prior to or after the war' (Sec. 7). The directive failed to say that the government had sold their assets at prices advantageous to Ethiopian buyers and that the proceeds from the compulsory sale of their property had been heavily taxed (see Chapter 2, 'Arbitration of war reparation claims before the EECC').

Box 4.3 Directive to Enable Eritreans Deported from Ethiopia due to the Ethio-Eritrea War [to] Reclaim and Develop their Property in Ethiopia

Whereas, it has become necessary to facilitate the condition whereby Eritreans who, due to the invasion of Ethiopia by the Eritrean government, were deported from Ethiopia upon being deemed a threat to national security could reclaim their properties which currently are under the custody of their agents in Ethiopia, under the administration of government organs and in blocked bank accounts as well as to settle the problems that had been encountered in this regard.

The Council of Ministers has issued this Directive.

1. Short Title: This Directive may be cited as the 'Council of Ministers Directive to Enable Eritreans Deported from Ethiopia due to the War Launched by the Eritrean Government on Ethiopia [to] Reclaim and Develop their properties in Ethiopia'.

2. Scope of Application:

1. This Directive is applicable to Eritreans who, due to the invasion of Ethiopia by the Eritrean government, were deported from Ethiopia upon being deemed a threat to national security.
2. Notwithstanding the provisions of sub-article one of this Article, this Directive is not applicable to Eritreans who have close ties with commercial or security entities which are particularly administered by the Eritrean Government.

3. Property Administration
Eritreans deported from Ethiopia who used to own property or a business enterprise in Ethiopia, can pursuant to Art. 5, carry on commercial activities upon presentation of the necessary proof, if the property or business has not been sold or wound up and it is being managed by their agents.

4. Money deposited in Banks
Eritreans deported from Ethiopia are entitled to:

1. Operate bank accounts wherein they have personally deposited money upon presentation of the relevant evidence;
2. Receive the proceeds from the sale of their property by government administration [organs] and deposited in blocked bank accounts without interest in Ethiopian currency on presentation of proof;
3. Property or money can be restituted pursuant to sub-articles 1 and 2 of this Article after government-owned debts are paid without interest and penalty.

5. Engaging in Investment
Eritreans deported from Ethiopia are:

1. Entitled to engage in commercial or investment activities as local investors in Ethiopia by virtue of Art. 5 of Proclamation No. 280/2002;
2. Duty bound to operate their money through accredited bank in accordance with the procedure to be laid down by the Committee established under Art. 8.

6. Issuance of Visa
The National Information and Security Service shall issue visa and residence permit to Eritreans deported from Ethiopia on the basis of the powers invested in it and its procedures.

1. People-to-people ties to be undertaken;
2. Devise implementation directives, work procedures and plans in respect of the Directive and implement the same; establish sub-committees necessary for the implementation of the Directive.

7. Identifying Eritreans not covered by the Directive
The National Information and Security Service shall investigate whether Eritreans who apply to benefit from this Directive used to or still work in collaboration with Eritrean commercial and security entities located in Eritrea or other countries prior to or after the war and submit [its findings] for decision to the Committee established under Art. 8; it shall implement this Directive in accordance with the Committee's decision.

8. Application of the Directive

1. Acts undertaken by the Government pursuant to the previous Directive shall remain legally valid;
2. A four-member Committee comprised of [representatives] from the Ministry of Foreign Affairs, who shall act as chair, the Ministry of Finance and Economic Development, the National Information and Security Service and the Federal Police shall be established to implement this Directive.

9. Powers and Duties of the Committee
The Committee shall have the power and duty to:

1. Adopt its own meeting and work procedures;
2. Deliberate on the implementation of this Directive and problems encountered and find solutions;
3. Provide explanations to raise the awareness of executive organs;

4. Collaborate with the relevant federal and regional government offices to facilitate the condition whereby tasks are undertaken jointly; follow up the implementation of this Directive;
5. Cause activities aimed at strengthening people-to-people ties to be undertaken;
6. Devise implementation directives, work procedures and plans in respect of the Directive and implement the same; establish sub-committees necessary for the implementation of the Directive."

10. Effective Date
The Directive shall enter into force as of May 15, 2009.

On 5 February 2010 I spoke informally with the Head of the Counsellor Section of the Embassy, who reiterated the position that, for the government, 'Eritreans were those individuals who had voted in the Eritrean referendum. The act of voting made them Eritrean'. With the outbreak of war the Ethiopian government faced a dilemma due to the presence of so many 'foreigners'. While all Eritrean officials, security personnel and many others had been deported, many Eritreans continued to live in Ethiopia. He felt that the 2004 directive was generous to them: they were allowed to remain, to work, to own a house etc. The only thing that they could not do, as with foreign nationals everywhere, was to vote in elections and participate in politics. He stated that the 2009 directive was the government's response to 'our brothers, the Eritrean people'; it allowed them to return and reclaim their property. In short, the directive was a signal to the international community that Ethiopia had moved on from the war.

My discussions with embassy staff made it clear to me that 'Eritreans' in Ethiopia were still perceived as foreigners/aliens and that the 2009 directive should *not* be seen in humanitarian terms and neither was it an admission that Ethiopia had violated international law when it expelled 'Eritreans'. Embassy officials could not, however, answer my questions about why the directive was not published neither were they able to say anything about how it was being implemented.

In April 2010 I travelled to Addis Ababa to meet the Director General of Political Affairs in the Ministry of Foreign Affairs, who is responsible for administering the 2009 directive. He told me that several months after the announcement of the directive the coordinating committee had drafted and released three application forms to be used to reclaim property: one for use by deportees residing overseas; a second for use by a deportee's 'agent' (an individual in Ethiopia with power of attorney to act for a deportee); and a third for use by a deportees' 'successor' (i.e. a member of a deportee's family who resides in Ethiopia). In late 2009 the ministry publicized information about the directive, including the procedure that an individual should follow to reclaim his/her property. Application forms were said to be available at embassies/consulates and at the Ministry of Foreign Affairs in Addis Ababa (where completed claims are filed).

The director general said that when a claim is received it is sent to the region where the expelled person claims to have lived and owned property (i.e. the *kebele* where s/he lived), to the federal police and to a bank for verification. The committee administering the directive – whose composition is set out at point 8 of the directive – is concerned only to let in Eritreans with no connection to *Shaebia*. But this is very difficult because 'they look like us'. How is this done? Embassies check applications but there is also a 'blacklist' of the individuals who were deported.

I was given conflicting information[13] about the number of claims that had been filed. As of April 2010 a total of 30 claims had been recognized (resulting in the return of their property) and a further 70 had been approved in principle (i.e. were awaiting a decision by ministers). The director general stated that 'no claims were refused'. However, no further information was made available to me nor was the ministry willing for me to speak to individuals whose property had been returned.

I asked the director general for information about the implementation of the 2004 decree. He told me that only the immigration division could answer my questions and he agreed to forward my queries and contact details to them. However, immigration officials failed to contact me.

Important unanswered questions remain about the directive. First, if it were a genuine effort to recompense deported Eritreans then implementation would surely be assigned to a department with fiscal responsibility and the capability of processing a large volume of applications and dealing with the complex issues arising from property claims, access to 'blocked' bank accounts etc. Secondly, the directive has never been published in the Ethiopian press or in the *Federal Negarit Gazeta* where all decrees, regulations etc. are published.[14] Finally there is the timing of the directive, which occurred shortly after the EECC decided that Ethiopia should compensate deported 'Eritreans' for their confiscated property. In short, everything points to the conclusion that the directive should be seen as an attempt to avoid paying $US46 million in damages to Eritrea (Yohannes Anberbir 2009). This conclusion is reinforced by the continued inability of 'Eritreans' in the UK and the USA to obtain a visa, enter Ethiopia and reclaim their property (see 'Conclusion').[15]

What then is the objective of this directive? My discussions with Ethiopian officials in London and Addis Ababa made it clear to me that it should be seen as an attempt to undermine the Government of Eritrea by encouraging *amiche* to leave. It is also a publicity stunt for foreign consumption.

I had anticipated that immigration officials would refuse to meet me and had identified a number of 'Eritreans' in Addis Ababa to speak to. I interviewed and/or obtained information from 16 individuals (and their families) including eight individuals who had been deported and eight who had remained in Ethiopia.

Very few of the 'Eritreans' I interviewed knew about the 2009 directive. Several individuals had heard about the directive while living in a refugee camp but officials had refused their request for a claim form. One person (Case 3) reported that several years after he returned to Ethiopia he discovered that his mother had been able to get from Eritrea to Khartoum, where she was issued a temporary entry visa allowing her to come to Addis Ababa to reclaim her house from an 'agent' (she still possessed the original title deed). His mother had filed a legal claim for immediate occupation but the outcome of the case was uncertain (it was also unclear whether she would be allowed to remain in Ethiopia). I was to learn that some designated 'agents' had facilitated the original owners' effort to reclaim their homes, but also that some 'agents' had sold the property and absconded with the money. A crucial element in establishing a property claim hinged upon whether the person still possessed the relevant documents (the majority of deportees were stripped of official documents when they were expelled). I did not hear of any cases where individuals had been able to obtain their assets from Ethiopian banks.

My contacts also provided a wealth of information about their current legal status and about how the 2004 directive had been implemented. Yohannes (Case 3) indicated that many 'Eritreans' had not registered in 1999 (or afterwards) out of fear. Cases 19 and 20 typify the situation of the Eritreans whose families were split up during the war and who were left behind.

Case 19

'Teodros' was born in Addis Ababa in 1975 to parents who had emigrated from Eritrea decades before his birth. In mid-1998 police came to the family home and arrested and deported everyone present (his father, mother, a sister and a brother). At the time, 'Teodros' and a second brother were out of the house and were not arrested. His father's business was taken over by a business partner and their government-owned house was allocated to another family.

Though his brother obtained a *kebele* ID card – with the 'help' of an Ethiopian family – and subsequently acquired an Ethiopian passport, 'Teodros' was afraid to approach the authorities and remained unregistered. In 2008 an Ethiopian family helped him to obtain a *kebele* ID card (by bribing officials), which he took to Immigration to obtain an Ethiopian passport so that he could join his family in North America. However, officials told him that his name was 'Eritrean' and he was arrested and detained in Maikalawi Prison in Addis Ababa (in the company of 20 other *amiche*, most of whom had returned from Eritrea). In violation of a judge's order, immigration officials detained him for three months before releasing him.

Despite important changes in the nationality law some 'Eritreans' continued to face political and legal obstacles preventing them from obtaining identity documents and passports, as indicated by Case 20.

Case 20

'Lebne' was born in Addis Ababa in 1986 to parents who had migrated to Ethiopia from Eritrea in the 1970s. After her parents divorced she lived with her father and his Ethiopian wife. In July 1998 her father was arrested and deported (the house remained with her adoptive mother). Shortly afterwards her birth mother was arrested and deported (her hotel and car were seized by officials).

Still only 12 years old, 'Lebne' stayed with her step-mother and attended school in Addis Ababa. In 2004 she heard about the Directive but out of fear did not register. Later she approached local officials for a *kebele* ID – which every 18-year-old is required to have – but was refused because they said her father was 'Eritrean'. The *kebele* then imprisoned her as an 'alien'. When her Ethiopian step-mother came forward to vouch for her she too was arrested. Several days later a judge came to the *kebele* and ruled that she had been legally adopted and that she should be given a *kebele* ID card (the two women were then released).

In 2007 she approached Immigration to request a passport. The official first disputed her age, then refused to accept a birth certificate, then told her she was 'Eritrean' and finally stated that they had documents on the deportation of her father. She returned to immigration with the court order stating that she was adopted and thus 'Ethiopian' but officials refused to issue the passport for a further six months. While 'Lebne' is now legally an Ethiopian she told me, 'I am not an Ethiopian and I do not accept to be one'.

Cases 9, 10 and 11 (in Chapter 1) clearly show that despite changes in the law resident 'Eritreans' were and are severely discriminated against. Many individuals face ethnic discrimination and harassment from the public and officials. Furthermore, many are temporarily detained and some have been dismissed from their jobs (and are unable to find other work). It is also the case that some 'Eritreans' are refused access to legal documents which establish their nationality and provide protection from the police and security forces. In short, despite having persevered in the face of extremely adverse conditions the lives of 'Eritreans' continue to be difficult and their basic rights continue to be disregarded. Case 21 illustrates how deportation tore a family apart and reduced them to a state of penury that took them many years to recover from.

Case 21

'Welete's' father was Eritrean and her mother Ethiopian. She grew up in Dire Dawa (Harar Region) where she and her four siblings were born. Her family were poor but until the outbreak of war they managed to get by because her father was employed by the government. In late 1998 police came to their house and arrested her father; two days later he was expelled. Her elder brother and his godfather were so angry that they asked the authorities to be sent to Eritrea (and have not been heard from since). During the war the family was called *Shaebia* and discriminated against. Her mother was reduced to peddling food which enabled the family to survive; fortunately they were left alone by the authorities. After the war ended ethnic and political tensions declined but in 2004 when the registration of Eritreans occurred she and her siblings hid because they did not want to be identified as Eritreans. Eventually, because their mother was Ethiopian, 'Lebne' and her sibling secured *kebele* ID cards (recently she obtained an Ethiopian passport).

The evidence from my interviews with 'Eritreans', in conjunction with information discussed in this chapter, indicates that a large number of 'Eritreans' who were entitled to register in 1999 and 2004 failed to and/or that they were denied the right to register. The brevity of the exercise, which lasted two weeks, together with the selective manner in which it was implemented by officials has compounded the situation of many 'Eritreans'. Furthermore, once the exercise ended the authorities refused to register other 'Eritreans'. The deeply flawed registration has significant implications for many 'Eritreans' including: (a) individuals who were under the age of 18 at the time of the registration exercise, who were not allowed to register; (b) the children of deportees (who were not allowed to register); and (c) individuals who for varying reasons were unable and/or afraid to register. Clearly many 'Eritreans' remain *de facto* stateless persons and are vulnerable to arrest and deportation as 'aliens'. Given the absence of any statistics on the registration exercise it is impossible to estimate the size of the unregistered population of 'Eritreans'.

What is the legal status of the *amiche* who fled from Eritrea back into Ethiopia over the past decade? The head of the immigration department stated in 2004 that only individuals who had been 'continuously resident' in Ethiopia would be allowed to register.[16] Perhaps the statement explains why, following their interview with ARRA (see Chapter 3) *amiche* are taken to a refugee camp and registered as an Eritrean refugee. In short, Ethiopian officials know the identity of *amiche* who were prevented from registering in 2004.

In April 2010 my informants in Addis Ababa suggested that 30 per cent of the refugees in the camps were *amiche*. There is indirect evidence to support this claim. ARRA created special 'urban refugee' permits, which were given to specified individuals permitting them to leave the camp and live in a designated town (where they registered with ARRA). The key condition for obtaining an 'urban refugee permit' was that the person had family in Ethiopia who would shelter and feed them. The US Department of State noted that there were 1,500 'urban refugees' in 2008 (2009: 19). The only conclusion permitted by the above facts is that most of the individuals given such a permit were *amiche* (though some Eritreans were also temporarily allowed out of the camps with support from UNHCR).[17]

Amiche are classified by Ethiopian officials as refugees who are placed in a refugee camp – though camp security is so poor that many regularly walk out – and who qualify for resettlement in the West. I interviewed several *amiche* who had been accepted for resettlement in the USA (see Case 17). In August 2010 the government announced that all registered Eritrean refugees could leave the camps and 'live in urban areas' providing that they 'are able to sustain themselves financially or have a relative or friend who commits to supporting them'.[18] However, permission to leave the refugee camps will not be an option for many Eritrean refugees unless they have their own income, neither does it provide significant relief to *amiche* who continue to face discrimination. The vulnerability of *amiche* is demonstrated by Case 17, who eventually fled back to Ethiopia in June 2004 to search for his youngest daughter.

Case 17 (Cont'd)

Within three days of being put into Shimelba and registered as a refugee, 'Yohannes' left camp without permission to find his child but was arrested on the way to Addis Ababa, jailed and returned to Shimelba camp. In March 2006 he once again left the camp without permission and travelled to Addis, where he located his daughter, who was still in the care of a neighbour. However, the family asked him not to speak to the girl at that time so he returned to Shimelba camp. He returned to Addis Ababa within a year but the family now refused him access to his daughter. He filed a court case against them to gain access and won, but they appealed – reportedly by bribing a judge – and overturned the initial decision. 'Yohannes' appealed against this decision but by the time it came to court in 2008 the family had fled to the USA, taking his child with them. He did not give up but returned to Shimelba, where he was interviewed and offered resettlement in the USA; in April 2009 he flew to the USA, from where he continued the search for his daughter.

There are an unknown number of *amiche* who have returned to Ethiopia from countries other than Eritrea and who are not registered refugees. These individuals are also *de facto* stateless persons who do not possess Ethiopian identity documents and who are, like Case 22, liable to arrest and expulsion.

Case 22

Born in Eritrea in 1935, 'Abebe' moved to Addis Ababa in the 1970s, where he married an Ethiopian woman and raised a family (their children were all born and raised in Addis Ababa). During the war the police arrested and deported him and two of his children and seized his metalwork shop. One daughter was living in the Middle East at the time; a second had been expelled to Kenya. His children managed to get him out of Eritrea and into Kenya, from where they obtained a temporary visa for him to enter Ethiopia for medical treatment (he has Alzheimer's disease). 'Abebe' was able to return to his home (which was registered in his wife's name) but is unable to renew his visa, which means that he is illegally resident in Ethiopia and can be arrested and deported at any time.

Despite normalizing the presence of many 'Eritreans' in the 2004 registration exercise, the government has refused to reopen registration to allow others the right to regularize their legal status. An unregistered person, who by definition lacks valid identity documents, remains stateless and is vulnerable to arrest and deportation as an alien. Rather than deal effectively with a serious human rights problem in the country, Ethiopia issued a directive in 2009 which ostensibly allowed deported Eritreans the right to return and reclaim their property. The evidence regarding this directive indicates that the vast majority of deported persons will never be allowed to legally return home or reclaim their property.

Conclusion

Simultaneously with their expulsion into Eritrea, the identity of *amiche* became linked to a range of socio-political problems that led officials to 'purge the visible attributes of their attachments to Ethiopia', which in turn created an atmosphere of hostility and mistrust that took the form of ethnic discrimination. During and after the war the very different cultural and political sensibilities of *amiche* came under growing scrutiny by officials as political difficulties mounted. Many *amiche* got into difficulties and in increasing numbers they have returned to Ethiopia, where they are registered as Eritrean refugees.

In the meantime, stateless 'Eritreans' in Ethiopia were subjected to violence, intimidation, rape and discriminatory administrative measures which seriously disadvantaged them. Ethiopia has issued various directives and proclamations since the war which have permitted some 'Eritreans' to reacquire their nationality, though a large number remain stateless. The 2004 directive was a half-hearted and semi-secretive effort to address the problem posed by the presence of tens of thousands of registered and unregistered 'Eritreans'. While the registration was publicly announced, the registration process was too brief and the discretionary power of officials too great, which meant that many individuals were excluded from the exercise. Furthermore, by refusing to reopen registration many children who were too young to register remain stateless, as of course do the people who were afraid to come forward.

Subsequent directives illustrate the way in which officials have carefully established new norms of citizenship by granting former refugees and certain honoured foreigners civic rights as 'Individuals of Ethiopian Origin' – complete with the issue of special certificates etc. – while refusing to countenance Somalis, resident 'Eritreans' and returning *amiche* as nationals. The registration exercise illustrates the way that autocratic states redraw the boundaries of citizenship to include new categories of persons and exclude citizens from state protection.

5   The illusion of refuge

The search for asylum and the failure of international law

Having examined the displacement and movement of people out of the Horn across Africa and the Middle East, and the precarious position of 'Eritreans' in Ethiopia, this chapter looks at what awaits the relatively few individuals who manage to reach the UK – a country with one of the best-resourced asylum systems in Europe[1] – and apply for asylum.

The first section, 'The asylum bureaucracy', sets out four fundamental aspects of Western asylum bureaucracies which asylum applicants must negotiate in their attempt to claim asylum, namely the refugee authority, lawyers, complex asylum/immigration law and the courts. The next two sections examine asylum policy and practice in the UK in considerable depth to illustrate how the asylum system works. Thus the section entitled 'UK policy and the 1954 Convention on the Elimination of Statelessness' examines how the UK's breach of its legal commitment to the 1954 Convention on the Elimination of Statelessness affects the manner in which asylum claims by stateless persons are processed and decided. The final section, 'How "Eritrean" claims alleging statelessness are decided in the British courts', examines two recent 'country guidance' asylum claims concerning stateless 'Eritreans' and shows how Home Office policy and judicial decision-making prevents/impedes 'Eritreans' – and other stateless persons – from obtaining status.

The asylum bureaucracy

Having reached a potential country of refuge, an asylum seeker must negotiate four hurdles if they are to be recognized as a refugee: (a) the refugee authority; (b) lawyers; (c) complex immigration law; and (d) judges. An individual must first file their asylum claim with the refugee authority. This involves one or more interviews conducted by immigration officials at the place where the person entered the country, i.e. the airport or port (applicants are increasingly interviewed in immigration detention centres). The interview provides an immigration officer with basic information about the claim and is used to decide whether the person will be allowed to enter the country to make a claim or whether they will be detained for making an 'unfounded claim'. For instance, when a person seeking asylum enters the EU their fingerprints are entered on a database to determine whether they have already made an asylum claim, whether they have a criminal record and/or whether they were previously the subject of a deportation order (Broeders 2007). If the individual has made an asylum claim elsewhere or has a criminal record etc. they will be detained pending deportation.

If the asylum applicant has what appears to be a potentially well-founded claim they are allowed to enter the country and make a formal application. However, even if an individual has no criminal record etc. they may still have to apply for release from detention via a bail/bond hearing,[2] which normally requires a citizen to stand bond (the detainee may then be released into their custody). Individuals in immigration detention can apply for asylum, but most can count on long periods of confinement as the state seeks to deport them (De Genova 2002; Gibney 2008).

For a variety of reasons – including resource constraints, institutional culture (Jordan, Strath and Trindafyllidou 2003), the discretionary power of officials and problematic policies – asylum procedures are seriously flawed. Frequently a state has failed to incorporate (and apply) international law into its domestic legislation but, just as importantly, staff are poorly trained and under pressure to meet management targets (which limit the amount of time they spend assessing an individual claim). The tendency is for officials to search for reasons to refuse a claim.

In the UK, one area of concern has been the poor quality of 'initial decisions' taken on asylum claims by Home Office case workers who consistently refuse between 66 and 88 per cent of all asylum applications (Smith 2004; Amnesty International 2004; Table 5.1). For well over a decade there have been calls to

Table 5.1 UK Home Office initial decisions on asylum claims, 2000–2007

Initial decisions	2000	2001	2002	2003	2004	2005	2006	2007
Applications made	109,205	120,950	83,540	64,940	46,020	27,395	20,930	23,430
Granted asylum	10,375 (11%)	11,450 (9%)	8,270 (10%)	3,865 (6%)	1,565 (3%)	1,940 (7%)	2,170 (10%)	3,545 (16%)
Granted exceptional leave to remain, humanitarian protection or discretionary leave	11,495 (12%)	20,190 (17%)	20,135 (24%)	7,210 (11%)	3,995 (9%)	2,800 (10%)	2,305 (11%)	2,200 (10%)
Refused	75,680 (78%)	89,310 (74%)	55,130 (66%)	53,865 (83%)	40,465 (88%)	22,655 (83%)	16,460 (79%)	16,030 (74%)
Applications withdrawn	1,720	2,400	1,490	1,835	2,205	2,545	1,780	1,230

Source: Freedom of Information request No. 78760 (1 November 2012) to the UK Border Agency. Figures are rounded to the nearest whole number. Because of the way UKBA record applications, the figures do not total 100%.

'front-load' resources into the bureaucracy to enable officials who undertake the initial assessment of asylum claims to be better trained and resourced, and thus better able to arrive at decisions which are in accord with the law and less likely to be overturned on appeal.

While not all of the Home Office's initial decisions are appealed against, on average about 20 per cent of all Home Office initial decisions appealed to the Asylum and Immigration Tribunal (AIT or Tribunal) are overturned (Information Centre about Asylum and Refugees [ICAR] 2009: 8). However, official statistics obscure important disparities. Thus as Table 5.2 shows, over a seven-year period appeals by individuals coming from the Horn of Africa are upheld at a substantially higher rate than for all nationalities combined.[3]

Despite substantial investment in 2007, with the creation of the 'New Asylum Model', the quality of initial Home Office decisions remains poor as suggested by the fact that: (a) at least 25 per cent of asylum applicants were not given an initial screening interview; (b) 20–25 per cent of the unit's decisions were overturned on appeal; (c) the unit was unable to handle an increase in asylum applications with the result that a growing backlog of applications remains to be assessed; and (d) a large percentage of 'legacy' cases are still undecided (National Audit Office 2009).

While resource constraints contribute to such problems, arguably the causative factor is the institutional culture of the refugee authority. For instance, the British Home Office/UK Border Agency (UKBA) uses more restrictive definitions than suggested by UNHCR to assess asylum applications. For example, officials rephrase UNHCR's definition of persecution 'in such a way as to encourage negative assessments of asylum claims' (Good 2007: 64). Equally troubling, Home Office Asylum Policy Instructions (APIs) create additional barriers to stateless persons (see 'UK policy and the 1954 Convention on the Elimination of Statelessness' in this chapter) and/or require asylum applicants to submit to 'language tests' in an effort, which lacks an objective basis, to detect fraudulent claims (Campbell 2013). Home Office 'Operational Guidance Notes' are also problematic. These notes provide a summary of legal and factual information to assist Home Office case owners to assess certain types of claims; however, all too frequently they provide a very selective summary of information which is not consistent with asylum policy or, occasionally, with case law (Immigration Advisory Services 2009a and b; see below).

The British Home Office spends massive amounts of public money to litigate against a wide range of asylum (and immigration) appeals (Table 5.3, and 'How "Eritrean" claims alleging statelessness are decided in the British courts' in this chapter). There does not appear to be a rational reason for this though it undoubtedly reflects media concerns about the arrival of immigrants and 'bogus' asylum seekers, which focuses public attention on the government's in/ability to enforce border controls. Expenditure on litigation may also reflect the desire to prevent a legal precedent from being made which might allow individuals, including individuals with valid asylum claims, to obtain status.

The use of public funds to litigate against asylum and immigration appeals has clearly escalated and it is noteworthy that step increases in expenditure have

Table 5.2 Immigration Asylum Tribunal/Asylum Immigration Tribunal decisions allowed on appeal by claimants from the Horn of Africa, 2005–2012 (percentages)

	2005–2006	2006–2007	2007–2008	2008–2009	2009–2010	2010–2011	2011–2012
All appeals	26	31	36	44	36	30	32
Eritrea	33	44	55	50	36	48	47
Ethiopia	32	34	33	42	22	0	20
Somalia	39	46	51	39	55	41	33
Sudan	23	69	53	53	23	15	56

Source: Freedom of Information request No. 78760 (1 November 2012) to the UK Border Agency.

Table 5.3 Cost of the UK Border Agency's litigation in asylum and immigration claims incurred by the government's Treasury Solicitor, 1997–2011

Year	Sum of fees (£)	Fees disbursed (£)	Number of claims	
			Administrative Court	*Court of Appeal*
1997	n/a	n/a	1743	No records
1998	887,563	942,604	1696	No records
1999	1,526,080	1,747,593	1884	No records
2000	1,406,206	1,789,156	2189	7
2001	1,675,818	2,634,688	2563	8
2002	2,431,695	1,715,361	3563	61
2003	3,438,280	2,323,992	3927	183
2004	4,425,485	3,000,438	2271	268
2005	4,851,675	2,975,922	3093	307
2006	5,991,371	2,307,500	4201	393
2007	8,897,959	3,191,052	4392	424
2008	10,864,021	2,875,581	4528	478
2009	14,227,846	4,322,190	1231 (to May)	2501
2010	16,871,652	5,143,279	n/a	609
2011	16,023,934	5,221,848	n/a	757

Source: Freedom of Information requests replied to by the UK Border Agency on 8 May 2009, 20 March 2012 and 15 November 2012.

occurred after national elections (in 1997, 2001, 2005 and 2010). The coalition government elected in 2010 has, in the wake of the current fiscal crisis, imposed budget cuts of 24 per cent, 27 per cent and 20 per cent on the Ministry of Justice, the Home Office and the UKBA, respectively.[4] Curiously there is no evidence that budget cuts have affected Home Office litigation, though cuts have seen a reduction in the number of senior barristers appointed to handle 'country guidance' asylum cases for the Home Office (see 'How 'Eritrean' claims alleging statelessness are decided in the British courts' in this chapter).

Once an asylum claim is submitted, good legal representation is required to ensure that the Home Office adequately assesses it and that an immigration judge properly decides it. In most countries asylum applicants do not have access to a lawyer. In the USA, for instance, the majority of asylum seekers either pay for an attorney or they file and argue their own claim (Lonegan 2004). As Box 5.1 indicates, when asylum applicants complete the form themselves it nearly always contains errors which can fatally undermine the appeal.

Box 5.1 Potentially fatal errors occur when appellants are unable to pay for an attorney in the USA

During the Ethiopia–Eritrea war Tedros Medhin was dismissed from a government job because he was 'Eritrean' and the police sought to arrest and question him. He fled to the US and completed his own asylum application in the US, which was found to contain ten potentially fatal errors which were corrected at his hearing. However the judges refused his appeal. They found that '[A]lthough severe, state sanctioned economic deprivation might rise to the level of persecution, Medhin has alleged only the loss of one job due to his ethnicity. At most he has suffered ethnic discrimination, and although deplorable discrimination is not persecution.' As a failed asylum seeker he was subject to deportation to Ethiopia.

Source: *Tedros Medhin* v. *John Ashcroft*, No. 02-4247 decided 1 December 2003 in the Seventh Circuit Court of the United States.

It is often the case, however, that access to a lawyer is not always helpful even when one is provided. For example in the UK, where the government provides legal aid to asylum applicants to cover the cost of initial legal representation, the quality of that representation varies considerably (Mayor of London 2005). The problem of poor legal advice arises for several reasons. For instance case workers may be poorly managed by more senior colleagues, they may lack sufficient skills (e.g. how to interview applicants, how to handle interpreters etc.), they may have insufficient time to prepare their client's case and they may wrongly refuse to represent their client after the initial Home Office decision (Asylum Appellate Project 2009). Poorly prepared appeals result in the case being refused by the Tribunal. Such problems might be mitigated if case workers instruct a good, independent barrister to handle the appeal because they will normally check the case file, request new witness statements and draw up better grounds for appeal.

Over the past decade the British government has introduced a number of measures intended to deter individuals from claiming asylum. For instance in 1999 a separate benefits system was created for asylum seekers – individuals are given £35 per week for food and are not allowed to work or study[5] – who are also compulsorily 'dispersed' across the UK to approved accommodation until their application is decided. However, in the socially deprived areas to which asylum seekers are dispersed there are no immigration/legal services, which seriously hinders asylum claim (Hynes 2006).

Access to immigration advice has been affected by progressive cuts to the legal aid budget. Today a fixed-fee system is in place which allows £450 for a 4–5 hour consultation with a case worker who takes a statement from an asylum applicant – using a translator – and writes and submits the claim to the Home Office. Cuts in legal aid have reduced lawyers' fees and have led to a drastic decline in the number of immigration lawyers.[6] In short, asylum applicants may not be able to access a qualified lawyer to take their claim and represent them. In the recent past it was rare to see an asylum applicant representing themselves in court, i.e. as a 'litigant in person'. However, cuts in legal aid have resulted in a substantial increase in the number of 'litigants in person' and thus in the time judges need to decide an asylum claim.[7]

Declining access to legal advice is compounded by the complex nature of asylum and immigration law, which has been the subject of extensive reform. Thus between 1997 and 2010 Parliament passed 11 major pieces of legislation which were intended to make it more difficult for individuals to claim asylum (Somerville 2007; Stevens 2004; see Chapter 6). Legislators have failed to 'consolidate' these laws which, together with growing case law, present a formidable challenge to lawyers and judges.

Among the measures introduced is the 'fast-track' detention and accelerated appeal system intended to shorten the time required to decide the asylum claims of persons held in immigration detention for a growing number of reasons[8] and thus the time required to deport/return the person to their country of origin (see Independent Chief Inspector of Borders and Immigration 2011; Immigration Law Practitioners Association 2008; Global Detention Project 2011). In fast-track detention:

> [T]ime is always against the asylum-seeker . . . The tight timescales are intended to minimise the unnecessary detention of asylum-seekers, yet Detention Action's research found that they were detained for an average of two weeks before the process even started. Nearly one in five waited for over a month. Most have no access to legal advice during this period. Yet when the process finally begins, its speed poses huge challenges for asylum seekers. Most meet their solicitor for a few minutes just before their interview, often without advance notice. 99% are refused asylum. They have two days to submit an appeal, for which 60% are unrepresented. Finally, after an asylum process at breakneck speed, they spend an average of 58 days in detention awaiting removal.
>
> (Detention Action 2011: 4–5)

In 1996, 1999, 2002, 2004, 2006 and 2009 the government reformed the Tribunal responsible for deciding asylum and immigration appeals with the result that the statutory regime became increasingly complex. At the same time important procedures have also been changed, not least the appeals procedure (ICAR 2009). As Thomas has observed there has been an increasing emphasis on efficiency and cost-effectiveness which has involved setting tight time limits and targets for assessing claims despite the fact that 'the speed at which the appeal proceeds . . . is entirely in the hands of the Home Office' (2005: 479, he is quoting Blake 1986).

Caught between demands for greater efficiency, delays created by the Home Office and problems with legal representation linked in part to reduced legal aid, decisions by the Tribunal on asylum claims have increasingly been subject to appeal (Tables 5.4 and 5.5). The increase in the number of appeals has, in turn, led the government to restructure the Tribunal to allow it to hear appeals against its own judges (thereby preventing appeals to the Administrative Court; Thomas 2005).

Given the extensive changes to the law etc. it is not surprising that immigration judges frequently err in deciding cases. Table 5.4 indicates that between 2005 and 2008 the High Court/Court of Appeal overturned between 28 and 44 per cent of

Table 5.4 The High Court/Court of Appeal's reviews of asylum appeals from the Asylum and Immigration Tribunal (AIT) on applicants from the Horn of Africa, April 2005 to June 2008

	Granted (%)	Refused (%)	Withdrawn (%)
Eritrea	41	59	0
Ethiopia	28	72	0
Somalia	35	65	0
Sudan	30	70	0

Source: Freedom of Information request to the AIT, Ref. FOI/56364/08/MB on 25 November 2008.

the Tribunal's decisions to refuse reconsideration (a grant means that the case is remitted/sent back to the Tribunal for a new hearing because the judge made a serious error of law). Overall, about 22 per cent of the decisions taken by immigration judges are overturned in the High Court, and 30–38 per cent of these cases are subsequently granted (ICAR 2009). In short, judicial decision-making is clearly a problem.

Table 5.5 indicates that nearly two-thirds of the appeals from the AIT which the Court of Appeal agreed to hear[9] between 2003 and 2009 were subsequently granted. These appeals are first made to the Tribunal and only if the Tribunal refuses to reconsider its decision can an application for an appeal be made to the English Court of Appeal. The high grant rate by the appellate court once again underlines the poor quality of Tribunal decisions.

In the USA there are huge disparities in the way that immigration judges decide asylum claims. TRAC[10] found that grant rates in the USA vary immensely by the nationality of the applicant, by court and by judge. TRAC analysed 297,240 asylum cases and found that the 'typical judge-by-judge denial rate' was 65 per cent (with grant rates ranging from 10 per cent to 98 per cent). The study found that an important factor which determined whether an applicant obtained asylum hinged

Table 5.5 Court of Appeal (Civil Division) cases appealed from the Asylum and Immigration Tribunal/Immigration and Asylum Tribunal by year and outcome, 2003–2009

Year	Total filed	Appeals disposed of by result					Total disposals
		Allowed	Dismissed	Dismissed by consent	Struck out	Otherwise disposed of	
2009	298	209	53	33	1	16	312
2008	395	276	67	40	–	18	401
2007	380	252	79	30	–	–	361
2006	341	235	77	25	2	1	340
2005	110	22	3	3	–	–	28
2004	150	24	27	21	–	61	133
2003	108	18	21	17	–	46	102
Total	1,782	1,036 (62%)	327 (19%)	169 (10%)	3	142 (8%)	1677

Source: Annual reports of the UK Ministry of Justice/Department for Constitutional Affairs.

upon whether they were legally represented: while 69 per cent of all claims were denied, 93 per cent of applicants without a lawyer were denied as opposed to 64 per cent of individuals who were represented by a lawyer.

A subsequent and more comprehensive study of asylum decision-making at all four levels of the US legal system – regional asylum offices, immigration courts, the Board of Immigration Appeals and US circuit courts – found that statistics on asylum adjudication:

> suggest that in the world of asylum adjudication, there is remarkable variation in decision-making from one official to the next, from one office to the next, from one region to the next, from one Court of Appeals to the next, and from one year to the next, even during periods when there has been no intervening change in the law. The variation is particularly striking when one controls for both the nationality and the current area of residence of applicants and examines the asylum grant rates of the different asylum officers who work in the same regional building, or immigration judges who sit in adjacent courtrooms of the same immigration court.
>
> (Ramji-Nogales, Schoenholtz and Schrag 2007: 302)

Serious disparities existed not only at regional asylum offices, immigration courts and the Board of Immigration Appeals but also across all the US circuit courts. Furthermore, as Table 5.6 indicates, the extent to which US circuit courts remanded, i.e. sent an asylum case back to the lower court for a fresh decision, varied immensely in 2004–2005.

So great were the disparities in the way that immigration judges, Tribunals and the courts decided asylum applications that the authors of the report were unable to offer a rational explanation. However, a careful regression analysis of decisions together with data on the biographic characteristics of the decision-maker revealed further, disturbing disparities (Box 5.2.).

Box 5.2 Refugee 'roulette' in the US courts

- 'Represented asylum seekers were granted asylum at a rate of 45.6 per cent, almost three times as high as the 16.3 per cent grant rate for those without counsel'.
- 'The number of dependents that an asylum seeker brought with her to the United States played a surprisingly large role in increasing the chance of an asylum grant . . . while asylum seekers with no dependents have a 42.3 per cent grant rate, having one dependent increases the grant rate to 48.2 per cent'.
- 'Female immigration judges granted at a rate of 53.8 per cent, while male judges granted at a rate of 37.3 per cent'.

Source: Ramji-Nogales *et al.* 2007: 340–42, 372.

Table 5.6 Remand rates (%) for asylum cases considered by the US circuit courts, 2004–2005

First	Second	Third	Fourth	Fifth	Sixth	Seventh	Eighth	Ninth	Tenth	Eleventh
7.7	17.4	11.4	2.5	4.1	9.9	31.2	11.1	22.1	9.1	3.8

Source: Ramji-Nogales *et al.* 2007: 366, Figure 48.

Ramji-Nogales *et al.* (2007) reservations about judicial decision-making in the USA would appear to be mirrored in the very different approaches taken by US circuit courts to the issue of 'persecution' as defined in the Refugee Convention. Box 5.3 sets out the contradictory way in which three circuit courts have interpreted the meaning of 'persecution' in claims arising out of the Eritrea–Ethiopia war.

Box 5.3 Refugee 'roulette' in the US circuit courts and the meaning of 'persecution'

- 'Eritreans' who fled in anticipation of being expelled by Ethiopia were found not to have been persecuted for a Convention reason (see *Senait Kidane Tesfamichael; Dawit Tessea-Damate*, petitioners, v. *Alberto Gonzales*, US Attorney General, respondent. No. 04-61180, US Fifth Circuit Court, 24 October 2006).

- Though a petitioner's evidence of being an ethnic Eritrean who was deported from Ethiopia was accepted, the court found that 'involuntary deportation' did not amount to persecution under the Convention (see *Nighisti Woldemariam, Issac Ghebretnsae Beletse*, petitioners v. *John Ashcroft*, US Attorney General, No. 03-4518 before the US Third Circuit Court).

- The Ninth Circuit Court of Appeal overturned an Immigration Judge's decision on Hannah M. Seid, an Ethiopian of Eritrean descent. It argued that the witness testimony and documentary evidence compelled 'the conclusion that if removed to Ethiopia, Seid will likely face arrest and imprisonment on the basis of her origin' because 'once her identity and that of her family is determined [by the Ethiopian authorities], it is likely that she will be imprisoned and subjected to severe mistreatment, because of her Eritrean origin.' (see *Hanane M Seid*, Petitioner v. *Eric Holder*, Attorney General, Respondent, US Court of Appeals for the Ninth Circuit, No. 05-72176, Filed 23 December 2009).

UK policy and the 1954 Convention on the Elimination of Statelessness

Evidence that decisions on asylum claims depend, whether in small or large part, on chance raises serious questions about the quality of justice. While chance cannot be discounted as a factor in the UK, the manner in which the claims of stateless persons are assessed depends upon whether a state has appropriate policies and mechanisms in place to identify and separately assess applications by stateless persons as required by international law.

Following Britain's accession to the 1954 Convention on Statelessness it adopted provisions which entitled stateless persons who were lawfully present in the UK to certain basic rights. These rights included the right to remain in the UK, to work, enjoy access to education, be issued with identity papers and the right not to be expelled except on national security or public order grounds. However, in 1978 a stateless Palestinian named Kelzani was found by the Tribunal to have violated the conditions of his admission with respect to his employment and was deported (McDonald 1983: 250–1).[11] The deportation violated the UK's obligations under Art. 31 of the 1954 Convention, which says that stateless persons could only be removed if the person was a threat to national security or public order.

In 1980, the Home Office used the AIT's decision upholding Kelzani's deportation to revise Immigration Rule HC82 by deleting 'provision 56', which stated that, 'where a person was stateless, full account was to be taken of the provisions of the relevant international agreement to which the UK was a party' (McDonald 1983: 250–1). The change to the immigration rule has meant that since 1980 the claims of stateless persons are no longer considered in light of the UK's international obligations, i.e. there are no legal provisions offering protection to stateless persons and, even where officials may identify a statelessness person, such persons no longer qualify for a grant to leave or remain in the UK.

The Secretary of State for the Home Department (SSHD) has the authority to grant leave to enter or remain to individuals on a 'discretionary' basis if s/he so chooses. It was apparently on this basis in 1998 that the Home Office operated a policy of granting indefinite leave to remain to stateless persons where 'he or she had no residence rights in any [other] countries and the UK was the most appropriate country for "resettlement"' (UNHCR and Asylum Aid 2011: 68). However, after 2002, and for reasons which remain unclear, the policy ended. This change of policy became clear in 2002 with respect to stateless Palestinians, when the Home Office published an API entitled 'UNRWA assisted Palestinians' which stated that, '[T]here is no provision in primary legislation, the Immigration Rules or Home Office published policies that require leave to be granted to a person on the basis that they are stateless'.[12] The API meant that stateless Palestinians claiming asylum in the UK were denied asylum/protection and were returned to their country of origin. The Home Office position on stateless Palestinians was reiterated in a February 2012 operational guidance note (OGN) entitled 'The Occupied Palestinian Territories' (UK Home Office 2012b), which states in part:

> 3.12.6 Conclusion. The UK is a signatory to the 1954 Convention on the Status of Stateless Persons, but that Convention does not require signatories to grant leave to stateless persons. *There is no provision in primary legislation, the Immigration Rules or Home Office published policies that require leave to be granted to a person on the basis that they are stateless.* A claim on this basis alone would therefore fail to be refused on the grounds that leave is being sought for a purpose not covered by the Immigration Rules.

3.12.7 No distinction is made between applications for leave to remain from stateless people and from people who have a nationality. *Stateless people whose applications are successful are granted leave to enter or remain in the usual way. Those whose applications fail are expected to leave the United Kingdom, usually to return to their countries of habitual residence.* The fact of being stateless is not, per se, a reason for granting leave to enter or remain in the UK, and would not give rise to a grant of asylum or Humanitarian Protection. [my emphasis]

This policy is at odds with Home Office policy, which allows the SSHD to grant discretionary leave to remain in the UK to stateless British overseas citizens (and other UK passport holders)[13] and it is at odds with an understanding reached between the Home Office and UNHCR/Asylum Aid when the latter reviewed Home Office policies on statelessness in late 2011. That study found major problems with Home Office procedures, which left a potentially large number of stateless individuals in the UK vulnerable to discrimination, immigration detention and deportation (UNHCR and Asylum Aid 2011; see Chapter 6). Phrased somewhat differently, in British policy 'statelessness has little bearing on [an individual's] . . . ability to access rights or other entitlements, despite the obligations of international law owed to them by the UK' (*ibid.*: 70).

On 6 April 2013 the Home Office finally announced a new Immigration Rule establishing a procedure for stateless persons resident in the UK to make a postal application for limited leave to remain.[14] Individuals must post an application, together with extensive supporting documents,[15] to the Home Office. This is a welcome step. However, given past practice and the evidentiary requirements that must be met by stateless persons, Asylum Aid notes that there are serious reservations about the potential unfairness of this policy:[16]

1. Under current government plans there will be no legal aid available to stateless persons to help them complete the required documentation and make a formal application.
2. The regulations do not stipulate a minimum or maximum time within which an official should arrive at a decision.
3. If officials assist applicants to identify the information required then there is some hope that stateless persons will benefit from the rule change; however, if officials are obstructive then the evidentiary requirements will be too high for most applicants to meet, and their applications will fail.
4. It appears that applicants will not have a right of appeal against a refusal of their application; if this is the case then their only solution will be to seek a judicial review (which requires legal advice).
5. Finally, the Home Office has identified a large number of conditions for applicants to meet, which places huge discretionary power in the hands of officials (in the past this power has been used to refuse applications).

The Home Office has not announced equivalent rules setting out guidance and the procedure for identifying and separately assessing the protection needs of stateless individuals seeking asylum in the UK.[17] Current practice is highly problematic because when an asylum claim alleging statelessness is made, the Home Office uniformly refuses the application; the claimant must then appeal to the Tribunal to overturn the decision.

The immigration judge (IJ) is tasked with determining a stateless person's nationality, but his/her approach to this issue can be problematic. First, officials, judges and lawyers draw upon public forms of discourse which imbue the meaning of 'race' with potentially conflicting and problematic meanings. The term 'nation' is derived from '*nationem*, Latin for breed, race, a term in common use from the 13th century originally with a primary sense of racial group rather than a political organized grouping' (Williams 1976: 213). Second asylum applicants *per force* employ the same terms to explain their case to the court, but their understanding of the terms is imbued with quite different cultural meanings. For the above reasons, terms like nation, nationalism, nationality and ethnicity carry complex and contradictory meanings that, if ignored or missed by a judge, can weigh against a claimant.

The court's interpretation of these terms is further complicated by the language of the Refugee Convention, which states that an individual claiming asylum must establish that they have a:

> well founded fear of being persecuted for reasons of race, religion, nationality, membership of a particular social group or political opinion, is outside the country of his nationality and is unable or, owing to such fear, is unwilling to avail himself of the protection of that country; or who, not having a nationality and being outside the country of his former habitual residence as a result of such events, is unable or, owing to such fear, is unwilling to return to it.
>
> (Art. 1 (A) 2 of the 1951 Geneva Convention)

Claims alleging that the individual was denationalized pose an additional problem to a judge who is required to determine the claimant's 'effective nationality'. The problem, and proper legal approach to this issue, is set out in the UNHCR Handbook (1992: ¶89) which states that an asylum applicant:

> may not know himself, or he may wrongly claim to have a particular nationality or to be stateless. Where his nationality cannot be clearly established, his refugee status should be determined in a similar manner to that of a stateless person, i.e. instead of the country of his nationality, the country of his former habitual residence will have to be taken into account.

In the UK the judicial task of determining a stateless person's nationality is further complicated by the Home Office practice of identifying an individual's nationality for the *administrative* purpose of 'returning'/deporting him should the asylum claim be refused.[18] In this way the Home Office deems that an applicant possesses 'dual nationality' (see UNHCR 1992: ¶106–7), which requires the applicant to seek 'national' (as distinct from international) protection because UNHCR distinguishes 'between the possession of a nationality in the legal sense and the availability of protection by the country concerned'. There would appear to be two procedures open to the court to determine which country an applicant may have a 'genuine and effective link' with. For instance, Art. 12, paragraph 4 of the International Covenant on Civil and Political Rights sets out guidance for states regarding 'freedom of movement' to 'everyone lawfully within the territory of the State'.[19] In a commentary on this article Human Rights Watch (2002b) observes that:

> The wording of article 12, paragraph 4, does not distinguish between nationals and aliens ('no one'). Thus, the persons entitled to exercise this right can be identified only by interpreting the meaning of the phrase 'his own country'. The scope of 'his own country' is broader than the concept 'country of his nationality'. It is not limited to nationality in a formal sense, that is, nationality acquired at birth or by conferral; it embraces, at the very least, an individual who, because of his or her special ties to or claims in relation to a given country, cannot be considered to be a mere alien. This would be the case, for example, for nationals of a country who have been stripped of their nationality in violation of international law, and of individuals whose country of nationality has been incorporated in or transferred to another national entity, whose nationality is being denied them. The language of article 12, paragraph 4, moreover, permits a broader interpretation that might embrace other categories of long-term residents, including but not limited to stateless persons arbitrarily deprived of the right to acquire the nationality of the country of such residence.

In short, the International Covenant on Civil and Political Rights adopts an 'inclusive interpretation that would protect stateless persons from being deprived of their nationality and from being removed from a country where they are legally resident, i.e. such as stateless persons in the UK. As such it offers a wider interpretation of the term 'genuine and effective link' – defined on the basis of identifiable factors such as place of birth, descent, family ties, participation in public life, attachments shown for a given country, residency etc. – than is set out in *Nottebohm* (*Liechtenstein* v. *Guatemala*).[20]

However, the British courts[21] apply a much more restrictive approach and consider only whether an individual may have a formal, legal entitlement to a nationality. Thus the Court of Appeal established the 'Bradshaw principle' [*1994 Imm AR 359*][22] which states 'that when a person does not accept that the Secretary of State is correct about his nationality, it is incumbent on him to prove it, if need be by making an application for such nationality' at an embassy (providing such an application does not put the person or their family at risk; Box 5.4). Thus an 'Eritrean' applicant is required to approach the Ethiopian embassy, the state which is alleged to have deprived him of nationality, to secure written documentation confirming that s/he is *persona non grata*; failing that s/he must approach the state of Eritrea, where the Home Office believes that s/he has a formal right of nationality (see Batchelor 1995:249–50). However, neither the Ethiopian nor the Eritrean authorities will confirm an individual's nationality.

Box 5.4 The 'Bradshaw principle' – 'when a person does not accept that the Secretary of State is correct about his nationality, it is incumbent on him to prove it'

T applied for a judicial review of the Tribunal's refusal to grant him leave to appeal against the judge's decision not to recognize him as a refugee. T's father was Eritrean and his mother was Ethiopian. He spent all his life in Ethiopia and had no family or friends in Eritrea. T was arrested because of his Eritrean origin but escaped to the UK. The issue was whether T was a national of Eritrea and whether he would be admitted. The Eritrea embassy indicated that in seeking citizenship T would need sworn testimony of his Eritrean paternity from three witnesses. The judge concluded that on the balance of probabilities T would be eligible for Eritrean citizenship. T argued that (1) he would not be able to obtain the necessary sworn evidence and (2) the judge had failed to evaluate his reasons for refusing to apply for citizenship in Eritrea, which was the risk that he would be required to undergo military service. The Tribunal refused T's application because T was not in a position to assert statelessness while eligible for citizenship in a country with which he had a close connection. If he was eligible he must apply for citizenship.

Source: *R (on the application of Tewolde)* v. *Immigration Appeal Tribunal* (Administrative Court, 28 January 2004).

Since at least 2002 there have been a continuous number of claims by stateless 'Eritreans' – many of whom have been deemed by the Home Office to be nationals of the state of Eritrea[23] – whose case has been refused on the basis of an administrative convenience, i.e. the Bradshaw principle, without attempting to examine the individual's effective nationality. Ironically the Tribunal's reliance on Bradshaw to define the nationality of Ethiopian-born ethnic Eritreans as Eritrean nationals has occurred at a time when Eritrean nationals cannot legally be returned to Eritrea due to the risk of persecution which confronts failed asylum seekers. In effect, reliance on Bradshaw produces a number of 'failed' asylum seekers who cannot be returned and who have no legal status in the UK (see Chapter 6).

To appreciate how the Home Office and the courts determine the asylum claims of stateless 'Eritreans' it is necessary to examine in some detail the two most recent cases which raised the issue of whether the state of Ethiopia has made ethnic Eritreans stateless.

How 'Eritrean' claims alleging statelessness are decided in the British courts

Both the asylum claims discussed here were listed by the Tribunal as 'country guidance' cases. This means that the decision reached in each case shall, in accord with 'Rule 12.2 of the Practice Directions'[24]:

be treated as an authoritative finding on the country guidance issue identified in the determination, based upon the evidence before the members of the Tribunal, the AIT or the IAT that determine the appeal. As a result, unless it has been expressly superseded or replaced by any later 'CG' determination, or is inconsistent with other authority that is binding on the Tribunal, such a country guidance case is authoritative in any subsequent appeal, so far as that appeal: (a) relates to the country guidance issue in question; and (b) depends upon the same or similar evidence.

When the claims are heard much of the background history/context is stripped away by the judge as s/he seeks to identify the key legal issue at the core of the claim (the wider context of both cases can be found in Chapters 1 and 2). In February 1999 'Medhin' (Case 5) returned home to learn that her husband had been deported to Eritrea. Friends assisted her to leave for Kenya, from where she travelled to the UK in 1999. On arrival she claimed asylum and gave her nationality as 'Eritrean' (which is the reason Ethiopian officials gave for wanting to expel her and her family); she claimed to fear persecution in Ethiopia *and* Eritrea. The Home Office refused her asylum application on the grounds that (a) she 'had not established a well-founded fear of persecution' and (b) that she could safely be removed to either Ethiopia or Eritrea. The Home Office set her 'removal directions' to Eritrea. By the time her appeal against the Home Office decision was heard in March 2002 Ethiopia and Eritrea had signed the Algiers Accord.

At her hearing 'Medhin' testified that: (a) she had been born and raised in Ethiopia to parents who had emigrated from Eritrea; (b) she had never lived in Eritrea; (c) she understood *Tigrinya* with difficulty; and (d) she had not been involved in Eritrean politics nor had she ever been issued with Eritrean identity documents. She also stated that her 'Eritrean' husband and son had been deported.

The judge accepted her evidence but dismissed her appeal. He found that she had a *formal entitlement* to Eritrean nationality and could 'return' there – the official euphemism for a forcible return or deportation –without risk. Because she held an Ethiopian passport the judge found that she was also a national of Ethiopia and could safely return there. Her counsel successfully appealed against that decision on the basis that, while she might be entitled to Eritrean citizenship if she choose to apply for it, 'that did not equate with a finding that she is a citizen of Eritrea currently'.

When the case was reconsidered in October 2002 the judge set aside an expert report that was three years old and a second report that was 'too general'. She also set aside a 'Note from UNHCR' because it 'did not relate specifically to the situation of this appellant'. The judge found that: (a) the appellant should have made a request for, and received a refusal of, protection from the Ethiopian *and* Eritrean authorities to establish that a given nationality was ineffective; (b) she was entitled to citizenship in Eritrea and would face no real risk if returned there; and (c) she was an Ethiopian national and could safely return there. This decision too was overturned on the basis that 'a lawful claim to Eritrean nationality meant that she would not be entitled to the protection of the Convention' and it was not clear 'whether she would in practice be afforded protection by the Eritrean authorities'.

At this point the SSHD changed 'Medhin's' removal directions to Ethiopia. At her August 2004 appeal[25] – which was listed for country guidance and 'joined' with two other claims that raised the same issue – her barrister argued that:

1. She was a former national of Ethiopia following the *de facto* removal of her nationality on the basis of discrimination. In short she was not an Eritrean national but rather a refugee under Art. 1(A) 2 of the 1951 Convention and she could not lawfully be removed to Eritrea.
2. Being an Ethiopian of Eritrean descent meant that, if she were sent back to Ethiopia she would face discriminatory withdrawal of her nationality and onward deportation to Eritrea. If she were returned to Ethiopia and allowed to stay, she would be transformed from a citizen into a registered alien.
3. Furthermore 'the fact that a claimant could seek another nationality would not disqualify him from protection under the Convention'. The issue was whether he already possessed such nationality. Citing an unreported Court of Appeal decision counsel argued that the failure of an appellant to make enquiries at the embassy for a passport or travel document 'was excusable where other credible evidence clearly showed that the result would be negative'.

Counsel for the SSHD – two barristers instructed by Treasury Solicitors (TSoL) to litigate on behalf of the Home Office – argued that there was no general risk for Ethiopians of Eritrean descent because hostilities had ended and 'The Convention provides that an asylum applicant must seek the protection of any country of which he is a citizen. The principle in Bradshaw should apply. . .' (see Box 5.4).

The Tribunal considered and dismissed a substantial body of evidence, including reports by Amnesty International and Human Rights Watch, as having little bearing on the current situation in Ethiopia. Two expert reports were set aside for similar reasons. The experts had argued that 'there has been no indication that either country is prepared to bring policies of deportation or repatriation, however implemented, to an end' and that 'there is no likelihood that they [deportees and other individuals who fled the country] would be allowed back or given identity documents'.

Accordingly the court decided that following the peace treaty of 2000 'Eritreans' were no longer at risk of being deported from Ethiopia. Furthermore it decided that the Ethiopian Directive of 2004 [see Chapter 4, the section entitled 'Ethiopia's unsatisfactory regularization of its resident "Eritreans"'] allowed 'Eritreans' to return to Ethiopia and that they would be recognized by the Ethiopian embassy and would be given travel documents allowing them to return. With respect to arguments about the approach that should be used in deciding 'dual nationality', the Tribunal found that 'the deprival of citizenship by itself is not necessarily persecutory' and that MA had not been deprived of her nationality. The Tribunal also relied on Bradshaw, stating, 'there is, on the face of the Eritrean legislation an entitlement to nationality . . . In fact [she] qualifies for Eritrean citizenship and there are no serious obstacles to their being able to apply for and obtain citizenship.' Yet again, 'Medhin's' counsel successfully appealed against the decision to the Court of Appeal (CoA) on the basis that the judges had made an error of law in considering her Eritrean – rather than Ethiopian – citizenship and whether she would be at risk if she were returned to Eritrea.

Her case was once again listed for country guidance but before it was reconsidered a related case was heard by the CoA which threw a very positive light on her claim. When MA's case was appealed to the CoA in 2004 it had been 'joined' with four related Ethiopian appeals. The parties to her case 'consented' (agreed) that her claim should be reconsidered by the Tribunal; at the same time the SSHD agreed to reconsider three other claims but she refused the claim of 'EB',[26] which was heard by the CoA in July 2007. In 'EB' the CoA found that (¶71):

> Ethiopia will not currently allow EB to be returned but the question must be answered now, not as at some date in the unknowable future when Ethiopia might change its mind and decide to re-admit EB for some reason which cannot be currently predicted. Once it is clear that EB was persecuted for a Convention reason while in Ethiopia, there is no basis on which it can be said that that state of affairs has now changed. I would therefore conclude that EB has a well-founded fear of persecution for a Convention reason and that she is now entitled to the status of a refugee.

This decision appeared to tilt the scales in favour of MA because the CoA had accepted the expert evidence which the Tribunal had dismissed when it decided 'Medhin's' 2004 reconsideration.

In the period leading up to her hearing the Home Office once again instructed, through the TSoL, two barristers to handle the litigation. Their case preparation, which occurred over five months and involved a 'case management review' with several departments in the Home Office, assessed the evidence submitted by 'Medhin's' counsel, decided what evidence the Home Office needed to produce, prepared the case and filed a skeleton argument with the court. The task, as the SSHD's legal team saw it, was to provide a more complete picture of the case and of the situation in Ethiopia, to argue that her case was materially different from that of 'EB' and to show that 'it shouldn't necessarily follow that a deprivation of nationality should lead to refugee status'.[27] The team, together with a Home Office Presenting Officer (HOPO), several barristers, a TSoL solicitor, produced four boxes of evidence for the two-day hearing.

'Medhin's' counsel prepared for her reconsideration and relied on 'EB', whose case he had argued, to 'sweep away' the previous Home Office argument on the issue of nationality. He assumed that the Home Office would argue that, as someone who fled Ethiopia in anticipation of arrest, she had not been denationalized. Based on the CoA's findings in 'EB' he believed that the expert evidence strongly supported his argument that 'Medhin' had been deprived of her nationality for a Convention reason. Going into the hearing he made several tactical decisions which may have affected the outcome of the case: (a) he relied heavily on international refugee law; (b) he did not call MA to testify (in order to preserve the credibility of findings from her testimony in earlier hearings); and (c) he submitted reports by two experts (but did not call them to give oral evidence).

When the case was heard in September 2007 the key issue was whether Ethiopia had deprived MA of her nationality and whether such an act amounted to persecution under the Convention. In short, if she could not be returned to Ethiopia then she was entitled to refugee status. Submissions were made on Ethiopian law, international law, domestic law, and the position of the Ethiopian embassy. A wide range of evidence – the findings of the EECC, evidence supplied by the SSHD on 'returns', human rights reports and expert reports – was submitted.

The expert evidence, the SSHD's rebuttal evidence and arguments about the role of the embassy were critical to the outcome of the case. The expert reports – based largely on interviews with 'Eritreans', access to key networks and documentary research – argued that deported 'Eritreans' were not allowed to return and that Ethiopian embassies/consulates refused to issue 'Eritreans' a travel document. In short, the experts argued that Ethiopia operated a policy of excluding deported Eritreans because officials saw them as having no entitlement to Ethiopian nationality.

The SSHD rebutted expert evidence with evidence by an official from the Home Office 'Returns Group Unit' who testified that the embassy in London accepted the majority of Ethiopians applying to return voluntarily via the IOM and would do so for the appellant if she made a *bona fide* application.[28]

Conflicting versions about the role of the embassy were presented. Counsel for MA argued that the embassy's failure to respond to his queries and the letters sent by the SSHD reflected a policy of excluding deportees/'Eritreans'. By contrast, the SSHD argued that while the embassy had failed to respond to its letters, this did not constitute evidence that the embassy would refuse to accept 'Medhin'.

The Tribunal argued that the first test in deciding whether a person was a national of a country was whether that person 'fulfils the nationality law requirements' of her country. Because she had reportedly travelled to the UK on an Ethiopian passport she was found to possess *de facto* Ethiopian nationality and, under Ethiopian law, she could not be deprived of her nationality.[29] The question of whether she had *de jure* nationality, said the Tribunal, rested on the factual question of whether the Ethiopian authorities will accept her. Unlike 'EB', the authorities had not removed her documents which, the SSHD argued, meant that she 'was not a person who was liable to be deported'.

The Tribunal rejected expert evidence to the effect that the human rights situation in Ethiopia had deteriorated since the war, that the authorities 'apply the laws in a highly arbitrary manner or openly violate them' and that it was a recurring practice of Ethiopian embassies and consulates to decline to recognize/assist 'Eritreans' (including individuals who had been deported and those who fled in anticipation of deportation). It was common ground that from 1998 until 2002–3 'the Ethiopian authorities would not accept an Ethiopian national of Eritrean parentage'. However, the Tribunal argued that (a) there were no current reports that Ethiopia discriminated against ethnic Eritreans and (b) the SSHD submitted rebuttal evidence to the effect that, 'as long as a person said they wanted to go back to Ethiopia and could show that they were *de jure* an Ethiopian national, they would be documented as an Ethiopian national and returned'.

We can now see how the Tribunal approached the case. Tellingly, counsel for 'Medhin' relied heavily on the case of 'EB' to support his argument about deprivation of nationality; in fact he submitted similar expert evidence in both cases. However, the judges set aside substantial elements of his argument and evidence on three grounds. First, they argued that the facts in MA were different from those in EB, i.e. the case of EB did not apply. Second, counsel for the SSHD rebutted MA's expert evidence with evidence that the London embassy accepted applications by Ethiopians wishing to return, i.e. she offered the court alternative evidence about the role of the embassy. Third, as her counsel later admitted, her solicitor had 'blinked' by failing to get her to make a *bona fide* application to the embassy, which would have countered the SSHD's assertion that she had only approached the embassy for 'the purpose of litigation'. The Tribunal found that if she had applied to the embassy in good faith she 'would be likely to be issued with emergency travel documentation allowing her to return'. On this basis it dismissed her appeal.

'Medhin's' barrister appealed against this decision but the CoA only agreed to hear the case on the basis that the Tribunal 'had erected a false distinction between *de facto* and *de jure* nationality'. After several hours of argument, the panel of three Lords Justices agreed[30] that while the Tribunal's approach to deciding nationality was flawed 'it did not erect any fresh legal analysis'. The CoA upheld the Bradshaw principle stating that, 'there is no reason why the appellant should not herself make a formal application to the embassy to seek the relevant documents'. On this basis her appeal was refused. Her counsel appealed 'on the papers' to the House of Lords but the appeal was refused; he subsequently advised her that she should make a fresh asylum claim (which succeeded).

In the ten years that her case had bounced back and forth in the courts, judges repeatedly erred in deciding it and they relied upon an administrative expedient in compelling her to approach the Eritrea embassy (a country that she had never lived in) and the Ethiopian embassy (which had deported her family). In short, rather than examine the arbitrary actions of the Ethiopian state or assess which country she had 'a genuine and effective link' to, the courts merely decided her formal entitlement to nationality.

The next country guidance case to be listed by the Tribunal on the issue of statelessness in Ethiopia was not heard until late 2010. This was the case of 'Solomon' (see Case 6) who was born in Addis Ababa in 1979 to an Eritrean mother and an Ethiopian father. In July 1999 his mother was seized and deported. Armed officers confiscated his identity card and detained him for a month during which time he was repeatedly interrogated and 'tortured' before being released on condition that he register with the police. With the assistance of his uncle he hid and was later helped to leave for the UK, where he claimed asylum in September 1999. However, the Home Office did not assess his asylum claim until January 2005, when they refused it.

His appeal against the Home Office was not heard until May 2008, when the IJ accepted evidence about the ethnic/national identity of 'Solomon' and his parents, his ill-treatment in custody and medical evidence that he had been physically ill-treated in detention. However, the IJ found that the objective evidence 'falls short of showing that those of part Eritrean descent face persecution'. The judge argued that 'there is a [legal] presumption that the appellant will be treated as a *de jure* national as one of its own' regardless of the refusal of the Ethiopian embassy in London to recognize him. The IJ argued that Ethiopia and Eritrea were no longer at war and '[T]here is an absence of objective evidence that the Ethiopian authorities harbour the same level of suspicion of those of part Eritrean descent now as they did in 1999'. On this basis the judge rejected his claim.

'Solomon's' counsel appealed against the decision on the basis that the IJ had: (a) to be satisfied that not even a reasonable likelihood existed that the appellant would be persecuted on return; (b) failed to consider relevant submissions in law; and (c) failed to address the expert evidence. The Tribunal refused to reconsider the case. Counsel therefore made an application 'on the papers' to the CoA (which was refused), following which he made an oral application which the CoA accepted. The CoA reasoned that the Tribunal had failed to assess possible persecution in the form of the deprivation of the appellant's Ethiopian citizenship.

The case was reconsidered in December 2008 by a senior IJ who, while noting the grounds for reconsideration, merely reviewed the previous decision without accepting new submissions or evidence. 'Solomon's' counsel appealed against this decision on the basis that the senior IJ had: (a) failed to assess whether persecution arose from the deprivation of Solomon's nationality; (b) failed to consider legal submissions; (c) had erroneously applied MA (Ethiopia) as if it were a country guidance; and (d) against a background of continued exclusion of individuals of part Eritrean descent, the senior IJ had failed to consider evidence which suggested that the appellant would not be allowed to return to Ethiopia and would not be allowed to register under the 2004 Directive.

The same senior IJ who had refused to reconsider the case in 2008 dismissed the appeal. Counsel again appealed 'on the papers' to the CoA in January 2009 but was refused. He made an oral application in March 2009 (amending the grounds to account for the CoA decision on 'Medhin'). The CoA decided that: 'In light of *MA (Ethiopia) [2009] EWCA Civ 289* there is a real prospect that the applicant will establish that both the IJ and senior IJ erred in law in applying a presumption that he was not at risk of being denied status as a national . . .'. The case was sent back to the Tribunal for reconsideration and was listed for country guidance.

Counsel for 'Solomon' instructed two country experts to prepare reports on related but distinct issues. It also transpired that prior to the hearing the government cut UKBA's budget, which meant that a senior HOPO (civil servant) handled the case rather than barristers. When the claim was heard in January 2011 the key issue was to ascertain whether the appellant who was 'entitled to Ethiopian nationality as a matter of international law . . . [had] been denied such nationality by the Ethiopian authorities'.[31] The hearing lasted three days and accepted submissions on the same issues as in MA's 2007 appeal.

It was common ground that the appellant was an Ethiopian national at birth and remained so until 1998–99. The Tribunal quoted Adjami and Harrison (2008) that deprivation of nationality 'must be accompanied by important procedural and substantive safeguards' – notably procedural fairness and due process together with a prohibition against ethnic discrimination – and reminded itself of the meaning of 'acts of persecution' as defined in Art. 1A of the Geneva Convention. Acts of persecution must:

a.   Be sufficiently serious by their nature or repetition as to constitute a severe violation of basic human rights, in particular the rights from which derogation cannot be made under Article 15(2) of the European Convention for the Protection of Human Rights and Fundamental Freedoms; or
b.   Be an accumulation of various measures, including violations of human rights which is sufficiently severe as to affect an individual in a similar manner as mentioned in (a).

Also acts of persecution can take various forms including:

a.   Acts of physical or mental violence, including acts of sexual violence;
b.   Legal, administrative, police, and/or judicial measures which are in themselves discriminatory or which are implemented in a discriminatory manner;
c.   Prosecution or punishment which is disproportionate or discriminatory;
d.   Denial of judicial redress resulting in a disproportionate or discriminatory punishment.

In light of accepted understandings of persecution, the Tribunal assessed the evidence before it, starting with the treatment of Ethiopian-born Eritreans in 1999. The Tribunal found that the removal of 'Solomon's' identity card constituted an act of persecution for a Convention reason because it was done on the basis of his 'race, nationality, membership . . .' The Tribunal then asked itself whether the events prior to his departure remain important today should he be returned. It noted that he had taken 'all reasonable steps' that could be asked of him in approaching the Ethiopian embassy and that the embassy had refused to acknowledge his entitlement to Ethiopian nationality. The court accepted that the reason for his exclusion arose from the arbitrary attitude of officials towards 'ethnic Eritreans' who 'blur the issues of ethnicity and nationality'.

Was it possible for the appellant to return to Ethiopia to reacquire nationality, live and work? Expert A argued – on the basis of transcribed interviews with Ethiopian officials at the London embassy, interviews with officials in Addis Ababa, with 'Eritreans' in Ethiopia and 'Eritreans' who had been deported to Eritrea that a large number of resident 'Eritreans' had not been registered under the 2004 Directive. Expert A also argued that it is no longer possible for 'Eritreans' to register, that unregistered 'Eritreans' currently resident in Ethiopia are 'stateless' and that Ethiopia would not accept that the appellant is entitled to nationality. Expert B argued that the authorities stipulate a four-year residence rule which effectively prevents an individual from applying for nationality from abroad. Both experts were unequivocal that: (a) the 2004 Directive only applied to 'Eritreans' who had been continuously resident in Ethiopia between 1993 and 2004; and (b) that 'Eritreans' who failed to register in 2004 were permanently excluded from reacquiring nationality.

In the absence of rebuttal evidence, the court accepted that the appellant was unable to make use of the 2004 Directive and unable to return to reacquire nationality. Finally the Tribunal concluded that 'looking at matters overall and acknowledging that the threshold for persecution is a high one, I have concluded that the state of affairs would be persecutory for the appellant'. 'Solomon' won his appeal and was granted refugee status.

Had the Home Office issued an initial decision on the two claims within a reasonable time – and prior to the Ethiopia–Eritrea peace accord of May 2000 – both individuals would very likely have been granted asylum. As it transpired, however, IJs erred repeatedly in deciding their claims: 'Medhin's' claim was heard six times while 'Solomon's' case was heard three times. A partial explanation for this relates to the fact that IJs have limited knowledge of and experience in dealing with complex legal issues like deprivation of nationality. Even so IJs tend to accept Home Office arguments rather than find in favour of appellants.[32]

The success of the SSHD in 'Medhin's' 2007 hearing arose from the fact that she offered the court rebuttal evidence about the role of the embassy and an alternative way of interpreting the principal legal and evidential submissions made on behalf of 'Medhin'. For instance the SSHD successfully argued that 'Medhin's' expert evidence was historic and did not address the current situation and that while the Ethiopian embassy may not have responded to a request for information there was other information indicating that the embassy allowed the majority of Ethiopians to return. In short, the court was given the opportunity to consider an alternative interpretation of the evidence before it. The SSHD's legal arguments concerning factual differences between Medhin and EB, and the nature of deprivation of nationality, provided sufficient grounds for the judges to dismiss 'Medhin's' appeal.

At 'Solomon's' 2011 hearing the SSHD was represented by a HOPO who failed to discredit the experts and failed to offer any rebuttal evidence. Once the Tribunal accepted the credentials of the experts it had to address their evidence (which was accepted). In point of fact expert testimony directly contradicted findings made at 'Medhin's' hearing about the role of the embassy, the effect of the 2004 Directive and findings about the likelihood of risk on return. The opinions of the two experts were adopted by the court, which was compelled to grant status to 'Solomon' and thus overturn prior case law on this issue.

Conclusion

Many 'Eritreans' (and other sojourners) are in transit across Africa and the Middle East, where they become 'bottled up' at various points. Most will never reach the West, but the few who escape Africa confront considerable difficulties in entering Europe and applying for asylum. There are four fundamental obstacles facing asylum applicants, which arise from the organization of the refugee determination system and the way it processes asylum claims. While some problems are exacerbated by resource constraints by far the more significant issues arise from the authority's 'institutional culture', its readiness to adopt and implement policies intended to deter/block valid claims and from problematic decisions by officials. If an asylum applicant is fortunate to be represented by a good lawyer s/he must navigate their way through complex laws and policies to appeal against a refusal of status by the refugee authority and to argue their case before an IJ (who frequently misjudge asylum claims). A great deal of public money is spent on refugee determination systems but one is left with the strong sense that the quality of justice available to vulnerable individuals in need of protection is so poor that obtaining a grant of status is a matter of chance. Above all one is left with a feeling that officials are indifferent to the fate of individuals fleeing persecution (as in Ethiopia, these officials are merely 'doing their job').

The seeming indifference of officials and of the public towards refugees is reinforced when we look at British policies and the way policies are implemented. Britain's long-term breach of its legal obligations under the 1954 Convention on the Elimination of Statelessness is a serious indictment of its commitment to uphold international law and the way it assesses asylum claims. This breach, together with the absence of policies capable of identifying and assisting stateless persons, has meant that some applicants have been wrongfully refused asylum while other stateless persons in the country lack legal status and rights. Furthermore, rather than operate an inclusive policy to assist stateless persons the UK adopts an exclusive policy by administratively determining an individual's formal entitlement to a nationality. The essential unfairness of the process is compounded by the poor quality of judicial decisions which transform valid asylum applicants into 'failed' asylum seekers who are subject to detention and deportation.

6 'Bare life'

The vulnerability and political significance of stateless persons

In previous chapters I have argued that UKBA policies and decisions, complex law and the work of lawyers and judges comprise key elements of an asylum system which impedes the ability of stateless 'Eritreans' (and many others) from obtaining asylum. In this chapter I look at the legal and socio-economic situation of individuals whose asylum claims are refused.

The first section, 'How policy creates "illegality" and how officials unlawfully implement policy', examines British policies aimed at rendering 'failed asylum seekers' destitute by denying them access to social welfare support in the hope that they will voluntarily leave the country. Rather than looking at legal arguments *per se,* I use legal cases to illuminate the effect of these policies and the unlawful actions of officials who implement them. The next section, entitled 'More than "bare life": Individual and collective strategies in the face of destitution', draws on a series of 'conversations' with failed asylum seekers to illustrate their efforts to rebuild their lives and communities in the UK. I conclude by arguing that the policies discussed in this chapter are poorly designed and poorly implemented, so much so that UKBA could be said to be operating a set of irrational and incompatible but also *ad hoc* and unlawful policies and positions.

How policy creates 'illegality' and how officials unlawfully implement policy

I begin by looking at legal challenges to key elements of British asylum and immigration policy which bear directly on individuals whose asylum claims have been refused, namely the removal of welfare support and the consequences of being 'temporarily admitted' into the UK and thus placed in a 'limbo' of non-existence, a 'bare life'.

Morris (2009) has analysed fourteen legal judgments beginning in 1996 with *R* v. *Secretary of State for Social Security ex parte JVWI, QBD* and ending with *R* v. *SSHD ex parte Adam, Limbuela and Tesema* in 2005, which focused on the right of the state to abolish access to benefits for 'late claimers' to asylum. Eleven of these legal cases went against the government. She concluded that during this period the judiciary increasingly drew on the 1998 Human Rights Act and case law from the European Court to question and expand the interpretation of key elements of government policy and statutory provision for asylum seekers (see also Dauvergne 2004).

The cases she examines span a period when the British courts moved from a reliance on common law through to the implementation of the 1998 Human Rights Act and the growing importance of the European Court of Human Rights. She argued that during this period there existed considerable scope for judicial interpretation of policy and statutory provision (legislation) which arose from growing attempts by officials to deter asylum seekers from entering and staying in Britain. Specifically, all the cases sought to contest efforts aimed at withdrawing social welfare provision from asylum seekers, i.e. the right to housing, health services, basic social benefits and the right to work.

The government reacted to this judicial activism by putting into place legislation – via the 1996 Immigration and Asylum Act, the 1999 Immigration and Asylum Act, the Nationality, Immigration and Asylum Act (2002), and the Asylum and Immigration (Treatment of Claimants) Act 2004 – which completely restructured social welfare provision for asylum seekers. By 2005 legislation had created a policy of deterrence linked to a highly stratified system of entitlements (Dwyer and Brown 2005). Thus:

1. Asylum seekers' rights varied depending on their date of entry into the UK (i.e. individuals making a claim more than 72 hours after entry had no right to public support or to family reunion).
2. Refugees (those whose asylum claims have been granted) enjoy the same welfare rights as nationals, plus the right to family reunion.
3. Individuals granted temporary protection – i.e. humanitarian protection/discretionary leave – are granted entry for up to three years (they enjoy the same welfare rights as citizens, including the right to work but not the right to family reunion).
4. Failed asylum seekers/over-stayers whose claims have been turned down have no right to remain, no recourse to social welfare and no right to work.
5. Failed asylum seekers being redocumented for voluntary return to their country of origin qualify for conditional, short-term assistance in the form of designated housing plus an 'entitlement card' (a cash benefit valued at 70% of what citizens are entitled to; see p. 147).

In short, while judicial activism in the late 1990s may have seen more expansive interpretations of the law, by 2005 there was significantly less opportunity for judicial challenge because key elements of a policy of deterrence were placed on a statutory basis which the courts are required to respect. In effect, the human and moral claims made on behalf of asylum applicants were, by Act of Parliament, unable to be transformed into a right. Phrased somewhat differently, when in 2003 Lord Justice Collins (in *R* v. *SSHD ex parte Q, EWCA* ¶3) rhetorically asked, 'Can the Secretary of State refuse support to the destitute without thereby subjecting them to inhuman treatment?', the Home Secretary was in a position in 2005 to answer with an emphatic 'Yes'.

In law an asylum seeker whose application is refused is considered to be an 'unauthorised migrant' who continues to be temporarily admitted (unless they are detained) until they leave Britain. Failed asylum seekers find themselves in a legal limbo because under section (4) of the 1971 Immigration Act they are considered to be temporarily admitted into the UK – they are *physically* present in the country but possess no legal rights (Sawyer and Turpin 2005). In effect, failed asylum seekers are transformed into a condition equivalent to statelessness because, 'while they might technically have a nationality yet [they] are not able to obtain or enjoy the concomitant benefits and protection' of nationality, i.e. they lack political rights, identity documents and are unable to obtain basic social services (Weissbrodt 2008: 84). The expectation is that when failed asylum seekers become destitute (Cholewinski 1998) they will voluntarily return to their country or origin or, failing that, the British government will detain and deport them.

Regardless of these measures, however, growing numbers of failed asylum seekers have remained in the UK because UKBA and the courts have taken a long time to process and decide their initial asylum claim *and* their subsequent fresh asylum application. In 2005 it was estimated that the number of illegal immigrants – many of whom are failed asylum seekers – was between 310,000 and 570,000. Despite promises by UKBA to substantially reduce if not eliminate this backlog of 'legacy' cases, the number continues to grow.[1]

As discussed in Chapter 5, by the late 1990s the government began to pursue a range of policies and initiatives to speed up asylum decision-making and to make life more difficult for those who remained in the UK on temporary admission. For instance: (a) fast-track detention and removal procedures were created; (b) a 'white list' of 'safe' countries began to be used to certify asylum claims as unfounded; (c) a large detention estate was created to ramp up the deportation of failed asylum seekers (including removing persons to a 'safe' third country where their initial asylum claim should be considered); (d) efforts have been made to limit appeals from the Tribunal; and finally (e) greater regulation has been imposed on immigration legal practitioners, whose numbers have dropped sharply due to continuous cuts in legal aid.

Additional efforts to deter 'bogus asylum seekers' included: (a) the creation of a new range of immigration offences which incur criminal sanctions[2] such as 'entering without leave' (section 24(1)(a) of the 1971 Act) and 'refusing to cooperate' with the authorities (in their efforts to redocument a person for removal; Immigration Rules part 9, paragraphs 320–2); (b) the imposition of further restrictions on asylum seekers access to health facilities; (c) the creation of a system to disperse asylum applicants across the UK; and (d) the creation of the National Asylum Support Service (NASS) as the sole institution responsible for supporting asylum seekers.

When asylum applicants are refused status they lose their right to shelter and food *and* they are subject to deportation. NASS offers a modicum of conditional, short-term assistance in the form of basic accommodation and a weekly 'entitlement card'/cash voucher to failed asylum seekers while they make arrangements to return to their country of origin. Called 'Section 4 support',[3] this assistance is available:

If your asylum application has been rejected and you have exhausted your appeal rights, you must make arrangements to return to your country of origin as soon as possible. However, you may be able to receive short-term support while you are preparing to return to your country. This is known as 'section 4 support', because it is given under the terms of section 4 of the Immigration and Asylum Act 1999. You must meet strict requirements in order to qualify for section 4 support. *You must be destitute* [my emphasis] and satisfy one of the following requirements:

(1) You are taking all reasonable steps to leave the UK or you are placing yourself in a position where you can do so; or
(2) You cannot leave the UK because of a physical impediment to travel or for some other medical reason; or
(3) You cannot leave the UK because, in the Secretary of State's opinion, no viable route of return is currently available; or
(4) You have applied for a judicial review of your asylum application and have been given permission to proceed with it; or
(5) Accommodation is necessary to prevent a breach of your rights within the meaning of the Human Rights Act 1998.

In short, Parliament passed legislation aimed at reducing the cost of supporting asylum seekers and at creating conditions so intolerable that failed asylum seekers would voluntarily leave.[4] However, this strategy is flawed: when individuals are unable to leave within three months – due to the well-known difficulties they face in obtaining travel documents – their entitlement to NASS support is withdrawn and they are again rendered destitute. Such decisions escalate the cost to the state and tax payer in as much as the cost of voluntary-assisted removal is far below the cost of finding, detaining and deporting a failed asylum seeker[5] (see Box 6.1). Furthermore this policy does not work: as of June 2012 there are an estimated 300,000 'illegals' believed to be residing in the UK, including 124,000 failed asylum seekers.[6]

It may well be the case that some refused asylum seekers do not wish to return to their country of origin and refuse to cooperate in the redocumentation process. However, it is also the case that some individuals cannot be returned because the Home Office has not worked out the logistics of their removal (e.g. to Somalia) or because the person's country of origin is affected by unrest/civil war which prevents individuals from being returned there. As Sawyer and Turpin note, 'Sometimes the person cannot be located in order to be removed, whether because they have been lost in the Home Office's filing system or because they have absconded. Alternatively, removal may be politically impossible' due to protests/campaigns by community organizations (pp. 699–700). It is also the case that: (a) individuals put on commercial flights for the purpose of removal have protested so vehemently that airlines have refused to transport them;[7] (b) that some countries have refused to accept failed asylum seekers;[8] and (c) that individuals who have been detained pending deportation face institutional problems[9] which contribute to prolonged periods of detention. All the above factors have contributed to a massive escalation in the cost of compulsory removal/deportation of failed asylum seekers (Box 6.1).

Box 6.1 The cost of removing failed asylum seekers from Britain

Between 2003 and 2010, £42 million was spent to remove/deport 306,535 individuals. In 2005/6 the average cost of removing an individual from the UK was £11,000, however by 2009/10 the average cost had risen to between £12,000 and £25,600 per person. Approximately £500,000 a month is spent on air travel for such persons; in 2009 the total annual cost to remove failed asylum seekers on 'special' charter flights was £10.4 million.

Source: '£42 million bill to remove failed asylum seekers: How taxpayer funding for secretive flights has quadrupled in past seven years', *Mail Online*, 29 December 2011.

As we saw in Chapter 5, when the Home Office issues a notice of removal in cases where there is a question of dual nationality, 'Eritrean' asylum seekers are required to go to the Eritrean *and* Ethiopian embassies to obtain a travel document and be redocumented. However, embassy officials refuse to recognize their entitlement to nationality and they refuse to provide a letter to the Home Office that the person has not been recognized. According to York and Fancott (2008) the Home Office is well aware of the situation but it nevertheless argues that the applicant has 'failed to cooperate' in being redocumented (an offence under Sec. 35 of the Asylum and Immigration (Treatment of Claims) Act 2004). The applicant is then refused access to NASS support and the Home Office seeks to remove the person regardless of the fact that removal to Eritrea has not been possible for many years because of a significant risk of persecution for a Convention reason[10] (Table 6.1).

Table 6.1 Removals and voluntary departures to Eritrea and Ethiopia, 2004–2012

Year	Eritrea		Ethiopia	
	Total voluntary departures	*Total asylum enforced removals*	*Total voluntary departures*	*Total asylum enforced removals*
2004	0	0	15	5
2005	0	1	32	17
2006	0	1	62	34
2007	6	2	95	32
2008	10	2	134	26
2009	8	0	85	13
2010	1	0	90	15
2011	1	0	185	9
Total	26	6	698	151

Source: UK Home Office 2012c.

There have been many attempts to judicially review decisions by officials implementing asylum and immigration policy on the basis that their decisions are irrational, unfair and/or illegal (Woolf 1998). In particular, judicial review applications have focused on the failure of officials to make a timely decision on the fresh asylum applications of failed asylum seekers, particularly where changes in case law provide a sound basis for a claim. In the context of the asylum claims discussed in Chapter 5, some 'Eritreans' whose claims were rejected prior to the decision in *ST (Ethnic Eritrean-nationality – return) Ethiopia CG [2011] UKUT 0025* (see pp. 138–141) are able to submit fresh asylum applications if their claim raised a similar issue, i.e. that they would become stateless on return to Ethiopia.

In *FH and Ors, R (on the application of)* v. *SSHD, CoA (Admin)*, Lord Justice Collins heard a case alleging that Home Office delay in processing a new asylum claim was unfair. He summarized the claim before him (¶23) as follows:

> It is submitted on behalf of the claimants that the system of dealing with the [asylum legacy] backlog is unfair and so unlawful. The delays are excessive. My attention is drawn to the requirement that applicants act in a speedy fashion in making their applications and in lodging any appeal. The Home Affairs Committee of the House of Commons in July 2006 identified delay as the cause of the vast majority of complaints. It concluded that the Home Office must address this problem. The new system attempts to do that and I am told that, albeit there remains a concentration on initial decisions, they now will be pursued to completion. Additional resources are also being injected into dealing with the backlog of incomplete cases.

He went on to conclude (¶30) that

> claims such as these based on delay are unlikely, save in very exceptional circumstances, to succeed and are likely to be regarded as unarguable. It is only if the delay is so excessive as to be regarded as manifestly unreasonable and to fall outside any proper application of the policy or if the claimant is suffering some particular detriment which the Home Office has failed to alleviate that a claim might be entertained by the court.

Unsurprisingly, a very large number of claims were subsequently filed which argued that the Home Office failure to acknowledge, much less decide, a fresh asylum application was indeed 'manifestly unreasonable'.

Among the many applications seeking to judicially review UKBA for excessive delay in considering a fresh asylum application was that of Mr Dawit Tekle, an Eritrean national (whose mother was Ethiopian and whose father was Eritrean). He fled Eritrea in 2001 following the deportation of his mother to Ethiopia and the detention of his father for supporting an opposition political party. His asylum application was dismissed. He made a fresh asylum application in April 2004 – based on a 2004 UNHCR paper on persecution in Eritrea and his inability to return to Eritrea – which the Home Office did not reply to. It was not until October

2007 that the Home Office wrote to him stating that his circumstances 'were not exceptional' and that he would have to wait until the backlog of cases was finally resolved in 2011.

His application for a judicial review was finally heard in late 2008 (*[2008] EWHC 3064 (Admin)*). At the hearing The Hon. Mr Justice Blake heard submissions from Mr Dawit (¶19):

> who for the past seven years has had no resources of his own, is prevented by refusal of permission from obtaining any resources of his own, employing his skills and personality in remuneration employment and prevented from leading something equivalent to a normal life whilst his eventual outcome is considered by the Home Office.

The Home Office merely argued that as a matter of general principle his case was not exceptional and did not merit special consideration. The judge, however, agreed with the applicant that his right to 'private life' under Art. 8 of the European Convention on Human Rights (ECHR) was infringed upon and that the Home Office refusal to consider his case amounted to a 'manifestly excessive delay' (¶22). The judge concluded (¶34) by stating that while:

> there is no right to a decision within a given period of time and no right to permission to work arises merely because of expiry of a particular period of time. However undue delay . . . both increases the right to respect to private life that is carried on of necessity during the period of delay, and can be said to diminish the strength of immigration control factors that would otherwise support refusal of permission to work.

Though the judge was unable to help Mr Dawit, he declared 'that the present policy is unlawfully overbroad and unjustifiably detrimental to claimants who have had to wait as long as this claimant has. . . I would expect the policy to be reviewed and reformulated [in] the light of this judgment within approximately three months' (¶54). In light of subsequent cases before the courts, however, it is clear that the Home Office did not review its policy.

Another judicial review application – based on the failure of the Home Office to acknowledge two fresh asylum claims – was filed on behalf of an 'Eritrean' woman in March 2007.[11] The woman had fled Ethiopia in anticipation of being deported but her asylum application and her appeal were refused in 2004. Two years later, and still in the UK, she was advised to approach the Ethiopian embassy to apply for a passport but the embassy refused to recognize her. Her lawyer wrote on her behalf to the Ethiopian and Eritrean embassies seeking to clarify her nationality but officials failed to reply. In the meantime the woman entered into a union with another failed asylum seeker from Ethiopia, had a child, and was now in need of essential medical treatment which would only be available to her if the Home Office recorded her outstanding asylum application and allowed her to be registered with NASS. Failing an acknowledgement of her application, and given that her partner had lost his job, she and the child would 'become unnecessarily destitute and without means of financial support'. In LJ Collins' terms, this woman was suffering a serious 'detriment' which only the Home Office could alleviate.

Her application was 'stayed' along with 'hundreds' of other 'Eritrean' cases behind the case of three failed asylum seekers – one of whom was 'Eritrean' – heard in the High Court in March 2009 by Mr Justice Cranston (*[2009] EWHC 1044 (Admin)*) who referred (¶2) to the individuals bringing the case as being stuck in a legal limbo:

> In Seamus Heaney's well known poem 'Limbo', he speaks of limbo as being 'a cold dark glitter of souls'. The claimants in this judicial review, two Palestinians and one claimant of Eritrean and Ethiopian ancestry, contend that by the decision of the Secretary of State for the Home Department they are effectively in limbo. One aspect is their limited entitlement to social and housing benefits. Their position results because of a decision of the Secretary of State to grant them temporary admission. Their claim is that this is unlawful and that I should make a declaration to that effect and also order that they be granted leave to enter. I am told that there are a number of other cases involving Palestinian and Ethiopian/Eritrean claimants whose cases have been stayed pending the determination of this case.

Justice Cranston noted (¶36) that the heart of the case is the 1971 Immigration Act, which provides for the 'temporary admission' into the UK of persons who:

> are subject to immigration control, who do not have leave to be here, but who cannot lawfully be detained, [and] are at large without there being anyway to keep track of them. The power to impose reporting and residence restrictions on asylum seekers and others while their claims to remain in the United Kingdom are being considered is for contact management purposes, and this power is dependent on there being a power to grant temporary admission or release.
>
> (he is quoting an explanatory memorandum of Sec. 67 of the 2002 Immigration and Asylum Act)

Despite finding that the Home Office's ability to remove the 'Eritrean' to Eritrea was 'at the borderline of being fanciful', he allowed the SSHD further time for her to be interviewed by the Eritrean embassy and, if necessary, for the Home Office to change removal directions to Ethiopia. However, he denied the other two claims (¶58) because:

> Temporary admission is a harsh regime. Although it may not be Seamus Heaney's 'cold glitter of souls', the claimants have been subject to a deprivation of rights as a result of their temporary admission. That has continued for a considerable period. However, that is the legislative regime. As a matter of law, I cannot find that temporary admission, in the circumstances of these claimants, is unlawful.

However, because there were hundreds of persons in a similar situation as the three applicants before him, Mr Justice Cranston allowed an appeal to the CoA, which was heard in late 2009. In *The Queen on the Application of MS, AR and FW and SSHD, CoA (Civil Division)*Lord Justice Sedley summarized (¶2) the issues before the court in the following way:

> The issue arises and is important because it concerns the grant of temporary admission to people who have no affirmative right to remain in this country but cannot for particular reasons be removed. Such people do not have to be detained, but they have to exist in a half-world (Cranston J called it limbo, but theologians have recently decided that there is no such place) in which they have £5 a day to live on, cannot take work, must live where they are required to, have access only to primary healthcare, can obtain no social security benefits or social services assistance and can study only in institutions that require no payment. In these respects, which are determined by law and are not simply discretionary conditions imposed by the Home Office, they may be no worse off than asylum-seekers (which all three of the present appellants initially were) but are markedly worse off than if they had formal leave to remain. Their case is that they are entitled to the latter.

The Lords Justices agreed that the difficulties facing the applicants were legal (not practical), which meant that any delays in their removal might become permanent and 'they can neither be removed nor lead a normal life in this country' (¶11). However, based on the arguments before the court, they upheld Mr Cranston's decision because refused asylum seekers are not able to challenge the legality of their treatment as set out in legislation.[12] The effect of the decision and the Home Office's continued reliance on a policy of temporary admission is that the pool of failed asylum seekers from Ethiopia, Palestine, Eritrea, Jamaica, Liberia, Somali, Sri Lanka and Sudan[13] continues to increase not because individuals refuse to cooperate in being redocumented (though of course some do) but because their country of origin refuses or is unable to identify and document an individual.

In late 2012 evidence about how UKBA had dealt with legacy cases of the type discussed above was published by the Independent Chief Inspector of Borders and Immigration (2012). The Chief Inspector found that UKBA had seriously misled Parliament – and by implication the courts via its submissions through TSoL – about its lack of progress in assessing and resolving the backlog of asylum and migration claims dating back to 2006. The inspector found that: (a) 'the programme of legacy work is far from concluded'; (b) that thousands of asylum applicants were 'disadvantaged' due to poorly communicated policy changes and poor decision-making; and (c) at least 150,000 claims had been wrongly archived without having been checked and resolved (Box 6.2). In short, there are tens of thousands of failed asylum seekers whose lives continue to be suspended in a limbo due solely to bureaucratic ineptitude and political indifference towards individuals who have been failed by the asylum system.

Box 6.2 UK Border Agency's (UKBA) poor handling of 'legacy' asylum and migration cases

- A review of UKBA's work found 'prominent organizational failings' including a lack of effective oversight and engagement at senior levels, an inadequate resourcing model, poor quality management information concerning the remaining caseload and ineffective handover processes.
- Limited resources created a significant impediment to case clearance.
- Effective decision-making was impaired by changing priorities (which were not clearly communicated to the unit), which led to inconsistent decisions regarding when to make a grant of discretionary leave.
- There were significant failures in checking case files, including undertaking security checks on key databases, with the result that 150,000 cases were incorrectly recorded as 'concluded' and wrongly 'archived'.
- A backlog of at least 100,000 pieces of correspondence about cases had been found in a back room.
- Case files were not updated as a result of correspondence.
- Despite the above failures, there was an increase in the number of cases granted leave since April 2011, which was believed to be related to a failure to consider new information and an agreement to come to a decision using the computer database (which was not fully updated with all relevant information).
- A check of cases which were refused suggested that while the decision to refuse was properly arrived at, officials failed to pursue removal in a large number of cases.

Source: Independent Chief Inspector of Borders and Immigration 2012.

A delay in responding to fresh asylum claims is but one, albeit very important, way that the state 'produces' failed asylum seekers. Quite apart from the effect of poor decision-making by the Home Office and the Tribunal, applicants face even greater problems if they are wrongly detained in fast-track procedures[14] where their case will be speedily and sometimes wrongfully decided (see Case 23).

Four months after 'Tiberh' was detained, her detention centre[15] was visited by a team offering free legal advice. Through a female interpreter she disclosed that when she was detained in Ethiopia she had been raped; a lawyer arranged a psychiatric assessment which confirmed that she was suffering from post-traumatic stress disorder linked to the rape. A fresh asylum application was made on her behalf which contained the medical report and new evidence in the form of an Ethiopian police report. In the face of a refusal by the Home Office to respond

Case 23

'Tiberh', an Ethiopian woman, was brought into the UK by an agent in October 2005 and abandoned in London. She claimed asylum the following day but within a week she was arrested and taken to an immigration detention centre, where she was subject to removal as an 'illegal entrant'. Her case was heard by a judge who – through a comprehensive attack on her credibility and a perfunctory reading of relevant case law – dismissed her appeal. An application was filed requesting reconsideration but this too was refused. Within 15 days of 'Tiberh's' initial hearing she had exhausted all legal remedies and was being held for deportation to Ethiopia.

to the fresh asylum application, her lawyer threatened to file a judicial review. Shortly afterwards she was released on bail, provided with food vouchers by NASS and she found a place to stay with a friend. Within two years her case had been reviewed and she was granted status.

Poor Home Office decision-making and record keeping can also have serious consequences for asylum seekers, as demonstrated in Case 24.

Case 24

'Gebriel' was born in Addis Ababa in 1976 to an Ethiopian mother and an Eritrean father (who died in 1998). At the height of the war with Eritrea his identity card was confiscated by officials and he was assaulted. In 2000 his mother, brother and sister were arrested (the latter two were deported). 'Gebriel' fled the country and arrived in the UK in mid-2000 and applied for asylum. The Home Office refused his application in November 2000 and he lost his appeal in January 2004 (which was linked to those of 'Medhin' and three other stateless Ethiopians, see p. 136). When his case was appealed to the CoA it was decided that it should be reheard because the Tribunal had failed to consider whether he had been arbitrarily deprived of his nationality. At his reconsideration hearing in March 2008 'Gebriel' was granted refugee status.

In the period between the refusal of his appeal in 2004 and the agreement to reconsider his case in 2007 he was denied welfare support and as a 'failed asylum seeker' was subject to arrest and removal. His initial difficulty with UKBA arose from their refusal to issue him a work permit in 2000 – which he was entitled to – while he waited for a decision on his asylum claim.[16] His difficulties were compounded when UKBA confused his case with another asylum applicant, which delayed consideration of his case. Between 2000 and 2005 he survived on £30 per week and lived in designated accommodation (until 2005 when a member of his church offered him accommodation).

In Chapter 1 I discussed the case of a young 'Eritrean' woman who, after being falsely imprisoned and raped by an Ethiopian official, escaped from a hospital and fled to the UK. I take up her story on arrival in the UK.

Case 8 (cont'd)

'Meriam' arrived in the UK in January 2002 and applied for asylum, but her application was refused in September 2002. At her July 2003 appeal the judge paradoxically accepted her evidence as credible, accepted that she had approached the Eritrean embassy and could not be returned there, and accepted that she had 'been stripped of her Ethiopian nationality'. Nevertheless he dismissed her appeal because, he argued, she was entitled to claim Eritrean nationality. The decision was successfully appealed against and her case was reconsidered in January 2005 but was once again dismissed. Successive attempts to file fresh asylum claims were made (which went unacknowledged) and it was not until a third application was made in 2009 that 'Meriam' was finally granted indefinite leave to remain. Her claim was allowed because of a judicial review on a related 'Eritrean' case that concluded: 'a determination of the "refugee" status of the claimant in accordance with Article 1 of the Refugee Convention was made by an appropriate Tribunal, the AIT. The decision is binding upon the defendant [i.e. UKBA] and affords the claimant the protection of Article 32(1).'[17]

In short, following her 2003 appeal she should have been granted refugee status but instead she was made to wait six years for that judicial decision to be overturned.[18] Following her unsuccessful appeal and in the period after each fresh asylum claim her benefits were removed and she was made destitute. She moved from northern England to London to obtain psychiatric therapy (and medication) from an NGO and spent varying periods of time in and out of official accommodation and on the street; at one point she slept in a church for two weeks. As a result of injuries and trauma suffered in Ethiopia, the refusal of the courts to grant her status and frequent eviction from official accommodation she was diagnosed as suffering from 'frequent episodes of loss of consciousnesses, olfactory hallucinations, post-traumatic stress disorder and depression. It was due to her own perseverance that she obtained medical treatment from an NGO, which contacted a lawyer who obtained status for her.

A final example of an irrational and unfair decision which affected many applicants relates to a change of policy in 2005 when the Home Office decided to replace permanent grants of residence with forms of temporary protection. The new policy recognized, however, that where an asylum appeal was significantly delayed it would be appropriate for the Home Office to grant indefinite leave to remain to a person.

A judicial review challenging the manner in which this policy was applied was heard in early 2009 (*[2009] EWHC 468 (Admin)*) on behalf of Mr Hailemariam, an 'Eritrean' who claimed asylum in November 2000. The Home Office failed to make a decision on his claim until December 2007. In the interim a series of administrative errors were made on his claim by the Home Office and the Tribunal. Despite these difficulties he successfully appealed against the Home Office refusal in 2007 and UKBA granted him five years' leave to remain in the UK (a temporary status). In light of the seven-year delay by the Home Office in dealing with his claim, and subsequent case law on statelessness (notably *EB (Ethiopia) v. SSHD [2007] EWCA Civ 809*), his counsel argued that Mr Hailemariam had suffered 'disadvantage' as a result of the delays and that the judge should quash the original order and instruct the Home Office to issue him with indefinite leave to remain (a permanent status). After hearing the evidence the judge agreed to this request.

More than 'bare life': Individual and collective strategies in the face of destitution

To understand the situation of failed asylum seekers we approached Refugee Community Organizations (RCOs) and our Ethiopian and Eritrean social networks in London, who helped us to identify and speak to 15 individuals. We spoke to all these individuals, some of them several times, between June and October 2008 (Table 6.2). It is important to note that the information made available to us comes from a series of conversations, not formal interviews.

As other researchers have found (Blitz and Otero-Iglesias 2011; Dwyer and Brown 2005), despite their ubiquitous presence in official statistics and press accounts such individuals are difficult to find. Furthermore, even when persons are identified they are, for obvious reasons, reticent to reveal much detail about their situation. To protect our informants' identities we did not take personal details and we have anonymized all the information they gave us. Because of the sensitivity of the issues we were unable to collect comparable information for all the individuals. Even with the above caveats, however, the information is very interesting. Our informants included 11 men and 4 women. The average period of residence in the UK was 8.7 years (the minimum was 3 years, the maximum was 14 years). Five were 'married' (two to a person with British nationality) and had families; two were in their mid-twenties and the rest were between 35 and 55 years of age.

Despite the precariousness of their lives they were all socially active in religious networks and RCOs; they do not conceal themselves but neither do they behave in ways that might bring them to the attention of the authorities (not only do they

Table 6.2 Summary of information on 'failed asylum seekers'

	Gender	Nationality	Years in UK	Working illegally	In reciept of benefit? claim?	Fresh asylum	Family
1	Male	Eritrean	3	Yes	Possibly	No	Wife and two children
2	Male	'Eritrean'	10	Yes	No	Yes	No
3	Male	Ethiopian	10	Yes	No	No	No
4	Male	Ethiopian	14	Yes	No	No	Wife and child
5	Female	Ethiopian	3	No	NASS	No	No
6	Female	Ethiopian	5	Yes	No	Yes	No
7	Male	Ethiopian	10	Yes	No	Accepted	Wife and child
8	Female	Ethiopian	9	[No data]	No	No	Husband and child
9	Male	Ethiopian	15	Yes	No	Yes	Wife and three children
10	Male	Ethiopian	4	[No data]	[No data]	Yes	Wife and children in Ethiopia
11	Male	Ethiopian	14	In and out of legal employment	Jobseekers allowance	Yes	No
12	Female	Ethiopian	3	Yes	No	No	No
13	Male	Ethiopian	10+	Yes	No	Yes	No
14	Male	Ethiopian	17	In and out of legal employment	[No data]	No	No
15	Male	Ethiopian	3	No	No	Yes	Not known

NASS, National Asylum Support Service.

Source: Fieldwork, June to October 2008.

avoid situations which might lead to arrest, they are extremely reticent to speak publicly about their treatment and situation). Furthermore nine had worked illegally; due to changes in their legal status two individuals had moved in and out of legal work; four individuals had not worked at all. Interestingly, while all of them would have been denied access to welfare benefits and would have been rendered destitute and homeless, only two persons spoke about that experience. Many of those we spoke to were attempting to legalize their presence in the UK: eight had made fresh asylum applications (one individual's application was accepted during our conversation with him).

This is not the place for a detailed analysis of the information they provided to us, but in view of reports about the abject condition of failed asylum seekers which lend support to official policies, it is worth making several observations. First, all of the individuals we spoke to – except the person who had just had his fresh application accepted – were living in the UK in a 'statelessness-like situation' in the sense of having no political rights; they were subject to immediate arrest and deportation. Paradoxically, however, all of them had access to primary health care and, through work and/or support from their social networks, to shelter (many were renting private accommodation but several individuals had not been evicted from NASS-supported accommodation despite the failure of their appeals).

They were acutely aware of their vulnerability as individuals without rights, as was made clear to us by one of those we spoke to:

Case 25

'Ermias' arrived in the UK in 2004 and after the first asylum application process he was sent to Ashford, Kent, for a couple of weeks. 'Then I was sent to Bolton and stayed there until my case was given the final decision. It is something around one year and some months when I got a refusal for my asylum application and [was] thrown out from the accommodation. I approached my lawyer who was here in London to start the appeal process but he declined [to help me] because I was not able to pay him. So I was left without support and legal advice and [I] also failed to proceed with the appeal . . . before the deadline. I had nothing and no where to live so I went to Manchester to be with friends. I stayed there for eight months without any support. Later on I came to London again to stay with friends. In the meantime I was advised to go to [an RCO] and seek advice . . . I went there and talked to one of the advisors . . . After consulting there I was sent to . . . [a] solicitor's firm and the solicitor started to follow my case. She managed to open my case and the appeal procedure [for] Section 4 entitlement. I was given a house [a place in a shared apartment/bed-sit] here in London.

[During this time] I was doing nothing except trying to follow my case and praying. The situation was not easy and it tests your ability to handle such difficult moments. I know there are a lot of people who have been left to depression and other problems. I was relatively strong and thank God I have managed to keep myself from such problems.

[. . .] It was not easy but I was not working. Well when I was in Manchester I have been working for sometime. It was for three months and except [for] that I didn't [work]. It is hard to be dependent on others but I had no choice and I was left to rely on others' support. I go to church, pray and some of them give me money for my transport; some offer me a place to stay . . . I had that support until I was placed on Section 4 support. The appeal process took some one year and some months and again I was refused and my support was terminated and I was thrown out of the accommodation for the second time. The good thing is my lawyer was still supportive and she advised me to get supporting documents to [make a] fresh application.'

He eventually filed a fresh asylum application and was once again provided support under Section 4, which is when we met him.

It was clear to us that most of the individuals we talked to could call upon support of varying types, though the amount and regularity of this support was highly variable. For instance, one young woman had this to say about her situation after her appeal was refused:

Case 26

'Serkalum': I have nothing. After the last decision I was asked [to] report to the police station and to bring with me two photographs. [After] asking advice people told me that it might not be good as they are preparing to deport you, so I decided to leave the accommodation and not to report to the police station. Since that time I have no accommodation, no financial support . . . I do not have contacts with officials and I am trying to stay away from them.

Q: Where and how are you living?

'Serkalum': Actually, my mother is living somewhere outside Ethiopia [in the Middle East] and she is supporting me financially. I also have some friends and family members here in the UK who are supporting me in one or another way. Well it is not something that you look for but when it is a problem and you have no other alternatives you turn your face for support. So I am living with friends and families. Here in [she names a town] I have a [British] friend to live with.

Q: How long do you think you can stay like this?

Serkalum: I know that is not good but I am afraid. I know someone who was in the same situation like me; he went to London and tried to get a lawyer. He was lucky and he got a lawyer and submitted a fresh application and at the moment he has been given accommodation and voucher and is living in Leeds . . . but I do not want [to] . . . give myself up to the authorities to be sent back whenever they want. I do not want to give myself to be deported.

There are, of course, individuals who have no support networks and who have been rendered destitute (poor administration by NASS staff has contributed to unnecessary destitution, see: Citizens Advice Bureau 2006; Asylum Support Partnership 2009; Asylum Support Appeals Project 2011; Lewis 2009; British Red Cross 2010). The extent to which policies create/reinforce destitution among failed asylum seekers – which degrades and debases the value of a life – is evident in the account of 'Haile' (Box 6.3).

The individuals who spoke to us were acutely aware of the inevitability of arrest and the abject state of destitution which could so easily be their fate. But curiously

---

Box 6.3 Haile: 'I don't feel like a human being'

Haile, who was taken to Tanzania by his Ethiopian parents as a boy, came to the UK as a stowaway on a boat in 2000. His asylum application was refused and UKBA have attempted to remove him to Tanzania even though it is highly unlikely that Tanzania would accept him. Without resources he is unable to leave the UK. One attempt was made to remove him but was cancelled at the last minute, following which he was released and left to survive on the street.

He has been homeless in central Birmingham for the past five years. He lives alone and for the past year has lived in a fenced-off doorway at the back of a hotel. The local authority has attempted to prevent him from staying there by erecting a sheet of chipboard over the doorway on which is posted a sign saying 'Trespassers will be prosecuted'. To enter he must climb over a ten foot metal fence. 'This is my sleeping bag, my table, my bed, blanket' he says through the fence. Pointing to one corner he says, 'my toilet'. Pointing to a heap of clothes on the ground: 'my clothes'. Piles of rubbish thrown by passers-by are also evident inside the doorway. He says he has problems with rats and foxes, but once inside he feels fairly secure. 'Sometimes I look and think it's like a prison. But no one can throw stones at me here. This is my mansion. I am a rich man.' Haile is clearly struggling to survive and to maintain his sanity. He says of himself, 'My life is wasted. My parents died. I don't have parents. I don't have a country. I don't feel like a human being anymore.'

Source: Gentleman, A. 'The asylum seekers who survive on £10 a week', *The Guardian* 16 June 2010.

---

none of them intended to voluntarily return to Ethiopia. While some individuals appeared to have a genuine fear of persecution on return (i.e. the 'Eritrean' case), some have married and raised families and they have all established a life in the UK and are hoping to be granted status. In short, the policy of enforced destitution has not compelled these individuals to leave. Part of the reason for this can be found in the inefficiency of the state: there continue to be long delays by the Home Office in considering fresh asylum applications (which allows failed asylum seekers to establish a 'family life')[19] and some government departments provide documents which make it possible for failed asylum seekers to work. A further factor at play is the availability of limited assistance – from refugees and from British people and institutions – in the form of food packages, temporary shelter and gifts[20] which allow individuals to survive. Finally, the fact that some employers do not check whether their employees have valid work permits also helps, and of course there is the flourishing informal economy which provides employment opportunities.

Fieldwork in London and south-eastern England helps to contextualize and make sense of the situation. While asylum applicants have been dispersed across the UK pending a decision on their claim, once their appeal is refused and welfare support is removed they rapidly move on. Many move to larger cities such as London, where they find a modicum of support from other asylum applicants, more established co-ethnics, RCOs created by co-ethnics and from 'black' Pentecostal and Protestant churches. Many Ethiopians are Orthodox Christians or Muslims and they find solace and support in their churches and mosques partly through familiar religious beliefs and practices but also through the vibrancy of transplanted social practices such as *idir* (an association of individuals who contribute to meet funeral costs), *ikub* (savings associations) and *mahiber* (irregular meetings of Orthodox Christians which take place on Saints days) as well as Eid and other Islamic festivals.

There is also a strong sense of the need to volunteer in, and support, RCOs. To give one example, an RCO founded in 1993 to assist Ethiopians who speak little or no English to receive medical treatment was dependent on six unpaid Ethiopian volunteers (including a failed asylum seeker). In 2008 this organization supported 312 Ethiopians via counselling, providing advice and interpreting. It is worth observing, however, that in 2008 we identified and spoke to 28 Eritrean RCOs and an equal number of Ethiopian RCOs in London (not churches, Christian associations or mosques). Nearly all of the RCOs were on the brink of collapse due to the dispersal of asylum seekers to areas outside of London (where new, poorly managed RCOs were started) and a major shift of government funding away from RCOs.

Indeed some of the individuals who have claimed asylum in Britain in the past decade have formed new associations, often in an attempt to assist failed asylum seekers and impoverished individuals who are granted status (Da Lomba 2010). For instance, stateless 'Eritreans' in the UK formed an association in 2002 which meets monthly to assist members.

Our evidence supports and expands the arguments of Zetter *et al.* (2006) regarding refugee social capital. First, successful *and* failed asylum seekers have created a 'vibrant' associational life, which is a strong indicator of the formation of social capital. These associations enable individuals to meet socially and pursue a range of shared social objectives. The associations occur because successful *and* failed asylum seekers seek out and interact with individuals with whom they have 'dense ties' based on shared bonds of kinship/ethnicity and/or shared political affiliation/identity. However, and contrary to the thrust of government policy on social cohesion, very few 'bridges' are being built with the host society or with state institutions. Instead refugees and failed asylum seekers are being 'absorbed' into the existing black and minority ethnic population who are themselves marginalized from mainstream white society by poverty, discrimination and racism.

Conclusion

Over the past 15 years British legislators have adopted a raft of laws which have reshaped the asylum system and reduced the level of protection and support offered to successful and unsuccessful asylum applicants. Thus Parliament now recognizes five different types of asylum applicant, each of which is entitled to different rights and a different level of support. In 2005 the entitlement of many successful asylum applicants to permanent/refuge protection was replaced by temporary protection (for one to three years) following which the person may be required to return to their country of origin. Parliament has also given its imprimatur to a policy of imposing enforced destitution on 'failed' asylum seekers in an attempt to force them to leave the UK. However, the number failed asylum seekers has grown because UKBA officials have consistently demonstrated their inability to implement asylum and immigration policies fairly, consistently and in a timely manner. For this reason the Home Office has earned the epithet, bestowed on it by a former Secretary of State, as 'not fit for purpose'.[21] As my analysis of judicial review applications has argued, officials have consistently decided cases and implemented policy in an arbitrary and unfair manner. Given the ability of the government to conceal its failures from the public, it has been left to the Independent Chief Inspector of Borders and Immigration (2012; Independent Chief Inspector of Borders and Immigration and HM Inspectorate of Prisons 2012) to reveal that the true extent of UKBA maladministration covers *all* areas of its work.

Rather than address the huge backlog of 'legacy' asylum (and migration) claims that take the form of fresh asylum applications UKBA has relied upon the policy of 'temporary admission', which places failed asylum seekers in a state of limbo, the parameters of which are marked by destitution and the absence of rights. While individuals are temporarily admitted and destitute, UKBA has slowly and ineffectively assessed some of their outstanding claims. In court, UKBA's defence has been that it was actively reviewing and resolving cases and that the majority of outstanding asylum claims were not exceptional and did not merit special consideration. Unfortunately the courts, who deferred to the Home Office, have been seriously misled on this issue.

Other Home Office policies are also flawed. Thus Home Office decisions to refer asylum applicants to the fast-track system, with its expedited system of appeals, has proved to be flawed, as is its ability to fairly and promptly decide fresh asylum claims and its ability to manage its paperwork. In short all these policies have delayed the assessment of claims and subjected individuals to prolonged destitution. In addition, the legal requirement that failed asylum seekers assist UKBA with their redocumentation is problematic because a growing number of individuals are not recognized by their embassies. Rather than taking these difficulties into account – for example by allowing such individuals access to minimal support from NASS or providing them with a grant of temporary protection – UKBA once again renders them destitute and subjects them to deportation. The net effect of this catalogue of errors and unlawful decisions is that UKBA 'produces' illegality on a massive scale: wrongful decisions, errors and indifference have transformed valid asylum claimants into illegal, deportable migrants.[22]

Though there is considerable information in the public domain about destitute and failed asylum seekers, researchers and the press have failed to examine how government policy is implemented and whether policy is effective. How else can we explain why the expenditure of vast amounts of public money has failed to reduce the number of 'illegal migrants'? The lack of information about the (in)effectiveness of asylum and immigration policies arises from the fact that the Home Office does not undertake or commission research into policy effectiveness and, to paraphrase De Genova (2007), because research has failed to examine the ways in which state practices produce 'culprits' for deportation.

Official discourse, including the many reports, official statements and videos of enforcement action contribute to a form of 'self-censorship' which obscures how the state treats illegals and how ineffective and poorly implemented policy really is. The failure to examine government policy and practice arises from official, discursive treatment of failed asylum seekers, who are said to be an affront to the nation – persons who have deservedly been placed outside the law and who are rightly condemned to 'inhuman treatment', incarceration and deportation. The individuals treated in this manner have effectively been silenced; they have learned to maintain a low profile and not to comment about how officials and the British public treat them. Media representations, official statements and the 'spectacle' of border enforcement (De Genova 2012), which portrays UKBA as effectively and efficiently deporting illegals, have contributed to a situation in which non-white asylum seekers have become the object of violence, racial abuse and discrimination. In effect, public and official discourse about illegals reinforces the 'natural' and self-evidently correct nature of policies aimed at protecting national sovereignty through raids, arrests, border controls, detentions and ultimately the deportation of 'illegal aliens'.

The limited information available from conversations with failed asylum seekers underlines their dignity as human beings *and* the poorly conceived nature of policies intended to compel them to leave. These individuals have endured destitution and public indifference/contempt and have rebuilt their lives (albeit at a level far below what they were conceivably entitled to given that many had a valid asylum claim or should have been given temporary status). Their continued presence among us should been seen as evidence of an effective political struggle for recognition as human beings and not as evidence of law breaking. Indeed their continued presence – on the streets and via strikes and demonstrations in immigration centres – poses a fundamental challenge to our impoverished conceptions of politics and citizenship. While stateless persons, including failed asylum seekers, have been placed in a state of exception outside the law, their struggles for recognition impose a duty on us to see them as human beings and to rethink asylum policies and the nature of democratic politics.

Conclusion

I conclude my analysis of the odyssey of denationalized 'Eritreans' by drawing together the different strands of my argument under four inter-related themes explored in this book, namely the illusion of nationalism, the illusion of return, the illusion of refuge and the illusion of justice/redress. The final theme compels me to anticipate the future of 'Eritreans' in the West. I begin this last task by looking at attempts by 'Eritreans' to use the law to obtain legal redress against Ethiopia, following which I look at the effect of a 'creeping amnesty' being implemented by the UK Home Office and ask whether this might assist stateless 'Eritreans' to obtain status. Finally, in light of this case study, I re-examine the link between sovereignty and statelessness.

The illusion of nationalism

Historical and political factors help explain the deep ideological divisions between the TPLF and the EPLF and Ethiopia and Eritrea. The two fronts have relied upon 'revolutionary' violence to survive and to seize and exercise power. Indeed both have drawn from Marxism–Leninism and to a much lesser extent neo-liberal economic notions to define their political vision, instil discipline and project the image that in government they merely implement their electoral mandate. However, the ease with which both states rely on violence to coerce, intimidate and/or secure compliance with policy decisions underlines the fact that in the Horn, law serves the interests of those who hold political power.

The lack of trust between the two ruling parties, and between each party and those they govern is reflected in the speed with which the political relationship between the two heads of state collapsed and war escalated in the 1990s. Rather than establish accountable institutions to address the politico-economic issues between their countries, the political leadership allowed events to escalate and they quickly used government-controlled media to give vent to old concerns and grievances about each other's conduct and the threat from the 'enemy within', i.e. so-called 'dual national' 'Eritreans' in Ethiopia and Ethiopians in Eritrea.

In an immediate response to Eritrean aggression – which its own forces triggered – Ethiopia escalated the conflict and arrested, detained and expelled 75,000 of its 'Eritrean' citizens. The decision to expel its nationals was well organized and occurred by targeting individuals on the basis of their presumed Eritrean ethnicity. The policy violated national and international law and Ethiopian courts watched in impotence as citizens were expelled. In a not too dissimilar fashion, Eritrea removed its protection from resident Ethiopians, which led first to the arbitrary detention of some individuals prior to a massive flight from the country (which after six months took place via organized repatriation programs). What we witnessed in the Horn was, to quote Arendt, 'the transformation of the state from an instrument of the law into an instrument of the nation' in which 'national interests had priority over law' (1968: 269). The use of mass denationalization by a state, which was a prominent characteristic of the inter-war period in Europe, reflected if not a totalitarian state then a state that 'would not tolerate any opposition and would rather lose its citizens than harbour people with different views' (p. 278).

Expulsion transformed this group of 'Eritrean' citizens into stateless persons, while at roughly the same time officials were formally denationalizing an even larger number of resident 'Eritreans'. In many ways Ethiopian policies were reminiscent of the denationalization of Jews in Nazi Germany: like Jews, resident 'Eritreans' were the subject of ethnic discrimination; they were stripped of their citizenship and associated rights and protections; their property was confiscated (if not transferred into private hands); they were compelled to register with the authorities (which put them at further risk of maltreatment) and they were issued special identity cards. Ethiopian officials also attempted, via the arrest and expulsion of adult males, to split up families and it pressurized remaining 'Eritreans' to 'voluntarily' leave. Unsurprisingly thousands of 'Eritreans' fled in fear.

While in retrospect it is not too surprising that the EPRDF and the PFDJ resorted to such policies, it is disturbing that so many citizens willingly supported these policies and helped to implement actions which clearly violated the basic tenets of law, not to mention respect for human dignity. Nationals in the Horn have clearly not understood that if their nation can create a political exception to justify the suspension of rights for 'Eritreans'/Ethiopians, it can act in a similar manner towards them.

Somewhat paradoxically, and seemingly oblivious to the violence on the battlefield and towards 'the enemy within', the international community sought to impose the terms of peace. While the fighting ended when both states signed the Algiers Agreement, the terms of the agreement and the stipulation that both states submit to binding international arbitration at The Hague was bound to fail. The idea that the Security Council could, through commissions at The Hague, impose a solution on Ethiopia and Eritrea that accorded with Western notions of a 'civilized' standard of inter-state behaviour was quickly proved wrong.[1]

The reason why The Hague proved to be an inappropriate forum is due to its procedural rules, which give it the power to decide the evidence and impose a binding decision. The rules redefine and transform the core political issues underlying the conflict into a matter of differing 'perceptions' or 'interests' which are subject to binding resolution. However, The Hague's decisions did not bind the parties. There are two possible explanations for the failure of The Hague. First, Ethiopia and Eritrea believe that law serves the interests of those who hold power. Neither state trusted the other to honour decisions by The Hague nor did they trust international law to find a solution to their dispute. Second, and equally important, binding arbitration might have had some purchase on the two states early in the conflict but, following Ethiopia's seizure of the disputed territory in mid-2000, arbitration could only be achieved at the expense of Ethiopia's costly victory over Eritrea on the battlefield.

In effect, by submitting the dispute to arbitration the political issues between the two states were left to The Hague to deal with or ignore at its own peril. It chose to ignore them. By failing to consider regional politics and the initial cause of the war, namely a military clash over the town of Badme, The Hague's decision was guaranteed to rebound against it. The situation was further compounded by the decisions of the EECC which, among other things, made a *jus ad bellum* finding that Eritrea caused the war.

The problems did not end there. Procedural rules required that both parties establish 'clear and convincing evidence' about violations which occurred in a 'frequent or pervasive manner'. Because this did not happen the EECC made relatively few 'findings of unlawful acts'. The problem arose from its role as the arbiter of truth: in the face of 'deep and wide ranging conflicts in the evidence', the absence of proof, and the failure of both parties to assist it to find the truth it was left to the EECC to define a 'truth'. In short, the arbitration process created a situation in which both parties had every reason to 'nationalize the truth' to prevent the commission from making findings of fact and deciding liability against it for breaching international law.

By 2002 Eritrea and Ethiopia had both refused to be bound by the findings of the EEBC. Well before the EECC issued its final decision in 2009, events in the Horn had completely undermined the Algiers Agreement and cost the UN dearly in prestige and money. Today the border remains un-demarcated, no compensation has been paid and Eritrean and Ethiopian troops once again face each other across a disputed border.

In some ways Ethiopia's policy toward its 'Eritrean' citizens conforms to Agamben's notion of the 'political exception' in the sense that a sovereign state dictated a policy that was ruthlessly and indiscriminately applied to a specific category of persons, i.e. 'Eritreans'. Contrary to Ethiopia's submission to The Hague that it had instituted due process to ensure that only 'dual nationals' were expelled, it is clear from the evidence that such was not the case: 'Eritrean' nationals of Ethiopia as well as 15,000 Ethiopian nationals were unlawfully expelled.

From the case studies it is also clear that despite the climate of fear and intimidation which prevailed at the time, 'Eritreans' did not quietly acquiesce. Some were detained and compelled to sign 'confessions'; others found a way to question or protest their innocence; some refused to register and some fled the country. Even though the police stood aside and watched, and the courts were mute about a policy dictated by the executive, nevertheless some Ethiopians assisted their 'Eritrean' friends and neighbours regardless of the possible consequences. However, given the organization and ideological underpinning of EPRDF political control and the lack of accountability of officials, it is not surprising that officials merely did their 'job' and implemented the prime minister's decision.

The illusion of return

The failure of the Algiers Agreement and continued political tension between Ethiopia and Eritrea brought the post-war ICRC repatriation program to an abrupt end in 2009 at roughly the same time that events in Eritrea were sending growing numbers of refugees to Ethiopia and the Sudan. It is notable that neither Ethiopia nor Eritrea assisted 'Eritreans' to re-establish their lives nor were they allowed 'home'.

The failure of the international community and of both states directly contributed to the flight of 'Eritreans' out of the Horn, where they joined thousands of other refugees and migrants moving along one of four transit corridors. Unfortunately the individuals travelling these routes have encountered serious problems, including death at the hands of smugglers and because states on the transit routes have instituted policies to prevent foreigners from entering. Officials along the routes have subjected these sojourners to arbitrary round-ups, arrest, extortion, torture, deportation and *refoulement*. Increasingly, regional states have adopted restrictive asylum policies aimed at preventing genuine refugees from registering and from being resettled in their territory.

The situation of *amiche* in Eritrea adds a further dimension to an already complicated situation. Simultaneously with their expulsion into Eritrea, *amiche* became linked to a range of socio-political problems which led officials to 'purge the visible attributes of their attachments to Ethiopia', which contributed to growing ethnic discrimination towards them. During and after the war the very different cultural and political sensibilities of *amiche* came under growing scrutiny by officials; *amiche* got into difficulties and in increasing numbers they have returned to Ethiopia, where they are registered as Eritrean refugees and treated as aliens.

In the meantime stateless 'Eritreans' in Ethiopia were subjected to violence, intimidation, rape and discriminatory administrative measures. Some years after the war Ethiopia issued various directives and proclamations that permitted some 'Eritreans' to reacquire their nationality, though a large number remain stateless. The 2004 Directive was a half-hearted effort to address the problem posed by the presence of tens of thousands of registered and unregistered 'Eritreans'. While the registration was publicly announced, the registration process was too brief and the discretionary power of officials too great, which meant that many 'Eritreans' were excluded from the exercise. Furthermore, by refusing to reopen registration, the children who were too young to register in 2004 remain stateless, as of course do those who were afraid to come forward.

Subsequent directives illustrate the way in which officials have carefully established new norms of citizenship by granting former refugees and honoured foreigners civic rights as 'Individuals of Ethiopian Origin' – complete with the issue of special certificates etc. – while specifically refusing to countenance Somalis, resident 'Eritreans' and returning *amiche* as nationals. The registration exercise illustrates the way that autocratic states redraw the boundaries of citizenship to include new categories of persons while specifically excluding others from state protection. The autocratic nature of state power was clearly demonstrated in September 2012 when, to mark the Ethiopian New Year, the prime minister pardoned 1,925 prisoners, including two Swedish journalists, from a total of 2,356 prisoners who had to ask to be pardoned.[2] By such actions nationals are made aware of the limited scope for political protest which, once crossed, will see them placed in a political limbo which Ethiopian law cannot extract them from. The prime minister's right to pardon criminals is written in the constitution and provides an example of how the 'political exception' works in Ethiopia, which is to say that it occurs outside the legal system/courts. It illustrates an element in the exercise of sovereignty which Agamben had not considered.

What do Ethiopian policies during and after the war tell us about citizenship? To paraphrase Abbink (2009) the 1994 Constitution 'looks great', particularly given its inclusion of the Universal Declaration of Human Rights and various other international legal principles. However, what is missing are institutions capable of making the executive publicly accountable. This situation arises for two reasons. First the EPRDF exercises considerable 'informal' influence on all areas of governance through its ability to make appointments, to interfere with the judicial process and to politically demote individuals using 'forced self-evaluation sessions (*gimgema*)' which rely upon party ideology and policy for their justification (Abbink 2009: 7–8). Secondly, the courts remain seriously defective because the legislature issues 'ouster clauses' to create institutions which operate outside the jurisdiction of the courts and because judges abdicate their power to review the executive (Assefa Fiseha 2011). A cynic might say that civic, political and human rights are worth less than the paper on which the constitution is written and they would not be wrong (though such a view would miss significant improvements in the administration of justice in other areas of social life).

The illusion of refuge

Many 'Eritreans' (and other sojourners) are in transit across Africa and the Middle East, where they become 'bottled up' at various points. Most will never reach the West, but the few who escape Africa confront considerable difficulties in entering Europe and applying for asylum. There are four fundamental obstacles facing asylum applicants, which arise from the organization of the refugee determination system and the way it processes asylum claims. While some problems are exacerbated by resource constraints by far the more significant issues arise from the authority's 'institutional culture', its readiness to adopt and implement policies intended to deter/block valid claims and from problematic decisions by officials. If an asylum applicant is fortunate enough to be represented by a good lawyer they must navigate their way through complex laws and policies to appeal against a refusal of status by the refugee authority and to argue their case before an immigration judge (who frequently misjudge asylum claims). A great deal of public money is spent on refugee determination systems but one is left with the strong sense that the quality of justice available to individuals in need of protection is so poor that obtaining a grant of status is a matter of chance. Above all one is left with a feeling that British/Western officials are indifferent to the fate of individuals fleeing persecution (as in Ethiopia, these individuals are merely 'doing their job').

The seeming indifference of officials and of the public towards refugees is reinforced when we look at British policies and the way policies are implemented. Britain's long-term breach of its legal obligations under the 1954 Convention Related to the Status of Stateless Persons is a serious indictment of its commitment to uphold international law and of the way it assesses asylum claims. This breach, together with the absence of policies capable of identifying and assisting stateless persons, has meant that some applicants have been wrongfully refused asylum while other stateless persons lack legal status and rights. Furthermore, rather than operate an inclusive policy to assist stateless persons the UK adopts an exclusive policy by administratively determining an individual's formal entitlement to a nationality. The essential unfairness of the process is compounded by the poor quality of judicial decisions which transform valid asylum applicants into 'failed' asylum seekers who are subject to detention and deportation.

Over the past 15 years British legislators have adopted a raft of laws which have reshaped the asylum system and reduced the level of protection and support offered to successful and unsuccessful asylum applicants. Thus Parliament now recognizes five different types of asylum applicant, each of which is entitled to different rights and different levels of support. In 2005 the entitlement of many successful asylum applicants to permanent protection was replaced by temporary, short-term protection, following which the person may be required to return to their country of origin. Parliament has also given its imprimatur to a policy of enforced destitution imposed on 'failed' asylum seekers in an attempt to force them to leave the UK. However, the number of failed asylum seekers has grown because UKBA officials have consistently demonstrated their inability to implement asylum and immigration policies fairly, consistently and in a timely manner. For this reason the Home Office has earned the epithet, bestowed on it by a former Secretary of State as 'not fit for purpose'.[3] As my analysis of judicial review applications in Chapter 6 argued, officials have consistently decided cases and implemented policy in an arbitrary and unfair manner. Given the ability of the government to conceal its failures from the public it has been left to the Independent Chief Inspector of Borders and Immigration (2012 and Independent Chief Inspector of Borders and Immigration and HM Inspectorate of Prisons 2012) to reveal that the true extent of UKBA maladministration covers *all* areas of its work.

Rather than address the huge backlog of 'legacy' asylum claims that take the form of fresh asylum applications, UKBA has relied upon the policy of 'temporary admission', which places failed asylum seekers in a state of limbo, the parameters of which are marked by destitution and the absence of rights. While individuals are temporarily admitted and destitute, UKBA slowly and ineffectively assesses some of their outstanding claims. In court, UKBA's defence has been that it was actively reviewing and resolving cases and that the majority of outstanding asylum claims were not exceptional and did not merit special consideration. Unfortunately the courts, who have deferred to the Home Office, have been seriously misled.

Other Home Office policies are also flawed. Thus Home Office decisions to refer asylum applicants to the fast-track system, with its expedited system of appeals, has proved to be flawed, as is its ability to manage its paperwork. In short, all these policies have delayed the assessment of claims and subjected individuals to prolonged destitution. In addition, the legal requirement that failed asylum seekers assist UKBA with their redocumentation is problematic because a growing number of individuals are not recognized by their embassies. Rather than taking these difficulties into account – for example by allowing these individuals access to minimal support from NASS or providing them with a grant of temporary protection – UKBA once again renders them destitute and deportable. The net effect of this catalogue of errors and unlawful decisions is that UKBA 'produces' illegality on a massive scale: wrongful decisions, errors and indifference have transformed valid asylum claimants into illegal, deportable migrants.

Though there is considerable information in the public domain about destitute and failed asylum seekers, researchers and the press have failed to examine how government policy is implemented and whether Home Office policies are effective. How else can we explain why the expenditure of vast amounts of public money has failed to reduce the number of 'illegal migrants'? The lack of information about the (in)effectiveness of asylum and immigration policies arises from the fact that the Home Office does not undertake or commission research into policy effectiveness and, to paraphrase De Genova (2007), because independent researchers have failed to examine the ways in which state practices produce 'culprits' for deportation.

Official discourse, including the many reports, official statements and videos of enforcement action, contribute to a form of 'self-censorship' which obscures how the state treats illegals and how ineffective and poorly implemented policy is. The failure to examine government policy and practice arises from official, discursive treatment of failed asylum seekers as an affront to the nation, as persons who have deservedly been placed outside the law and who are rightly condemned to 'inhuman treatment', incarceration and deportation. The individuals treated in this manner have effectively been silenced; they have learned to maintain a low profile and not to comment about how officials and the British public treat them. Media representations, official statements and the 'spectacle' of border enforcement (De Genova 2012), which portrays UKBA as effectively and efficiently deporting illegals, has contributed to a situation in which non-white asylum seekers have become the object of violence, racial abuse and discrimination. In effect, public and official discourse about illegals reinforces the 'natural' and self-evidently correct nature of policies aimed at protecting national sovereignty through raids, arrests, border controls, detentions and ultimately the deportation of 'illegal aliens'.

It appears that Britain's and the West's approach to refugees and stateless persons has come full circle from 1930 when, as Arendt noted over 50 years ago, 'the one question' asked at all international conferences was, 'How to make the refugee be made deportable again?' (1968: 284). In the inter-war period when the country of origin of a refugee refused to take them back this question was answered by creating internment camps into which refugees were incarcerated. Does the existence of so many immigration detention facilities today testify to our failure to learn from history?

If we acknowledge the failure of asylum and immigration policy and reject the discursive treatment of refugees as deserving culprits for deportation, we are not left with 'open-borders' (Hayter 2004). Foremost, it is important to see refugees, stateless persons and failed asylum seekers as fellow human beings. The aim of the expanding number of strikes and demonstrations in immigration detention facilities worldwide is to protest against the inhumane treatment meted out to detainees and to be accorded basic human rights.

It is in this light that conversations with 'failed' asylum seekers have underlined not merely the injustice of being subjected to destitution but also the need to see them as human beings. The 'Eritreans' who are the subject of this book were taken from their homes and, together with their families, expelled into an unforgiving land where they sought without great success to re-establish their lives, find family members and take refuge. In Eritrea they were unable to re-establish their lives, neither have they achieved this goal as they transit Africa and the Middle East. The relatively small number of individuals who make it to the West and who apply for asylum are denied refuge and as failed asylum seekers they have faced the vicissitudes of 'bare life'/destitution and illegality. Remarkably, and despite all the obstacles placed in their way, many individuals have rebuilt their lives and demonstrated their dignity.

Their presence among us should be seen as evidence of an important political struggle for recognition as human beings and not as evidence of law breaking. Indeed, their presence poses a fundamental challenge to our impoverished conceptions which link the right to participate in politics with (increasingly impoverished rights granted to those who hold) citizenship.

The illusion of justice/redress

In Chapter 2, I examined The Hague's assessment of conflicting legal claims and briefly noted that Eritrea had entered a claim on behalf of six individuals. In August 2009 the EECC awarded limited damages to these individuals on the basis that they were prevented from gaining access to their bank accounts and/or because their property had been unlawfully appropriated. Thus Hiwot Nemariam and Belay Redda, husband and wife, were awarded $US319,615; Sertzu Gebre Meskal was awarded $US1.5 million; Fekadu Andemeskal's claim was dismissed for lack of proof; Mebrahtu Grebremedhin was awarded $US21,250; and Mebrat Gebreamlak was awarded $US225,000. The awards were far less than the value of the property they lost and, in any event, both states refused to honour the decision. In short, international law did not permit these individuals redress against Ethiopia for the wrongs committed against them.

In June 2000 a small number of 'Eritreans' attempted to sue the Ethiopian government in the US District Court for confiscating their property.[4] Hiwot Nemariam[5] and five others sought to use US law to obtain redress against Ethiopia and the

Commercial Bank of Ethiopia (CBE), which they alleged had 'retained their funds and 'exchanged them for other assets'. They argued that because they had been 'expelled without due process' they were unable to access their bank accounts, which could only be done in person.[6] In August 2001 their claim was dismissed because Ethiopia argued that the court did not have jurisdiction and that the EECC was the appropriate court to deal with the issue.

The district court's decision was overturned because the EECC could not make an award directly to individuals. However, in November 2005 the court once again dismissed the case for lack of jurisdiction. A further appeal was made on the basis that the Foreign Sovereign Immunities Act (1976) gave US courts 'jurisdiction over a civil action against a foreign sovereign for any claim with respect to which a foreign state is not entitled to immunity'. Since the CBE and Ethiopia did not dispute the appellants' factual allegation, the circuit court reviewed the case. It found that the appellants had 'failed to demonstrate that the CBE had owned or operated their bank accounts'. Rather, the bank had neither taken possession of nor exerted control over the appellants' contractual right to the funds, but together with the Ethiopian government it had prevented them from accessing the account. This action was not viewed by the court as equivalent to expropriation. With respect to a new submission by the appellants that they be given access to the bank accounts holding the proceeds of the compulsory sale of their property, the court dismissed this claim because the issue had not been argued in, and thus was not appealed from, the lower court. So ended efforts in the USA to obtain redress against Ethiopia.

In early 2011 a group of 'Eritreans' in England met to discuss the possibility of filing a claim in the British courts against Ethiopia to obtain compensation for the property and assets that had been taken from them. Because not everyone in the group had had their property expropriated or bank account frozen, agreement on the purpose of the claim was reached with some difficulty.[7] Once a decision was made to move forward a meeting was held with a law firm, which identified a number of legal and practical problems. First, in British courts, private individuals cannot sue a foreign nation because of the principle of sovereign immunity (unless that state gives its permission). This meant that they would have to file a claim in an Ethiopian court. Such a case was not entirely out of the question but it did raise further questions: (a) who would collate and document all the evidence?; (b) could a reliable lawyer could be found to file their claim in Ethiopia?; and finally (c) would the Ethiopian courts agree to hear it? Also if the case was heard, would they as the appellants be able to attend the hearing to give evidence? Just as important, the cost of preparing and arguing the case could be quite high while the chance of winning the case was low. Nevertheless they decided to persevere. Following a meeting with an experienced Ethiopian judge, however, the group realized just how difficult it would be to file a case in Ethiopia because reliable Ethiopian lawyers were scarce (and would be wary of filing a case against the government) and the case would be difficult to win. Reluctantly, the idea of taking Ethiopia to court was dropped.

Ten months later, and partly in response to the failure to initiate a legal case, a representative of an association of deportees comprising one-hundred families approached the Ethiopian ambassador in London to discuss their concerns. Following the meeting a petition was sent to the embassy in February 2011 for onward submission to the Ministry of Foreign Affairs. The petition stated that the association:

> welcomed the move by the Federal Republic of Ethiopia to grant deported Eritreans the right to reclaim the assets left behind as a result of the war [as stated in the 2009 Council of Ministers Directive].
>
> However we would like to meet with officials to discuss the way in which the 2009 Directive affects our members. Indeed, we see a discussion as the only way we . . . are able to address the needs of our members and assist in the effort to foster a positive relationship between the people of the two countries.
>
> The problems that our members face are as follows:
>
> 1. In applying to the Ministry to return to Ethiopia to claim our property . . . many of us are denied an entry visa and . . . [are] unable to make a claim.
> 2. Following the seizure of our property some of our homes were publicly auctioned, allegedly to pay outstanding debts. We ask to see the evidence indicating the nature of our debts.
> 3. Many members worked in Ethiopian government service for decades and would like to be able to claim their pensions. How can we work together to resolve this problem.
> 4. Several members owned commercial trucks which were confiscated and apparently parked in a government lot. We have papers of ownership but are unable to come to Ethiopia to establish a claim. . . How can we resolve this issue?
> 5. Many of us have not been given permission to access our bank accounts. As you will know the accounts were frozen and interest is not paid on our deposits. We have documents which prove ownership but have not been allowed entry into Ethiopia to make a claim.
> 6. The Directive says that we should be able to reclaim our homes and business property which were confiscated at the time of our arrest/deportation. We have documents proving ownership but are unable to come to Ethiopia to make a claim.

There has been no reply to their petition. The embassy has disclaimed all responsibility for the lack of progress and has blamed the problem on the government in Addis Ababa.

It seems that there is no prospect of obtaining redress in Western courts for the wrongs committed against 'Eritreans' and no prospect that the Ethiopian government will unblock bank accounts or return confiscated property belonging to 'Eritreans'. As a result of the inability of law to provide redress, it has become clear to 'Eritreans' that they have no choice but to remain in the West, which means that they must have legal status. In the UK, individuals whose asylum claim was granted prior to 2005 were able to take advantage of the 'family reunion' policy which allowed them to bring dispersed family members to the UK. Furthermore, and as a result of prolonged legal residence in the UK, this group of refugees and their families have been able to obtain indefinite leave to remain or British nationality. However, individuals granted humanitarian protection or a form of temporary status after 2005 have no entitlement to family reunion nor are they able to obtain permanent residence. There are also a considerable number of failed asylum seekers in the UK whose status will not be secure unless they make a successful fresh asylum application.

In 2006, gossip about a 'creeping amnesty' began to circulate among British refugee lawyers with respect to the outstanding fresh asylum claims of their clients, which were slowly being resolved by the Home Office with grants of indefinite leave to remain. In fact, the British government has resolutely refused to offer an amnesty to individuals, fearing that it would encourage more asylum seekers to come to Britain and because an amnesty would alienate support for the governing political party. What has happened is that in dealing with the backlog of asylum and migration claims the Home Office quietly granted status to 36 per cent of those with an outstanding claim, which represents 172,000 individuals (including family members). At the same time the Home Office refused eight per cent of outstanding claims (for 37,500 persons who were reportedly removed; UK House of Commons Home Affairs Committee 2011). However, as the Independent Chief Inspector's report made clear (2012), UKBA has failed to assess tens of thousands of cases, which leaves open the prospect that a large number of failed asylum seekers will – either as a result of a proper review of their application by the Home Office or by court action – be granted indefinite leave to remain. No doubt some in Britain will object to failed asylum seekers being granted status, but it should be noted that if and when such a grant is made it comes not as a result of an 'amnesty'[8] – i.e. a measure granted indiscriminately to individuals residing unlawfully in the country – but because these individual have valid asylum claims.[9]

Sovereignty and statelessness

The creation of stateless 'Eritreans' and their treatment in Africa and in the West has demonstrated how the exercise of sovereignty is fundamentally implicated in the enduring nightmare which stateless persons endure. A state's right to legislate its own nationality laws is based in international law, but this fact fails to explain why states consistently refuse to address and remedy the situation of stateless persons in their jurisdiction. It fails to explain why Arendt's trenchant observation in 1948 remains true today, namely that:

> Once they had left their homeland they remained homeless, once they had left their state they became stateless; once they had been deprived of their human rights they were rightless, the scum of the earth.
>
> (Arendt 1968: 267)

Clearly the problem arises from human indifference and from the idea that the role of law consists merely in the mechanical application of rules to a case. This dogmatic approach to law has clearly failed to provide justice to those most in need and it needs to be replaced with a 'purposive approach to interpretation', which involves a transformation:

> from a preoccupation with classification and a strict adherence to formal rules to focussing on principled modes of weighing up the competing interests as triggered by the facts of the case and assessed in the light of the values of an open and democratic society.
>
> (Justice Albie Sachs 2009: 205)

Justice Sachs' realization of the role that law *had* to play in the new South Africa returns us to our starting point, namely the exercise of sovereignty. I began by setting out Agamben's concept of the 'political exception', which he saw as the defining principal of modern sovereignty. However, an ethnographically informed study of the 'Eritrean' odyssey has led me to revise his concept to accommodate political reality and everyday life. While it is correct to say that when refugees, migrants and stateless persons are placed outside the state/polity they are deprived of the 'right to life' – in Foucault's sense of the right 'to one's body, to health, to happiness' etc. – the concept is problematic for three reasons not envisaged by Agamben.

First the concept is trite because all individuals convicted of serious criminal offices are sanctioned in a similar manner (how else can we explain life sentences or capital punishment). Furthermore, the implications of 'bare life' are contingent on factors other than an exercise of 'political exception'. To put it in different terms, the 'life' to which an individual is sentenced by the law varies. Thus even though asylum seekers are finding it increasingly difficult to reach a safe country and obtain recognition as a refugee, nevertheless their moral and legal right to asylum is embodied in the Refugee Convention, which requires signatories to create a refugee determination system that conforms to basic conditions.

Unfortunately, very few states recognize the rights of migrants, in particular the rights of individuals who have illegally entered a country and those who, through no fault of their own, have had their contractual rights abruptly terminated and who find themselves in a legal limbo. An important step would be for states to become a signatory to the International Convention on the Protection of the Rights of All Migrant Workers and Members of Their Families[10] followed by the adoption of safeguards against the prolonged detention of migrants and policies that would ensure that migrants would not become stateless (see pp. 176–177).

It is true, however, that the two statelessness conventions have not prevented states from refusing to recognize and assist stateless persons. Indeed, this study found that unlawful decisions by UKBA has sustained the situation of stateless persons. While the prevailing political climate in the UK does not support the adoption of policy reforms – not to mention reforms in the way that policies are implemented – that would recognize the rights of refugees and stateless persons, I am hopeful that sustained pressure by NGOs and UNHCR might bring the British government back into line with its international legal obligations under the 1954 Convention Related to the Status of Stateless Persons.

This study has found that *all* states constantly redraw the political boundaries to exclude as well as include certain categories of citizens, criminals, political dissidents, terrorists, refugees, stateless persons, aliens, skilled migrants, honoured foreigners etc. Indeed the political exception can exclude, and later, as occurred in Ethiopia, may allow some of those excluded and made stateless to register and reacquire citizenship. Crucially, even those individuals who were denied the possibility of reacquiring their formal rights have not given up. Rather they continue to struggle against the very real constraints and disadvantages imposed on them to earn a living, rebuild their lives and find a way to cope with if not negate their lack of rights. This study also suggests that while changes in the situation of stateless persons are slow in coming, Agamben's conception of stateless persons etc. as lacking political agency and as socially dead is wrong. Such individuals are seriously constrained by their lack of rights but their struggle to survive puts them in a situation which directly challenges the state.

It appears that authoritarian and democratic states exercise sovereignty in slightly different ways. In authoritarian states where politicians/officials contrive to exercise absolute power their reach is not total nor, despite their undisputed ability to incarcerate and torture, can they extinguish a person's worth as a human being. In more democratic states there is the expectation, not always found in reality, that the rule of law will constrain the power of the executive and protect the rights of citizens. However, where the courts fear the executive and/or where they dogmatically apply rules to a case, the rule of law does not exist.

How do the above observations apply to the way that states create and sustain statelessness? When the Ethiopian prime minister decreed in 1998 that its ethnic Eritrean citizens 'live in Ethiopia because of the good will of the Ethiopian government' he was articulating a sentiment towards an ethnic minority that was employed by Nazi Germany in the 1930s (towards Jews); in contemporary Kenya (towards Nubians), in Myanmar, Bangladesh and Malaysia (towards the Rohingya), in Israel (towards Palestinians and African refugees), in the Arabian Peninsula (towards the Bidoon), in Bhutan (towards ethnic Nepalese), in Syria (towards Kurds) and in the Czeck and Slovak Republics (towards Roma) to name but a few contemporary examples. Similarly, the ease with which Ethiopia denationalized its citizens, i.e. without providing an independent right to review executive policy/decisions, is also found in Kenya, Botswana, Liberia and many other countries (Manby 2009a: 81 f.).

Where discrimination towards ethnic and religious minorities contributes to the creation of statelessness it is often the case that citizenship laws only recognize the right of a citizen-father to pass citizenship on to his child. In short, women married to foreigners are unable to pass their nationality to their children (who may become stateless). Today, Burundi, Guinea, Kenya, Liberia, Mali, Mauritania and at least seven other African countries 'still discriminate on the grounds of gender in granting citizenship rights to children' born in their mother's country of origin or overseas (Manby 2009b: 34). Similarly many states refuse to recognize individuals with dual nationality (i.e. people who are citizens in two countries). While some countries like Ethiopia adopt this rule to explicitly exclude certain groups, other African states refuse to recognize dual nationals in its diaspora (Manby 2009a: 63).

In addition to adults, many children are stateless. Thus in Ethiopia an entire generation of 'Eritrean' children are not recognized as nationals. Likewise children born to sojourners living illegally in foreign countries, or where nationality does not accrue on the basis of birth in a country (*jus soli*), are also stateless. In many African countries the state does not register births (or issue birth certificates), which can result in a child being discriminated against on the basis of their ethnicity or religion and excluded from education, health services etc. because they cannot prove their entitlement (Bhabba 2011). If undocumented children migrate with their parents – or on their own – the lack of documentation may cause them serious difficulties: they may be prevented from accessing basic services such as primary health care or shelter and they may be subject to arrest and deportation as an undocumented alien (either as a child or as a dependent of a parent who is an alien).

Discrimination may arise from the way that state policies are implemented. For example, regulations may be introduced which make it impossible for a specific group to access their rights and/or there may be a requirement for individuals to prove their identity to be allowed to vote, access school etc. While such actions may not have been undertaken with the aim of discriminating against a specific group, nevertheless they often result in discrimination. For example in Kenya, officials developed their own criteria to screen individuals for inclusion onto a nationality register; in the process they excluded Nubians (Sing'oei 2011). An example of an explicit attempt to exclude a group is Ethiopia's Proclamation No. 378 (2003) which redefined the right to nationality (as originally set out in the 1994 Constitution) to exclude 'Eritreans'. Another example comes from the Republic of Slovenia where officials 'erased' the names of Yugoslav migrants and some Slovene citizens from the register of permanent migrants to ensure that they were not registered as citizens; their actions transformed 25,000 individuals into stateless persons (Zorn 2011).

As Manby (2009b) has noted, many states either do not provide mechanisms for non-nationals to naturalize (acquire nationality) or they adopt preferential rules[11] (for specific types of person) or barriers which prevent certain categories of person from naturalizing; for example in Ethiopia, a four-year legal residence rule and fluency in a national language screen out applicants. One major exception to the rules for naturalization these days has been to provide an opportunity for special categories of persons – skilled migrants, entrepreneurs etc. – to emigrate and 'earn' citizenship.

The situation confronting stateless persons in the West is little different to that which prevails in developing societies. Thus in the UK, Canada and the USA an unknown number of stateless persons are resident, all of whom lack political rights (UNHCR and Asylum Aid 2011, Brouwer 2003, Price 2012). The majority of these persons are either stateless persons who entered the country legally, or undocumented migrants and failed asylum seekers who cannot be returned to their country of origin. All these persons are vulnerable to removal and, because they cannot afford legal counsel, they are prone to lengthy periods of immigration detention. Such persons are easily exploited by landlords and employers, they cannot fully integrate into society because they lack documents and legal status, and their children are usually unable to attend secondary school or university. In short, the status and situation of stateless parents is inherited by their children.

Indeed even where human rights are entrenched in law (and denationalization is prohibited) as in the EU and North America, it is nevertheless the case that new forms of vulnerability are constantly being created 'along the fault lines of perceptions of state security, race and ethnicity, ideal workers, and gender' (Kerber 2005: 744). Indeed, in the USA efforts are underway to introduce a limited principle of *jus soli* to prevent the children of illegally resident aliens from obtaining American nationality. However, if this principle is introduced it will almost certainly have the effect of extending statelessness to:

> second or subsequent generations, as well as create statelessness for some children even though their parent has a recognized nationality. The US would create a new class of persons who cannot be deported, thereby frustrating the primary objective of restrictions on birthright citizenship.
>
> (Price 2012: 3)

States are constantly reconfiguring their laws to defend national interests and, in the process, they sustain existing forms of statelessness and create new forms. The problem cannot easily be resolved. Acceding to the Conventions on Statelessness may help reduce the extent of statelessness, but it will not provide an adequate solution for resolving it. What is required is an international proscription against creating statelessness, not merely a request to 'consider sympathetically' granting status to stateless persons. Furthermore, all states should be required to put into place: (a) effective policies to identify and assist stateless persons; (b) a more inclusive approach to identify a stateless person's 'real' nationality; (c) policies which prevent stateless persons from being made destitute; and (d) measures which prevent stateless persons from being detained when there is no prospect of removing them from the country. In short, nothing less will do than to transform a nation, currently hostage to narrow national interests, back into a state capable of upholding the law and respecting the rights of all human beings.

Appendix

**Letter from Berhanu Kebede, Ethiopian Ambassador to the
United Kingdom, to Dr J. Campbell. Ref. deported Eritreans
(2 December 2009).**

የኢትዮጵያ ፌዴራላዊ ዴሞክራሲያዊ ሪፐብሊክ ኤምባሲ
ለንደን

Embassy of The Federal Democratic Republic of Ethiopia
LONDON

Our Ref. 223/4/27/2002
Date: 02 December 2009

Dr. John Campbell
Department of Sociology and Anthropology
University of London
School of Oriental and African Studies
Thombaugh Street
Russell Square, London
WC1H OXG

Dear Dr. Campbell,

I refer to your letter of 25 October 2009, addressed to H. E. Mr. Meles Zenawi, requesting information on the Council of Ministers Directive regarding Readmission of Deported Eritreans back to Ethiopia: i.e. the May 2009 Council of Ministers Directive to Enable Eritreans Deported from Ethiopia due to the War Launched by the Eritrean government on Ethiopia Reclaim and Develop their properties in Ethiopia.

This Directive has become in to force as an integral part of Ethiopian Law since May 2009 when it was issued.

In this regard, steps have been already taken to implement the directive. For instance, necessary visas have been issued by the Ethiopian Immigration, Ethiopian Embassies and consulates abroad.

As you may be aware,

- Ethiopia deported: Eritreans who were being deemed a threat to national security during the 1998–2000 Ethio-Eritrean war, the war that was launched by the Eritrean government,
- When Eritreans were deported, Ethiopia made sure as much as possible, that every deportee delegated an agent who can administer his/her property in Ethiopia,
- In the absence of such agent/representative in Ethiopia, deported Eritreans have been administering their properties in Ethiopia by delegating somebody of their choice who is in Ethiopia. This process requires the individual to provide power of attorney at the Ethiopian Embassies or consulate abroad.
- After a decade, when it is felt that the threat of most of these people to Ethiopia's national security is felt to be minimum or manageable, the Government of Ethiopia issued directives that will allow deportees to claim properties which were under the custody of their agents in Ethiopia, under the administration of government organs (where the deportee has not had agent at all and the government organs have been looking after the property), and in blocked accounts (as banks kept their money in safe place, i.e. blocked accounts.)

Ethiopia did not deport its own nationals, nor was there any property of Ethiopians confiscated. If we have some Eritreans who were deported and still they claim to be Ethiopians, then we will be forced to consider them as Eritreans as dual citizenship is not permissible under the current nationality laws.

Ethiopia did not confiscate Eritrean deportees' property. There may be cases where government organs undertook over the custody of such property in the absence of any legal representative of the deportee for the safe upkeep of the property and that has been in the interest of the owner of the property and that property will be reclaimed and developed by the rightful owner upon presentation of the necessary proof.

As the deportees were Eritreans as the time of deportation, they will be considered to be Eritreans unless and otherwise to have acquired citizenship of other countries. Request for Ethiopian citizenship shall proceed in accordance with the current Ethiopian Nationality law. Eritreans opting for Ethiopian citizenship shall be treated accordingly.

Dear Dr. Campbell, please find the Amharic version and the unofficial English translation of the Directive.

In case you want further clarification on this matter, please don't hesitate to contact Mr. Haileselassie Subba, Second Secretary and head of International Organizations and Legal Affairs section at the Embassy.

With regards,

Berhanu Kebede
Ambassador

Glossary

ADR	Alternative dispute resolution.
AIT	Asylum Immigration Tribunal (UK). See also 'Tribunal'.
Algiers Agreement	The agreement imposed by the international community on Eritrea and Ethiopia in 2000; the peace treaty which both states ratified.
alien	A person from a foreign country; one who is not a naturalized citizen of the country in which they reside.
Amharic	An Ethiopian language.
amiche	A colloquial term coined in Eritrea which refers to a class of persons who were assembled (i.e. grew up) in Ethiopia but exported (deported) during the war to Eritrea (i.e. those Ethiopian-born ethnic Eritreans who were expelled by Ethiopia).
API	Asylum Policy Instructions are issued by the UK Home Office to case workers undertaking the initial assessment of an asylum claim. They summarize the current legal position on key aspects of an asylum claim.
ARRA	National Intelligence and Security Service, Administration of Refugee and Retournee Affairs, Addis Ababa.
asylum	Formal protection granted to a person recognized as having fled 'persecution' in their country of origin.
asylum seeker	An individual who is making an asylum claim.
bare life	A term coined by Agamben to refer to individuals whom the state places outside of society; it denotes mere biological existence.
birr	Ethiopian currency.
cessation clause	Article 1C of the 1951 Refugee Convention sets out the basis on which UNHCR can determine that situations in which refugee status properly and legitimately granted comes to an end.
CoA	The Court of Appeal (England).
de facto stateless persons	Persons outside the country of their nationality who are unable or, for valid reasons, are unwilling to avail themselves of the protection of that country.

de jure stateless persons	A person who is not considered as a national by any state under the operation of its law, e.g. individuals who do not possess or are not issued identity documents, birth certificates or other documents attesting to their nationality etc.
denationalization	When a state removes the citizenship of a national of the country. The act makes the person stateless.
deportation	When a state compulsorily removes an individual from its territory by an act of compulsion. See also 'return' and '*non-refoulement*'.
Derg	The Amharic name for a self-appointed council of Ethiopian military officers who came to power in 1975 via a *coup d'état* and who governed until they were ousted from power in 1991.
discretionary leave	A grant of leave to enter made to an asylum applicant who is not recognized as a refugee but who cannot be returned to their country of origin without breaching Art. 8 of the European Convention on Human Rights. It is conferred in exceptional circumstances. The grant is for three years or less.
dual nationality	Possessing more than one nationality.
durable solution	UNHCR's mandate is to promote durable solutions to the plight of refugees via: (a) voluntary repatriation to their country of origin in conditions of safety and dignity; (b) local integration in a host country; and (c) resettlement in a third country.
ECHR	European Convention on Human Rights.
EEBC	The Eritrea–Ethiopia Border Commission was convened at The Hague to assess competing claims and demarcate the international border between the two countries.
EECC	The Eritrea–Ethiopia Claims Commission was convened at The Hague and heard state claims for compensation arising from the Eritrea–Ethiopia war.
effective nationality	In international humanitarian law, the principle that 'in cases of plural nationality a person is to be considered as having the nationality which in fact he exercises'.
EPLF	Eritrean People's Liberation Front. The liberation front which succeeded in wresting Eritrea from Ethiopia in 1991. It became the People's Front for Democracy and Justice (PFDJ) in 1993 and has governed Eritrea ever since.
EPRDF	Ethiopian People's Revolutionary Democratic Front; the political party which has governed Ethiopia since May 1991.
EPRP	The Ethiopian People's Revolutionary Party; a leftist-inspired political party opposed to the Derg

Eritrean	A citizen/national of the country of Eritrea.
'Eritrean'	The quotation marks indicate that the person is of Eritrean ethnicity and was born in the state of Ethiopia.
ERREC	Eritrea Relief and Refugee Commission.
estoppel	Estoppel prevents a party from denying or alleging certain facts that are inconsistent with the party's previous positions if others relied upon those positions.
expulsion	When an individual is expelled from a country. See also 'return' and '*non-refoulement*'.
'failed' asylum seeker	An individual who applied for asylum but whose claim was refused by the courts; they have no legal status and are subject to immediate 'return'.
fast-track asylum procedures	In the UK the process by which asylum seekers are detained during their application for asylum and any subsequent appeal, which is supposed to be processed quickly under accelerated procedures. Typically individuals are detained if officials believe that their claim is unfounded, i.e. they come from a country on a 'safe list'.
Federal Negarit Gazeta	The official newspaper in which the Ethiopian government publishes laws, decrees etc.
geographical limitation	When the 1967 Protocol to the Refugee Convention was adopted it permitted signatories the option of adopting a geographic limitation that meant that only Europeans would be accepted as refugees.
giffa	A sweep or military round-up (Tigrinya).
HOPO	Home Office Presenting Officer. A junior official with limited legal training who represents the Home Office in asylum and immigration appeals.
HP	Humanitarian protection. A status granted to asylum applicants who do not qualify for refugee status but who cannot be returned to their country of origin owing to a serious risk to life or person. It is a grant of indefinite leave to enter the UK for five years.
HRW	Human Rights Watch.
IAT	Immigration Asylum Tribunal (UK).
ICJ	International Criminal Court at The Hague.
ICRC	International Committee of the Red Cross (Geneva).
IDP	Internally displaced person.
IHL	International humanitarian law is a set of rules which seek, for humanitarian reasons, to limit the effects of armed conflict. It protects persons who are not or are no longer participating in the hostilities and restricts the means and methods of warfare. International humanitarian law is also known as the law of war or the law of armed conflict.

immigration detention	The practice of detaining asylum seekers and migrants by a government to resolve their immigration claims, facilitate their removal or establish their identity. See also 'fast-track asylum procedures'.
integration	The process by which individuals granted refugee/permanent status integrate into their host country.
IOM	International Organization for Migration (Geneva).
judicial review	In British administrative law, a court proceeding in which a judge reviews the lawfulness of a decision or action made by a public body. A judicial review is a challenge to the way in which a decision has been made, rather than the rights and wrongs of the conclusion reached.
jus ad bellum	The branch of law that defines the legitimate reasons a state may engage in war and focuses on certain criteria that renders a war just.
jus in bellow	The law that governs the way in which warfare is conducted. International humanitarian law is purely humanitarian, seeking to limit the suffering caused. It is independent from questions about the justification or reasons for war, or its prevention, covered by *jus ad bellum*.
jus sanguinis	Latin for 'right of blood', it is a principle of nationality by which citizenship is determined by descent, i.e. by having one or both parents who are citizens of a nation.
jus soli	Latin for 'right of soil', it is the conferment of nationality based on place of birth, regardless of the nationality of one's parents.
kebele	The lowest level of the political administration in Ethiopia, also called urban dwellers associations.
kebessa	The northern highlands of Eritrea, heartland of the EPLF.
legacy cases	In the UK, asylum claims made before 2007 and which are still awaiting a decision by the Home Office.
mixed flows	A mixed composition of population movement containing refugees and 'economic' migrants. See also 'transit migration').
nakfa	Eritrean currency.
NASS	National Asylum Support Service, established in 1999 to be responsible for managing the dispersal and support of asylum seekers across the UK.
national/citizen	A citizen of a country.
non-refoulement	Under Art. 33 of the Refugee Convention, the right of individuals to leave their country in search of asylum and not to be sent back to where their lives or freedom may be in danger.
OAU	Organization of African Unity (1963–2002); replaced by the African Union.

OGN	Operational guidance notes are published policy instructions issued to British Home Office officials.
PCA	The Permanent Court of Arbitration at The Hague.
persecution	Subject to prolonged ill-treatment. The term takes its meaning from Art. 1(A)1 of the Refugee Convention as in 'owing to well-founded fear of being persecuted for reasons of race, religion, nationality, membership of a particular social group or political opinion.'
PFDJ	People's Front for Democracy and Justice; the ruling party in Eritrea (formerly the EPLF).
preclusion	Preclusion generally bars the re-litigation of claims that produced a final decision on the merits in an earlier proceeding.
RCO	Refugee community organization.
refugee	An individual whose asylum claim was recognized and who now has legal status in a host country.
refugee status	A grant of status conferred on an individual who has established a well-founded fear of persecution within the meaning of the 1951 Refugee Convention. Prior to 2005 this was a grant of permanent residence/protection; individuals are now granted indefinite leave to enter the UK for a period of five years.
resettlement	One of the UNHCR's durable solutions which allows refugees for whom neither repatriation nor local integration in their first country of asylum is possible the opportunity to resettle in a third country. For these refugees permanent resettlement in a third country may be the most appropriate and, in some cases, the only durable solution.
return/deportation	The compulsory return of an individual who has no legal status to their country of origin.
self-determination	A principle recognized in international law in which a 'people' or 'nation' decides to be independent.
Shaebia	'People' or 'popular' (Arabic). A term coined by the EPLF to refer to their secessionist struggle against Ethiopia. The term is also derogatively used by the EPRDF to describe the current government in Asmara.
SINIT	A group composed of stateless Ethiopians and their families, most of whom were deported by Ethiopia during the war. They currently reside in south-east England
SIRRA	The Department for Immigration and Nationality Affairs (Addis Ababa).
Sojourn(er)	A temporary stay; a person constantly on the move.
sovereign immunity	A judicial doctrine that prevents a government or its constitute departments, agencies etc. from being sued

	without its consent. The doctrine stems from the ancient English principle that the monarch can do no wrong.
SSHD	Secretary of State for the Home Department (the UK Home Office).
stateless	Not being considered a national by any state (see Art. 1(1) of the 1954 Convention on Statelessness). See also '*de facto* statelessness' and '*de jure* statelessness'.
stateless person	A individual without legal status; a person made stateless by his/her country of origin; a person who is not returnable to their country of origin.
status	Short for immigration status. A grant of, for example, refugee status, humanitarian protection or discretionary leave made by a refugee authority to an asylum applicant.
tegedalie	Eritrean freedom fighters belonging to the EPLF.
Tigrean	Members of the Tigray ethnic group.
Tigrinya	The language of Tigrayans; one of two national languages spoken in Eritrea and Ethiopia.
TMZ	Temporary security zone. Established by the UN Security Council as a buffer between Eritrea and Ethiopia; UN troops were stationed there to police the border pending its demarcation by the EEBC.
TPLF	Tigrayan People's Liberation Front. A liberation front/ guerrilla movement in Ethiopia which came to power in Ethiopia in 1991 and formed the EPRDF.
transit migration	A problematic, policy-based term used to describe very different migrant processes and types of sojourners who are said to have the common goal of reaching Europe. See also 'mixed flows'.
Tribunal	In the UK the first-tier court that decides asylum and immigration appeals. See also 'IAT' and 'AIT'.
TSoL	Treasury solicitors (UK) undertake litigation on behalf of the SSHD (UKBA).
UKBA	United Kingdom Border Agency.
UNHCR	United Nations High Commissioner for Refugees.
UNMEE	The United Nations Mission to Eritrea and Ethiopia, which attempted to police the disputed border between the two countries.
uti possidetis	Latin for 'as you possess'. In international law the term signifies that the parties to a treaty are to retain possession of what they have acquired by force during war.

Notes

Introduction

1 Source: Interview 6 February 2011, London. Further details in Case 1.
2 Following Jenkins (1994), a social category is a class whose nature and composition is externally defined by, for instance, state officials. It may be, and often is, at odds with how individuals placed in this category see themselves.
3 See Bachelor (1995, 1998) and Massey (2010) for a discussion about drafting the two statelessness conventions For an excellent online resource on this and related issues see: http://untreaty.un.org/cod/avl/ha/cssp/cssp.html.
4 The first statistics on statelessness are reported by UNHCR (2007) for 2006; the report records no figures for Ethiopia or Eritrea (Tables 1 and 14) – clearly an error as this book will demonstrate – and only 204 stateless persons in the UK (Table 14). In July 2010, UNHCR-London and Asylum Aid initiated a scoping exercise to assess the number of stateless persons in the UK. It is noteworthy that the British government does not have reliable statistics on the number of stateless persons residing in the UK (UNHCR and Asylum Aid 2011).
5 In 2010 the UK announced that it would be monitoring performance of the multilateral institutions that it funded with a view to cutting assistance to institutions who do not 'demonstrate value for money' (UK Department for International Development 2011).
6 An important exception is work on stateless Palestinians, e.g. Feldman 2007.
7 See: 'Tough times ahead for western scholars studying Ethiopia', *Addis Neger Online* 5 July 2010. Even if access is not denied, officials refuse to speak to foreign researchers.

1 Nationalism, the 1998–2000 Ethiopia–Eritrea war and the denationalisation of 'Eritreans'

1 Because the boundary between Eritrea and Tigray had never been demarcated, the Mareb river, which transects the region, was understood as the boundary.
2 See: 'Rebels pledge democracy in Ethiopia: US-brokered talks end in agreement after fall of capital', *The Baltimore Sun* 29 May 1991; 'Eritreans declare autonomy from Addis Ababa', *The Baltimore Sun* 30 May 1991; Banks and Muller 1998.
3 For an unofficial English version see: http://www.wipo.int/wipolex/en/details.jsp?id=7438.
4 See: http://www.unhcr.org/refworld/docid/3ae6b4e026.html.
5 Agreement on Security and Related Matters signed in Addis Ababa on 13 May 1994 by Kuma Demeska, Minister of Internal Affairs (Ethiopia) and Naizghi Kiflu, Vice Minister of Internal Affairs (Eritrea), Art. 2.1.
6 In 2000, the TPLF was reported to be 'gerrymandering Tigray's borders at the expense of Amhara and Afar regions and diverting national resources to develop war-devastated

Tigray' ('IRIN Focus on Assab', *IRIN* 5 June 2000. Available at: http://www.irinnews.org/Report/15484/ERITREA-ETHIOPIA-IRIN-Focus-on-Assab-5-June-2000).

7   To see an image of the map and of the 100-birr note see: http://www.eritrea.be/old/eritrea-ethiopia.htm.

8   Prime Minister Meles of Ethiopia was held to account for his 'pro-Eritrean' policies at a meeting of the TPLF in May 1998 but was able to muster support for his position 'At the price of accepting the expulsion of Eritreans and a continuing military build-up' ('Brothers at War', *Africa Confidential* 1998; 39(18): 5).

9   Under Haile Selassie and the *Derg* there had been a consistent policy of de-industrializing Eritrea through enforced closure of Eritrean businesses, which pushed the relatively better educated Eritreans and better capitalized Eritrean entrepreneurs into Ethiopia. It is also worth noting that in the late 1970s the *Derg* embarked on a policy to liquidate Eritrean army officers and officials (Firebrace *et al.* 1984; Resoum Kidane 1999).

10 I have relied upon Plaut (2005) for details of the conflict and peace negotiations; see also Gilkes and Plaut (1999), Tekeste Negash and Tronvol (2000) and Jacquin-Berdahl and Plaut (2005).

11 See: 'Press release: Precautionary measures taken regarding Eritreans residing in Ethiopia' (12 June 1998) issued by the Ministry of Foreign Affairs, available at: http://www.geocities.com/dagmawi.geo/News_Jun12_EthioPressRelease.html; and Daniszewski, J. 'Ethiopia sees threat in resident Eritreans', *Los Angeles Times* 19 June 1998. Available at: http://articles.latimes.com/1998/jun/19/news/mn-61535.

12 The speech is quoted in Asmeron Legasse 1999.

13 For additional interviews that support those cited here see: Eritrea 2002 ¶1.13–f, ¶2.55–2.78 and Amnesty International 1999.

14 I have a copy of a registration document issued to an 'Eritrean' expelled into Eritrea, which says in Tigrinya: 'Deported by the Weyane regime on January 27 1999'.

15 This information is taken from a 2001 report by the Commercial Bank of Ethiopia entitled 'General report on Eritrean expellees bank loan collection process and its result', which can be found in Eritrea 2004a.

16 Deportees are still denied access to their bank accounts (see Chapter 2).

17 Source: Affidavit of Tekle Tekea, dated 19 December 2003, submitted in Ethiopia's Counter-Memorial and contained in Eritrea 2004a.

18 See: 'Plight of the stranded Eritreans', *BBC News* 4 November 1999. Available at: http://news.bbc.co.uk/1/hi/world/africa/504784.stm.

19 See: UNDP 1998; Klein 1998; Calhoun 1998; Eritrean Relief and Refugee Commission 1998; Asmeron Legasse 1998, 1999, 2000; Human Rights Watch 1999; Amnesty International 1999, 2000; Wilson 1999; Byrne 2002; and Global IDP 2003.

20 The Ministry of Foreign Affairs was identified as the source of this paper by Novogrodsky (1999). A formal statement was made in July 1999 that none of the individuals expelled 'over the course of the past year' were nationals of Ethiopia, rather 'they are Eritrean citizens because they registered to vote in Eritrea's 1993 referendum on independence' (HRW 2003a: 20).

21 The author of the statement failed to acknowledge his reliance on, and plagiarization of, Ibrahim Idris (1990), whose paper was altered to fit official requirements.

22 This probably occurred because officials used lists of names provided by neighbours and informants.

23 Ethiopia's actions directly contravened: the Ethiopian Constitution (Art. 33); the Universal Declaration of Human Rights (Arts. 15 and 17[2]); the International Convention on the Elimination of All Forms of Racial Discrimination (Arts. 2 and 12 [5]); and the African Charter on Human and People's Rights. Ethiopia was a signatory to all the above conventions/instruments at the time it arrested and expelled ethnic Eritreans.

24 See: 'Eritreans begin registering as aliens in Ethiopia', *Associated Press* 16 August 1999. Available at: http://www.geocities.com/dagmawi.geo/NewsAug99/News_Aug17_Ethio-Eritrea.html.

2 Politics, law and the limitations of international arbitration at The Hague

1 For information about UNMEE see: http://www.un.org/en/peacekeeping/missions/past/unmee/.

2 The agreement can be accessed at: http://www.pca-cpa.org/showpage.asp?pag_id=1150.

3 According to the International Criminal Court of Justice, 'It is a principle of general scope, logically connected with the phenomenon of the obtaining of independence, wherever it occurs. Its obvious purpose is to prevent the independence and stability of new States being endangered by fratricidal struggles provoked by the challenging of frontiers following the withdrawal of the administering power. The fact that the new African States have respected the territorial *status quo* which existed when they obtained independence must therefore be seen not as a mere practice but as the application in Africa of a rule of general scope . . . The principle of *uti possidetis juris* accords pre-eminence to legal title over effective possession as a basis of sovereignty. Its primary aim is to secure respect for the territorial boundaries which existed at the time when independence was achieved.' (Case Concerning the Frontier Dispute [Burkina Faso/Republic of Mali] Judgment of 22 December 1986, III. (2), p. 172).

4 For information about The Hague see van Haersoltevan Hof 2007 and http://www.pca-cpa.org/showpage.asp?pag_id=363.

5 The procedural rules can be found at: http://www.google.co.uk/url?sa=t&rct=j&q=&esrc=s&source=web&cd=2&ved=0CCoQFjAB&url=http%3A%2F%2Fwww.pca-cpa.org%2Fshowfile.asp%3Ffil_id%3D195&ei=nZlRUJycHYmN0wXw5ICQCA&usg=AFQjCNHkoCE4JaY0o02ROndyKjFZvAn4KQ

6 Parties submit evidence without the rules of admissibility which prevail in other jurisdictions. The arbitration rules do not define the 'burden of proof' which applies in its hearings; indeed, the 'burden' may vary but, in general, 'it is close to the balance of probabilities', i.e. 'each party has the burden of proving the facts relied on to support its claim or defense' (von Mehren and Salomon 2003: 291).

7 Contrast this with litigation which, while messy and confrontational, proceeds through a fair and open hearing to examine the issues at the heart of the dispute.

8 The decisions of the EEBC and all related correspondence can be found at: http://www.pca-cpa.org/showpage.asp?pag_id=1150.

9 In this way 'stronger evidence' was found for the claim of Ethiopian sovereignty over the 'Endeli projection' and for Eritrean claims regarding much of the 'Bada region', including the town of Badme (pp. 52–5).

10 The failure to identify the location of Badme on EEBC Map C is very surprising. In fact the town is located on the Eritrean side of the border about 60 km from 'point 6' moving north-east to 'point 9', and about 10 km inside the border.

11 Source: Transcript of a press conference compiled by UNMEE on 13 April 2002 reported in Healy and Plaut 2007: 4.

12 See note 1, 'Facts and Figures' at: http://www.un.org/en/peacekeeping/missions/past/unmee/.

13 All the documents issued by The Hague, and associated correspondence, can be found at: http://www.pca-cpa.org/showpage.asp?pag_id=1151.

14 The EECC's 'Decision no. 8', which reiterated Art. 5(8) of the Algiers Agreement, stated that both states had agreed that given the number and complexity of claims which could be filed by individuals that each state would instead either file claims on behalf of individuals who were their nationals (which Eritrea did on behalf of six named individuals), or that a state's claims would include claims for damages on behalf of individuals. If an individual's claim was upheld, compensation would not be awarded to that person but used instead for relief or development programs.

15 Art. 3 of the Algiers Agreement assigns the task of assessing the origins of the conflict to another, undefined, institution.

16 See: http://www.crimesofwar.org/a-z-guide/jus-ad-bellum-jus-in-bello/.

17 For instance, Ethiopia's expulsion of individuals after the peace treaty (see Won Kidane 2007: 44–51) and Gray (2006: 705).

18 Art. 5(8) of the Algiers Agreement stipulated that a state could make a claim on its own behalf and on behalf of individuals but that individuals could not bring a claim before the Commission. Why Ethiopia did not submit individual claims is unclear.

19 It also applied Art. 75 of Protocol I, the Protocol Additional to the Geneva Conventions of 12 August 1949. See: http://www.icrc.org/eng/assets/files/other/additionnal_proto-cols.pdf.

20 Eritrea's legal counsel adopted the approach used at the International Criminal Tribunal for Former Yugoslavia.

21 The database did not contain the names of all rural expellees who left their homes along the border at gunpoint or those who fled to third countries. Thus there was no record of the people who were deported at Addis Ababa airport or who fled from or were deported by Ethiopia to Sudan and Kenya.

22 In addition to Art. 32 of the Ethiopian Constitution, which states that 'no Ethiopian national shall be deprived of his or her Ethiopian nationality against his or her will', Eritrea also cited Public Rights Proclamation no. 139 of 1959 which states that '[n]o Ethiopian subject may be banished from the Empire' (Eritrea 2002: ¶2.41).

23 Later in the war the Ethiopian passports of 'Eritreans' were stamped 'expelled, never to return' as the individuals were forced across the border (Eritrea 2002: ¶2.107).

24 The Commission set aside the theory of 'dominant and effective nationality', which is based on the 1955 case of Nottebohm decided by the ICJ, and accepted instead the 'theory of non-responsibility' (Won Kidane 2007: 54–55).

25 Regarding 'Eritrea', HRW's 2003 report is the principal source of data. It reported that in 1998 'thousands' of Ethiopians fled across the border without waiting to be repatriated (p. 32); that an unknown number of persons were expelled (p. 33) and that a total of 18–19,000 persons were repatriated by the ICRC (p. 33). In its 1999 report (p. 34) 1800–2500 Ethiopians were reportedly interred and the ICRC repatriated a further 12,000 Ethiopians. In 2000 HRW reported that 7,500 individuals were expelled between May and June (p. 35), that a further 3,342 persons were expelled in July to August (p. 36) and that the ICRC repatriated 12,000 persons (p.36). HRW reported that in 2001 the ICRC repatriated a further 21,255 persons (p. 36). ICRC-published reports on repatriations are only available from 2002 onwards. Regarding Ethiopia: HRW (2003) states that there had been 75,000 expulsions (p. 5) without specifying dates, places or the exact number of people affected. Likewise, reports by Amnesty International only provide a global figure of 54,000 expulsions with no details about specific dates, places etc. (1999, 2000).

26 Eritrea submitted a Counter-Memorial to 'Ethiopia's claim 5: Ethiopian nationals in Eritrea' which disputes Ethiopia's evidence. For instance, it argues that Ethiopia's sub-missions fail to differentiate between nationals and aliens, fails to offer independent corroboration for its assertions (instead it relied upon travel guides) etc. Eritrea also questions Ethiopia's 'credibility gap' due to deliberate misrepresentations, the submis-sion of statements from unreliable witnesses, misrepresentations about conditions in detention and about the seizure of property etc. In a nutshell, Eritrea argued that 'To take Ethiopia's "witness statements" as *prima facie* convincing, simply because they are sworn and signed, and to place the burden on Eritrea to come up with a convincing refutation is to turn one's back on a clear pattern of wilful dishonesty' (Eritrea 2004b: ¶1.24).

27 See the EECC's discussion of this issue and the evidence before it (EECC 2004b: ¶83–90).

28 And also the drowning of six women attempting to cross the Mereb River and an inci-dent in which some women were transported by sea to Djibouti.

3 Flight from the Horn: Transiting Africa to find refuge

1   See: 'Eritrea: authorities terminate ICRC role in repatriations of Ethiopians', International Committee of the Red Cross news release 09/149, 3 August 2009. Available at: http://www.icrc.org/eng/resources/documents/news-release/2009-and-earlier/eritrea-news-030809.htm.

2   There were many misleading stories about the prospect of resettlement which may have encouraged people to depart, e.g. 'Eritrea refugees at Shimelba refugee camp will be resettled in the US of America' (14 September 2008) at: http://redsea1.websitetoolbox.com/post/Eritreans-Refugees-in-Shimelba-refugee-camp-will-be-resettled-in-the-U.S-of-America-2988449. Details of the US resettlement plan (with no indication about the number of persons who would be accepted) can be found at: http://www.state.gov/j/prm/releases/factsheets/2009/181065.htm.

3   Source: http://www.unhcr.org/4b1e7c5a9.html.

4   See: 'Ethiopia: Eritrea's hard road to independence', *Africa Confidential* 1992; 33(6): 7 and 'Ethiopia: Asmara looks inwards', *Africa Confidential* 1992; 33(11): 11.

5   Assuming they had not acquired other rights to protection. The cessation documents can be accessed on UNHCR's Refworld at: http://www.unhcr.org/cgi-bin/texis/vtx/refworld/rwmain.

6   See: 'Human Rights Alert: Eritreans and Ethiopians detained in Sudan face risk of detention, torture and execution if returned home', 8 January 2008. Available at: http://www.soatsudan.org/public/Press%20Releases%202008.asp (accessed 1 September 2009).

7   In July 2012, 51 Eritreans were arrested in Sudan for illegal entry. The authorities immediately deported six into Eritrea ('Sudan urged by Amnesty to stop deporting Eritrean asylum seekers', *Bloomberg News* 16 August 2012, in *Fahamu Refugee Legal Aid Newsletter* October 2012).

8   Such actions violate Art. 15 of the Universal Declaration of Human Rights, and Arts 5 and 12 of the International Convention on the Elimination of All Forms of Racial Discrimination, which both Ethiopia and Eritrea have signed.

9   See: 'Sudanese refugee protest at UNHCR-Cairo ends tragically', *RSD-watch* 10 March 2006. Available at: http://rsdwatch.wordpress.com/2006/03/10/sudanese-refugee-protest-at-unhcr-cairo-ends-tragically/.

10 See: 'Eritrea asks Israel to deport "deserters"', *Haaretz* 25 March 2008. Available at: http://www.ehrea.org/eritrean_refugees_in_israel.html.

11 See: 'Eritreans risk death in the Sahara', *BBC News* 25 March 2007.

12 See: 'Eritrea: Refugees involuntarily repatriated from Libya', 3 Aug 2004. Available at: http://hrw.org/english/docs/2004/08/03/eritre9178.htm.

13 See: '60 Eritreans deported from Libya are granted asylum in Sudan', UN Radio 7 September 2004 (available at: http://www.un.org/radio/260.asp) and 'Libya slammed for expelling Eritrean refugees', *afrol News* 21 September 2004 (available at: http://www.afrol.com/articles/14248).

14 The humanitarian crisis which unfolded in Libya in early 2011 engulfed migrants as well as Libyan nationals. See: 'Humanitarian crisis grows on Libya–Tunisia Border', *PBS News* 1 March 2011. Available at: http://www.pbs.org/newshour/rundown/2011/03/crisis-on-libya-tunisia-border-as-huge-crowds-flee.html. For details about the repatriation of migrants, including a small number of Ethiopians and Eritreans, see: http://www.migration-crisis.com/libya/page/index/1.

15 In *Hirsi Jamaa and Others* v. *Italy* the European Court ruled that in 2009 Italy violated the human rights of 24 Eritrean and Somali migrants fleeing Libya when it returned them to Libya without assessing their asylum claims. See: http://www.statewatch.org/news/2012/feb/ecj-italy-libya-judgment.pdf.

16 See: 'Italy: Over 100 reportedly "pushed back" at sea', Amnesty International public statement, 30 August 2011. Available at: http://www.amnesty.org/en/library/asset/

EUR30/017/2011/en/bdf6924e-4ddb-4e56-bf81-870b232bcf6b/eur300172011en. html.

17 See: '57 Eritrean asylum-seekers reported saved from a sinking boat but secretly incarcerated in Libya', 26 May 2007 (available at: http://www.ehrea.org/57libya.htm) and 'Doomed to drown: The desperate last calls of the migrants no one wanted to rescue', *The Independent* 25 May 2007.

18 See: 'Malta: The government should suspend deportations of Eritreans', Amnesty International, 11 October 2002 (available at: http://www.amnesty.org.uk/news_details. asp?NewsID=13608) and Elsa Chyrum 'Testimony of Eritreans deported from Malta, jailed at Dhalak', 2 July 2005 (available at: http://www.awate.com/artman/publish/article_4190.shtml).

19 See:'SpaintoprovisionallytakeinEritreanimmigrants'.Availableat:http://216.239.59.104/ search?q=cache:gKljwAK0wJgJ:www.eubusiness.com/afp/060721180502.r3y8oiqp+E ritreans+in+Libyaandhl=enandclient=firefox-aandgl=ukandstrip=1 (accessed 1 September 2009).

20 See: http://www.thepetitionsite.com/takeaction/490908132#body. The Djibouti government currently detains 334 Eritrean army deserters and an unknown number of Eritrean soldiers captured in a border conflict between Eritrea and Djibouti ('Petition presented to the Djibouti delegation attending the UN meeting in New York, concerning Eritreans detained in Djibouti', 1 October 2012, in *Fahamu Refugee Legal Aid Newsletter* October 2012).

21 See: 'Thousands gather in Somalia port for Gulf of Aden sailing season', UNHCR, 31 August 2007. Available at: http://www.unhcr.org/news/NEWS/46d816664.html.

22 See: 'Somali deportations' [1300 Ethiopian migrants handed over], reliefweb, 10 October 2006. Available at: http://www.reliefweb.int/rw/rwb.nsf/db900sid/AMMF-6UFG JA?OpenDocumentandquery=forced%20returns%20from%20bosaso. In August 2012 dozens of Ethiopians were reportedly refouled back to Ethiopia ('Somaliland: Stop deporting Ethiopian refugees' (4 September 2012) reported in *Fahamu Refugee Legal Aid Newsletter* (October 2012).

23 UNHCR Global Appeal 2008–9: Yemen (available at: http://www.unhcr.org/home/ PUBL/474ac8d90.pdf) and Gemund 2007.

24 See: *2005 UNHCR Statistical Yearbook* Country Data Sheet: Yemen. Available at: http://www.unhcr.org/cgi-bin/texis/vtx/home/opendocPDFViewer.html?docid=4641b ed30&query=UNHCR%20Statistical%20Yearbook%20Country%20Data%20Sheet: %20Yemen.

25 See: 'Ethiopia: Cautionary migration tales are no deterrent', *IRIN* 22 November 2011 (available at: http://www.irinnews.org/Report/94279/ETHIOPIA-Cautionary-migration-tales-are-no-deterrent). Ethiopians are arrested and deported from Yemen without being allowed to access the asylum process.

26 See:*2005 UNHCR Statistical Yearbook Country Data Sheet: Saudi Arabia*, p. 481. Available at: http://www.unhcr.org/statistics/STATISTICS/4641bebf11.pdf.

27 See: 'Turkey sticks to "limited" application of the Geneva Convention', *bianet* 1 August 2011 (available at: http://bianet.org/english/world/131856-turkey-sticks-to-limited-application-of-the-geneva-convention) and Gusten, S. 'As refugees flood Turkey, asylum system nears breakdown', *New York Times* 25 September 2012.

28 UNHCR recorded the presence of 400 Eritreans and 300 Ethiopians seeking refuge in Uganda in 2005 (see: *UNHCR Global Report 2006: Uganda*. Available at: http://www. unhcr.org/home/PUBL/4666d26b0.pdf) but accounts from Ethiopian refugees suggest that the number is higher.

29 See: 'UNHCR head accepts Nairobi corruption report', *IRIN News* 28 January 2002. Available at: http://www.irinnews.org/report.aspx?reportid=29962.

30 See: 'Mozambique/Tanzania: Horn migrants beaten, deported, imprisoned', *IRIN News* 19 September 2001. Available at: http://www.irinnews.org/Report/93759/MOZAMBIQUE-TANZANIA-Horn-migrants-beaten-deported-imprisoned.

31 See: 'Tanzania: Migrants die in truck', *BBC News Africa* 27 June 2012. Available at: http://www.bbc.co.uk/news/world-africa-18606620.
32 See: 'Migrants drown in Lake Malawi in Karonga District', *BBC News Africa* 21 June 2012. Available at: http://www.bbc.co.uk/news/world-africa-18531470.
33 See: 'Zimbabwe: South Africa deports illegal local immigrants', *The Herald* 12 October 2011. Available at: http://allafrica.com/stories/201110130422.html.
34 See: 'Home Affairs asylum changes', *news24* 14 April 2010. Available at: http://www.news24.com/SouthAfrica/News/Home-Affairs-asylum-changes-20100414.
35 In 2011 '64 percent of migration was intraregional and employment-related' (IOM 2011: 62).

4 The illusion of citizenship and of return: Politics and persecution in the Horn

1   See: 'Ethiopia hits at bases run by militants in Eritrea', *New York Times* 15 March 2012. Available at: http://www.nytimes.com/2012/03/16/world/africa/ethiopian-troops-enter-eritrea.html?_r=0
2   Riggan's informants returned to Eritrea prior to the war, whereas my informants had all been deported to Eritrea.
3   I have a copy of a registration certificate in my possession for two children deported from Ethiopia in 1999 entitled, 'Form for under age Eritreans deported by the Weyane Government'.
4   See: Kebrab 2009.
5   See for instance: 'Eritrea: Two students die in government clampdown', *World Socialist Web Site* 24 August 2001. Available at: http://www.wsws.org/articles/2001/aug2001/erit-a24.shtml.
6   Source: Interview with the Director General of the Ethiopian Expatriate Affairs Division, Ministry of Foreign Affairs, 21 April 2012.
7   See: http://www.unhcr.org/refworld/country,,,LEGISLATION,ETH,,409100414,0.html.
8   See: http://www.unhcr.org/refworld/country,,,LEGISLATION,ETH,,48abd56c0,0.html.
9   See: ¶23 of http://www.unhcr.org/refworld/pdfid/467bcd292.pdf and CERD's 2009 reply to Ethiopia's belated report, which failed to answer the specific query about the legal status of 'Eritrean' children whose parents had been deported at: http://www.unhcr.org/refworld/publisher,CERD,,ETH,4abc820f3,0.html.
10 See the evidence of Mr Gunter Schroder on this issue in: 'ST (Ethnic Eritrean – nationality – return) Ethiopia CG [2011] UKUT 00252(IAC)'. His evidence and my own is summarized in Appendix A at: http://www.asylumlawdatabase.eu/sites/asylumlawdatabase.eu/files/aldfiles/Judgment_6.pdf
11 I have a photocopy of such a passport in my possession.
12 See: 'Eritrean President says peace prospects good in Horn of Africa', *Associated Press* 16 August 1999 (available at: http://www.oocities.org/~dagmawi/NewsAug99/News_Aug17_Ethio-Eritrea.html) and the Eritrea–Ethiopia Claims Commission's final report on reparations (EECC 2009: ¶331–340).
13 I was told that the total number of applications was 800; this was adjusted to 300 and then to 212. I was unable to clarify this discrepancy.
14 I was told by embassy officials in 2009 that the directive would be placed on embassy websites, but this has not happened and neither has it been published on the website of the Ministry of Foreign Affairs.
15 Embassy officials exercise a huge amount of discretion in deciding to allow a deportee to make a claim. Some individuals in the USA and UK – including individuals with valid travel documents and title deeds – have been refused outright. I am aware of cases where the Ethiopian-national spouse of an 'Eritrean' has been allowed to return to reclaim a house.

16 See: 'Recently issued directive will benefit only Eritreans who lived in Ethiopia permanently' at: www.dehai.org/archives/dehai_news_archive/jan04/0423.html (accessed 6 November 2006). This speech was also picked up by a German news service – see: 'Aiszuge aus Ethiopia Seven Days Update', 24 March 2004, at: http://www.deutsch-aethiopischer-verein.de/Infobl-Maerz-2004-010304.pdf (accessed 23 May 2009).

17 Eritreans were allowed out for medical reasons, special training and to ensure their security.

18 See: 'Eritrea-Ethiopia: Refugees embrace life "out of camps" ', *IRIN* 30 August 2010. Available at: http://www.irinnews.org/report.aspx?ReportId=90334.

5 The illusion of refuge: The search for asylum and the failure of international law

1 The UK also has one of the highest asylum grant rates in the European Union. See: http://epp.eurostat.ec.europa.eu/statistics_explained/index.php/Asylum_statistics#Main_statistical_findings.

2 In the period January 2007 to July 2008 the AIT heard 1,554 bail/bond applications: 308 (20%) were granted, 661 (43%) were refused and 584 (37%) were withdrawn. Source: FOI request (FOI/55519) to the AIT on 16 September 2008.

3 The reasons why Home Office decisions are overturned include: (a) a decision based on an error of law and (b) changed conditions in the applicant's country of origin since the initial decision was made etc. In 2004 the National Audit Office found that Home Office case workers were too sceptical in assessing an applicant's credibility; some did not make a proper assessment concerning whether the individual would face persecution on return and some made mistakes in drafting refusal letters (National Audit Office 2004: 31).

4 See: 'Justice budget will fall to £7 billion in four years', *Law Society Gazette* 20 October 2010 and 'Spending review: What it means for the Home Office', *The Telegraph* 20 October 2010.

5 See: Barkham, P. 'The asylum seekers facing a Kafkaesque legal nightmare', *The Guardian* 4 August 2011. Available at: http://www.guardian.co.uk/uk/2011/aug/04/asylum-seekers.

6 In 2008 it was estimated that one in five community law centres faced closure and 49% were in serious debt (cited in J. Robins, 'Denying child asylum seekers a legal lifeline', *The Guardian* 16 June 2010). In 2011 it was estimated that legal aid cuts would result in the closure of a third of existing law centres ('One in three centres set to shut down', *The Law Gazette* 4 August 2011). Indeed, evidence indicated that cuts had created large geographic areas in England and Wales where no legal advice was obtainable (see: Justice for All 'Impact of proposed reductions in legal aid funding for not-for profit agencies' (2011) at: http://www.justice-for-all.org.uk/dyn/1319033794772/jfa_SWL_viabilitybyarea2.pdf (accessed 11 September 2011).

7 See: 'Litigants in person set to rise', *The Law Society Gazette* 20 January 2011. Available at: http://www.lawgazette.co.uk/news/litigants-person-set-rise.

8 The reasons include: having an 'unfounded claim'; coming from a 'white list safe country'; failing to cooperate with official efforts to obtain a travel document; arriving with false documents; arriving via another European country; entering the country illegally; overstaying their visa and/or other breaches in the conditions of their stay etc.

9 The appellate courts also act as a 'filter' by holding 'permission hearings' to decide whether to hear an appeal from the AIT. At permission hearings held between April 2005 and June 2008, 41% of Eritrean claims, 28% of Ethiopian claims, 35% of Somali claims and 30% of Sudanese claims were allowed. Source: FOI/56364.08/MB to the Tribunal Service dated 25 November 2008.

10 Transactional Records Access Clearinghouse (TRAC) is a data gathering, data research and data distribution organization at Syracuse University, USA. Its purpose is to provide the American people – and institutions of oversight such as Congress, news organizations, public interest groups, businesses, scholars and lawyers – with comprehensive information about staffing, spending and enforcement activities of the federal government. This includes data about decision making by officials such as the Bureau of Immigration Affairs and judges. It obtains its data via use of the Freedom of Information Act and statistically analyses and reports on federal decisions etc. See: 'Judges show disparities in denying asylum' (July 2006) available at: http://trac.syr.edu/immigration/reports/160/.

11 See: *Kelzani* v. *SSHD (7 Nov. 1978) Imm. A.R.193.*

12 See: Home Office API, 'UNRWA Assisted Palestinians' at: http://www.ukba.home-office.gov.uk/sitecontent/documents/policyandlaw/asylumpolicyinstructions/apis/unrwa.pdf?view=Binary, p. 3.

13 See: Immigration Directorate's Instructions (July 2006), Chapter 7, Sec. 3: 'EEA Nationals and Family Members' available at: http://www.ukba.homeoffice.gov.uk/sitecontent/documents/policyandlaw/IDIs/idischapter7/section3/section3.pdf?view=Binary.

14 See: http://www.ukba.homeoffice.gov.uk/sitecontent/documents/policyandlaw/statementsofchanges/2013/hc1039.pdf?view=Binary.

15 See: http://www.ukba.homeoffice.gov.uk/visas-immigration/while-in-uk/stateless/.

16 See: http://www.asylumaid.org.uk/data/files/publications/214/STATELESSNESS_BRIEF.pdf.

17 It is understood that the new policy, which has not yet been announced, will only come into effect when an asylum claim is withdrawn from the asylum process or possibly when it has been determined (Chris Nash, personal communication 11 April 2013). Clearly, it will be essential to monitor how officials use the new policy and guidance in order to ensure that the UK complies with its international legal commitments.

18 This policy is set out in an API entitled, 'Disputed nationality – allowed appeals' dated November 2005. Available at: http://www.ukba.homeoffice.gov.uk/sitecontent/documents/policyandlaw/asylumpolicyinstructions/apunotices/disputednatallowedappeals.pdf?view=Binary.

19 See: http://www.ohchr.org/EN/ProfessionalInterest/Pages/CCPR.aspx; also see the Human Rights Commission's comments on Article 12 at: http://www.unhchr.ch/tbs/doc.nsf/MasterFrameView/6c76e1b8ee1710e380256824005a10a9?Opendocument.

20 The case can be found at: http://www.icj-cij.org/docket/index.php?p1=3&p2=3&code=lg&case=18&k=26.

21 In the USA the authority for this approach is found in U.S.C. 1101 (a)(42)(A); in Australia, statutory authority is found in subsection 36(2) of the Act, qualified by subsections 36 (3), (4) and (5)1 (which commenced on 16 December 1999).

22 The principle is spelled out in *YL (Nationality – Statelessness – Eritrea – Ethiopia) Eritrea CG [2003] UKIAT 00016*at ¶44.

23 In effect the Home Office is asserting that an ethnic Eritrean, though born and raised in Ethiopia, has an entitlement to Eritrean nationality based on Proclamation No. 21 of 1992. Relevant case law includes *BG [Removal to Eritrea of Ethiopia/Eritrea] Eritrea CG [2003] UKAIT.*

24 See: http://www.judiciary.gov.uk/Resources/JCO/Documents/Practice%20Directions/Tribunals/IAC_UT_FtT_PracticeDirection.pdf.

25 See: *MA and others (Ethiopia – Mixed ethnicity – dual nationality) Eritrea [2004] UKIAT 00324.*

26 See: *EB (Ethiopia)* v. *SSHD [2007] EWCA Civ 809.*

27 Interview with one of the barristers representing the Home Office, London, 25 September 2007.

28 The SSHD produced an email from the IOM concerning applications for voluntary assisted return made to the Ethiopian embassy, but it was not clear whether some of the individuals who were issued a travel document were deported 'Eritreans'.

29 There was ample evidence presented to the court from the Eritrea–Ethiopia Claims Commission that Ethiopia had indeed breached domestic and international law by arresting and expelling its 'Eritrean' nationals. However the Tribunal set this evidence aside and ruled that because deportations had ceased it was now safe to return.

30 See: *MA (Ethiopia)* v. *SSHD [2009] EWCA Civ 289.*

31 See: *ST (Ethnic Eritrean-nationality – return) Ethiopia CG [2011] UKUT 0025,* ¶2.

32 Between 2000 and 2004 'a much larger percentage of appeals brought by the Home Office were allowed' in comparison to appeals made by counsel for the appellant (ICAR 2009: 13; Chart 9).

6 'Bare life': The vulnerability and political significance of stateless persons

1 See the Home Affairs Committee report on the work of UKBA for April–June 2012 at: http://www.parliament.uk/business/committees/committees-a-z/commons-select/home-affairs-committee/news/121109-ukba-rpt-published/.

2 For a list of these offences see: http://www.cps.gov.uk/legal/h_to_k/immigration/.

3 Source: http://www.ukba.homeoffice.gov.uk/asylum/support/apply/section4/.

4 The Refugee Convention protects refugees and those who have filed an asylum claim but *not* failed asylum seekers (Sawyer and Turpin 2005: 721; Weissbrodt 2008: 125).

5 In 2010, individuals returning to their country of origin via the Voluntary Assisted Return Program operated by the IOM were flown home and entitled to assistance valued at about £4,300 per person (IOM 2010). While the cost of identifying and arresting failed asylum seekers is not known, the cost of detaining such a person in 2007 was between £511–1,344 per week, depending on which detention centre the person was held at (Migration Observatory, 2012).

6 See note 1.

7 See question 52 of the Parliamentary Home Affairs Committee minutes of evidence, 'The work of the UK Border Agency (April–June 2012)', HC 603. Available at: http://www.publications.parliament.uk/pa/cm201213/cmselect/cmhaff/603/120918.htm.

8 See for instance: 'Iraqi parliament refuses to accept nationals deported from Europe', *The Guardian* 2 July 2012.

9 A recent report on immigration detention found that in two-thirds of the cases it investigated the absence of a travel document arose because UKBA 'lacked a strategic approach' in managing such cases, which resulted in prolonged and possibly unlawful detention. Furthermore, changes in legal aid had substantially reduced the availability of legal representation to immigration detainees to 30 minutes (including interpreting time) (Independent Chief Inspector of Borders and Immigration and HM Inspectorate of Prisons 2012).

10 This is established in British case law in *MO (illegal exit – risk on return) Eritrea CG [2011] UKUT 00190 (IAC).*

11 I am grateful to Sheona York, at that time a solicitor at Hammersmith and Fulham Law Centre, for an interview on 19 March 2007. We spoke about this case and she provided me with copies of the case material.

12 The LJs suggested that it might be possible to challenge the Secretary of State for the Home Department using sec. 3 of the 1998 Human Rights Act to argue that treatment of failed asylum seekers was a disproportionate interference with their private life.

13 See: Bail for Immigration Detainees at: http://www.biduk.org/543/country-information/country-information.html.

14 There are many reports of individuals who have wrongfully been put into fast-track detention, including individuals who had been tortured and whose asylum claims were

too complex to be properly decided in the speeded-up procedures available in detention. See: http://www.freedomfromtorture.org/news-blogs/6334.

15 The immigration detention centre where this woman was placed has been the focus of hunger strikes against substandard health care and the detention of children etc. (see: 'Hunger strike at Yarlswood Detention Centre', *The Guardian* 18 June 2009). Strikes and protests in British, Spanish, French, Polish etc detention centres have substantially increased in recent years and have provided 'illegals' with a focus and a means of publicly commenting on their treatment.

16 The practice of the Home Office to refuse applicants a work permit while they waited for a decision on their claim, or indeed on a fresh claim, for longer than 12 months was the subject of litigation (see: *R (on the application of ZO (Somalia) and others) (Respondents)* v. *Secretary of State for the Home Department (Appellant) [2010] UKSC 36*) which ended the policy because it violated the European Directive on the reception for asylum seekers.

17 See: *[2008] EWHC 3162 (Admin)* ¶22 heard on 19 December 2008.

18 Interestingly, 'ST (Eritrea) was later overturned in the CoA and in the Supreme Court. See: *R (on the application of ST (Eritrea)) (FC) (Appellant)* v. *Secretary of State for the Home Department (Respondent) [2012] UKSC 12*.

19 Article 8 of the European Convention on Human Rights (Right to respect for private and family life) states that: (a) everyone has the right to respect for his private and family life, his home and his correspondence and (b) there shall be no interference by a public authority with the exercise of this right except such as is in accordance with the law and is necessary in a democratic society in the interests of national security, public safety or the economic well-being of the country, for the prevention of disorder or crime, for the protection of health or morals, or for the protection of the rights and freedoms of others.

20 Despite the very clear level of destitution reported for failed asylum seekers only one of the individuals we spoke to relied on churches or NGOs for shelter and food packages, although we are aware of many individuals who are destitute.

21 See: 'System "not fit for purpose" says Reid', *The Guardian* 23 May 2006.

22 This is not the place to address De Genova's arguments (2002, 2007) on this issue though clearly the revolving door of immigration policy which 'produces' illegal migrants for deportation is part of the wider picture in the UK.

Conclusion

1 See Arendt's analysis of the failure of international efforts to create/impose peace in Europe following World War I (1968: Chap. 9)

2 Source: 'A week in the Horn, 15 September 2012', which is produced by the Ministry of Foreign Affairs, Addis Ababa.

3 See: 'System "not fit for purpose" says Reid', *The Guardian* 23 May 2006.

4 According to the terms of the Algiers Agreement all legal claims filed in other jurisdictions before 12 December 2000 should be heard.

5 See: *491 F.3d 470, Hiwot Nemariam et al., Appellants* v. *The Federal Democratic Republic of Ethiopia and the Commercial Bank of Ethiopia, appellees. No. 05-7178.* Decided on 22 June 2007 in the US Court of Appeals, District of Columbia.

6 They also claimed that their businesses, houses, cars and other property were seized and auctioned below market value.

7 One individual had been able to reclaim part of his property, others had given an 'agent' authority to manage their assets, still others discovered that their 'agent' in Ethiopia had sold their property etc.

8 In 2006 the Institute of Public Policy Research estimated that an 'amnesty' would bring in £1 billion in extra taxes and would save an estimated £4.7 billion from the cost of removing failed asylum seekers.

9 As set out in Immigration Rule 395C, which states that, 'Before a decision to remove under section 10 is given, regard will be had to all the relevant factors known to the Secretary of State, including: (i) age; (ii) length of residence in the United Kingdom; (iii) strength of connections with the United Kingdom; (iv) personal history, including character, conduct and employment record; (v) domestic circumstances; (vi) previous criminal record and the nature of any offence of which the person has been convicted; (vi) compassionate circumstances; (vii) any representations received on the person's behalf. In the case of family members, the factors listed in paragraphs 365–368 must also be taken into account.' Of particular relevance in family cases is paragraph 367 (i), which states that in the case of a child of school age, the effect of removal on his education is to be taken into account. For an explanation of the current situation see: http://www.gherson.com/news-articles/paragraph-395c-of-the-immigration-rules-deleted-3138/.

10 For the text of this convention see: http://treaties.un.org/UNTC/Pages/ViewDetails.aspx?src=TREATY&mtdsg_no=IV-13&chapter=4&lang=en. Clearly, there is an important distinction between signing up to the convention and implementing it.

11 Even where the procedure is available and the rules are fair, the actual process may be highly problematic.

Bibliography

Abbink, J. 'The impact of violence: The Ethiopian "Red Terror" as a social phenomenon', in P. Braunlein and A. Lauser (Eds), *Auf dem Weg zu einer Ethnologie des Krieges und des Friedens: Hindernisse, Annäherungen. Krieg und Frieden – Ethnologische Perspektiven*: Bremen; 1995, pp. 129–45.

Abbink, J. 'Ethnicity and constitutionalism in contemporary Ethiopia', *Journal of African Law* 1997; 41: 159–74.

Abbink, J. 'Briefing: The Eritrean–Ethiopian border dispute', *African Affairs* 1998; 97: 551–65.

Abbink, J. 'The Ethiopian second republic and the fragile "social contract"', *Africa Spectrum* 2009; 44(2): 3–28.

Adjami, M. and J. Harrison. 'The scope and content of Art. 15 of the Universal Declaration of Human Rights', *Refugee Survey Quarterly* 2008; 27(3), 93–109.

Agamben, G. *Homo Sacer: Sovereign Power and Bare Life*. Stanford University Press: Stanford; 1998.

Albahari, M. 'Death and the modern state: Making borders and sovereignty at the southern edges of Europe'. Working Paper 137. Centre for Comparative Immigration Studies, University of California: San Diego; 2006.

Alemseged Abbay. 'The Trans-Mareb past in the present', *The Journal of Modern African Studies* 1997; 35(2): 321–34.

Alemseged Tesfai. 'The cause of the Eritrean–Ethiopian border conflict'. Undated. Available at: http://www.dehai.org/conflict/analysis/alemsghed1.html

Amnesty International. *Ethiopia and Eritrea: Human Rights Issues in a Year of Armed Conflict* (AFR 04/03/99). 21 May 1999.

Amnesty International. *Ethiopia/Eritrea: Cease Fire and Human Rights* (AFR 04/01/00). 2000.

Amnesty International. *Eritrea: Country Report 2002*. London; 2003.

Amnesty International. *Getting it Right. How Home Office Decision Making Fails Refugees*. London; 2004.

Amnesty International. 'Immigration cooperation with Libya: The human rights perspective. 12 April 2005. Available at: http://www.amnesty.eu/static/documents/2005/JHA_Libya_april12.pdf.

Amnesty International. *Forcible Return/Torture and Ill Treatment* (UA235/07). 2006.

Aregawi Berhe. 'The origins of the Tigray People's Liberation Front', *African Affairs* 2004; 103(413): 569–92.

Arendt, H. *The Origins of Totalitarianism*. Houghton Mifflin Harcourt: New York; 1968.

Asmeron Legasse. *The Uprooted: Case Material on Ethnic Eritrea Deportees from Ethiopia. Concerning Human Rights Violations.* Eritrea Relief and Refugee Commission: Asmara, Eritrea; 1998.

Asmeron Legasse. 'Prime Minister Meles Zenawi's interview with Radio Ethiopia (Appendix 3), 9 July 1998' in *The Uprooted (Part II)*. On Behalf of Citizens for Peace in Eritrea: Asmara, Eritrea; 1999.

Asmeron Legasse. *The Uprooted (Part III): Studies of Urban Eritrean Expelled from Tigrai and Communities in Eritrea Displaced by Bombardment*. On Behalf of Citizens for Peace in Eritrea: Asmara, Eritrea; 2000.

Assefa Barigaber. 'States, international organizations and the refugee: reflections on the complexity of managing the refugee crisis in the Horn of Africa', *Journal of Modern African Studies* 1999; 37(4): 597–619.

Assefa Fiseha. 'Separation of powers and its implications for the judiciary in Ethiopia', *Journal of Eastern African Studies* 2011; 5(4): 702–15.

Asylum Appellate Project. 'Second Year Report'. 2009. Available at: http://www.icar.org.uk/11265/research-directory/asylum-appellate-project-second-year-report.html

Asylum Support Appeals Project. *No Credibility: UKBA Decision Making and Section 4 Support*. London; 2011.

Asylum Support Partnership. 'The second destitution tally: An indication of the extent of destitution among asylum seekers, refused asylum seekers and refugees'. Policy Report. London; 2009.

Bakewell. O. and H. de Haas. 'African migrations: continuities, discontinuities and recent transformations', in Patrick Chabal, Ulf Engel and Leo de Haan (Eds), *African Alternatives*. Brill: Leiden; 2007, pp. 95–118.

Baldwin-Edwards, M. 'Between a rock and a hard place: North Africa as a region of emigration, immigration and transit migration', *Review of African Political Economy* 108(33): 311–24.

Banks, A. and J. Muller. 'Ethiopia', in *The Political Handbook of the World*. CSA Publications: Binghamton NY; 1998, pp. 303–12.

Barnes, C. and H. Hassan. 'The rise and fall of Mogadishu's Islamic courts'. Briefing Paper AFP BP 07/02. Chatham House: London; 2007.

Bascom, J. 'The long, 'last step'? Reintegration of repatriates in Eritrea', *Journal of Refugee Studies* 2005; 18(2): 165–78.

Batchelor, C. 'Stateless persons: some gaps in international protection', *International Journal of Refugee Law* 1995; 7(2): 232–59.

Batchelor, C. 'Statelessness and the problem of resolving nationality status', *International Journal of Refugee Law* 1998; 10(1/2): 156–82.

Baxter, P. 'The creation and constitution of Oromo nationality', in K. Fukui and J. Markakis (Eds), *Ethnicity and Conflict in the Horn of Africa*. J. Currey: Oxford; 1994, pp. 167–86.

Bhabba, J (Ed). *Children Without a State. A Global Human Rights Challenge*. MIT Press: Cambridge, MA; 2011.

Blake, C. 'Immigration appeals: the need for reform', in A. Dummett (Ed), *Towards a Just Immigration Policy*. Cobden Press: London; 1986.

Blitz, B. 'Statelessness, protection and equality'. Forced Migration Policy Briefing 3. Refugee Studies Centre, University of Oxford; 2009.

Blitz, B. and M. Lynch (Eds). *Statelessness and the Benefits of Citizenship: A Comparative Study*. Geneva Academy for International and Humanitarian Law and International Observatory on Statelessness: Geneva; 2009. Available at: http://www.nationalityforall.org/pubs

Blitz, B. and M. Lynch (Eds). *Statelessness and Citizenship: A Comparative Study of the Benefits of Nationality.* Edward Elgar: Cheltenham, UK; 2011.

Blitz, B. and M. Otero-Iglesias. 'Stateless by any other name: Refused asylum seekers in the UK', *Journal of Ethnic and Migration Studies* 2011; 37(4); 657–73.

Boswell, C. 'The "external dimension" of EU immigration and asylum policy', *International Affairs* 2003; 79(3): 619–38.

Bozzini, D. 'Low-tech surveillance and the despotic state in Eritrea', *Surveillance and Society* 2011; 9(1/2): 93–113.

Brewer, K. and D. Yukseker. 'A survey of African migrants and asylum seekers in Istanbul'. Migration Research Program, Department of Sociology, Koç University: Istanbul; 2005/6. Available at: http://portal.ku.edu.tr/~mirekoc/reports/2005_2006_kelly_brewer_deniz_yuksekeker.pdf

Brietzke, P. 'Ethiopia's "leap in the dark": Federalism and self-determination in the new constitution', *Journal of African Law* 1995; 40: 19–38.

British Red Cross. *Not Gone, But Forgotten: The Urgent Need for a More Human Asylum System.* London; 2010.

Broeders, D. 'The new digital borders of Europe: EU databases and the surveillance of irregular migrants', *International Sociology* 2007; 22 (1): 71–92.

Brouwer, A. 'Statelessness in Canadian context'. Discussion Paper. UNHCR: Ottawa; 2003.

Brown, N., S. Riordan and M. Sharpe. 'The insecurity of Eritreans and Ethiopians in Cairo', *International Journal of Refugee Law* 2004; 6(4): 661–701.

Bryne, H. *Eritrea and Ethiopia: Large Scale Expulsions of Population Groups and Other Human Rights Violations in Connection with the Ethiopia-Eritrean Conflict* (QA/ERI/ETH/02.001). INS Resource Information Centre: Washington, DC; January 2002.

Calhoun, C. 'Ethiopia's ethnic cleansing', *Dissent* 1998 (Winter); 47–50.

Campbell, J. 'The enduring problem of statelessness in the Horn of Africa: How nation-states and Western courts (re)define nationality', *International Journal of Refugee Law* 2011; 23(4): 656–79.

Campbell, J. 'Language analysis in the United Kingdom's refugee status determination system: Seeing through policy claims about "expert knowledge"', *Ethnic and Racial Studies* 2013; 36(4): 670–90.

Campbell, J., H. Yaron and N. Hashimshony-Yaffe. '"Infiltrators" or refugees? An analysis of Israel's policy toward African asylum seekers', *International Migration.* Forthcoming.

Cholewinski, R. 'Enforced destitution of asylum seekers in the UK: The denial of fundamental human rights', *International Journal of Refugee Law* 1998; 10(3): 462–98.

Citizens Advice Bureau. 'Shaming destitution: NASS Section 4 support for failed asylum seekers who are temporarily unable to leave the UK'. London; 2006.

Clapham, C. 'Indigenous statehood and international law in Ethiopia and Eritrea', in A. De Guttray, H. Post and G. Venturini (Eds), *The 1998–2000 War Between Eritrea and Ethiopia: An International Legal Perspective.* T. M. C Asser: The Hague; 2009, pp. 159–70.

Clay, J. and B. Holcomb. *Politics and the Ethiopian Famine 1984–85.* Cultural Survival: Cambridge, MA; 1985.

Collier, J., B. Maurer and L. Suarez-Navaz. 'Sanctioned identities: Legal constructions of Modern Personhood', *Identities* 1995; 2(1–2): 1–27.

Collyer, M., F. Duvell and H. de Haas. 'Critical approaches to transit migration', *Population, Space and Place* 2012; 18(4): 407–14.

Cooper, D. *Urban Refugees: Ethiopians and Eritreans in Cairo.* American University in Cairo Press: Cairo; 1992.

Crisp, J. 'Briefings: The politics of repatriation: Ethiopian refugees in Djibouti, 1977–83', *Review of African Political Economy* 1984; 39: 73–81.

Crisp, J. 'A state of insecurity: The political economy of violence in Kenya's refugee camps', *African Affairs* 2000; 99(397): 601–32.

Da Lomba, S. 'Legal status and refugee integration: A UK perspective', *Journal of Refugee Studies* 2010; 23(4): 415–35.

Das, V. and D. Poole (Eds). *Anthropology in the Margins of the State*. J. Currey: Oxford; 2004.

Dauvergne, C. 'Sovereignty, migration and the rule of law in global times', *Journal of Modern Law* 2004; 67(4): 588–615.

De Genova, N. 'Migrant "illegality" and deportability in everyday life', *Annual Review of Anthropology* 2002; 31: 419–47.

De Genova, N. 'The production of culprits: From deportability to detainability in the aftermath of "Homeland Security"', *Citizenship Studies* 2007; 11(5): 431–48.

De Genova, N. 'Border, scene and obscene', in T. Wilson and H. Donnan (Eds), *A Companion to Border Studies*. Blackwell: Oxford; 2012, pp. 492–504.

Detention Action. 'Fast track to despair: The unnecessary detention of asylum seekers'. London; 2011. Available at: http://www.irr.org.uk/pdf2/FastTracktoDespair.pdf

Dwyer, P. and D. Brown. 'Meeting basic needs? Forced migrants and welfare', *Social Policy and Society* 2005; 4: 4: 369–80.

Emebet Kebede. 'Ethiopia: An assessment of the international labour migration situation: The case of female labour migrants'. GENPROM Working Paper No. 3, Series on Women and Migration. International Labour Office: Geneva; undated.

Equal Rights Trust. 'Project "Stateless Persons in Detention"'. Legal Working Paper: The Protection of Stateless Persons in Detention. London; 2009.

Eritrea Department of External Affairs. *Eritrea: Birth of a Nation*. Asmara, Eritrea; 1993.

Eritrea. 'Memorial of the State of Eritrea. Eritrea's claims nos. 15, 16, 23, and 27–32: Expellees, civilian detainees, and persons of Eritrean national origin remaining in Ethiopia'. 15 November 2002. Submitted to the Eritrea–Ethiopia Claims Commission. The Hague; 2002.

Eritrea. Case-in-Chief Judge's Folder. 16 March. Submitted to the Eritrea–Ethiopia Claims Commission. The Hague; 2004a.

Eritrea. 'Counter-Memorial of the State of Eritrea. Ethiopia's Claim no. 5: Ethiopian nationals in Eritrea'. 14 January. Submitted to the Eritrea–Ethiopia Claims Commission. The Hague; 2004b.

Eritrea. 'Counter-Memorials of the State of Eritrea. Ethiopia's allegations about the *jus ad bellum* /Ethiopia's claim no. 7; Ethiopia's claim no. 6 (ports); Ethiopia's claim no. 8 (diplomatic); Ethiopia's claim nos. 1–3 (Western and Eastern Zones)'. 17 January. Submitted to the Eritrea–Ethiopia Claims Commission, The Hague; 2005.

Eritrea. 'Memorial of the State of Eritrea, Damages (Group 2)'. Submitted to the Eritrea–Ethiopia Claims Commission. (15 December). The Hague; 2007.

Eritrea. 'Counter-Memorial of the State of Eritrea. Damages (Group 2)'. 17 March. Submitted to the Eritrea–Ethiopia Claims Commission, The Hague; 2008.

Eritrea–Ethiopia Boundary Commission (EEBC). 'Decision on delimitation of the border between Eritrea and Ethiopia'. Chapter 4. The Hague; 2002.

Eritrea–Ethiopia Claim Commission (EECC). 'Prisoners of war. Eritrea's claim 17'. The Hague; 2003.

Eritrea–Ethiopia Claim Commission (EECC). 'Partial award: Civilian claims. Eritrea's claims 15, 16, 23 and 27–32'. The Hague; 2004a.

Eritrea–Ethiopia Claim Commission (EECC). 'Partial award: Civilian claims. Ethiopia's claim 5'. The Hague; 2004b.

Eritrea–Ethiopia Claim Commission (EECC). '*Jus ad bellum*. Ethiopia's claims 1–8'. The Hague; 2005.

Eritrea–Ethiopia Claim Commission (EECC). 'Final award: Eritrea damages claims. Between the State of Eritrea and the FDR of Ethiopia'. The Hague; 2009.

Eritrean Relief and Refugee Commission. *A Preliminary Report on the Eritrean Nationals Expelled From Ethiopia During June–July 1998*. Asmara, Eritrea; 1998.

Ethiopia, Reports Submitted by State Parties Under Article 9 of the Convention. Information provided by the Government of Ethiopia on the implementation of the concluding observations of the Committee on the Elimination of Racial Discrimination, CERD/C/ETH/CO/15/Add.1.2008.

Feldman, I. 'Difficult distinctions: Refugee law, humanitarian practice, and political identification in Gaza', *Cultural Anthropology* 2007; 22(1): 129–69.

Firebrace, J., S. Holland and N. Kinnock. *Never kneel down: Drought, development and liberation in Eritrea*. Spokesman: Nottingham; 1984.

Fortress Europe. 'Escape from Tripoli: Report on the conditions of migrants in transit in Libya'. October 2007. Available at: http://www.statewatch.org/news/2007/nov/fortress-europe-libya-report.pdf.

Foucault, M. *The History of Sexuality* (Vol. 1). Random House: New York; 1976.

Fransen, S. and K. Kuschminder. 'Migration in Ethiopia: History, current trends and future prospects'. Migrant and Development Country Profiles. Maastricht Graduate School of Governance; 2009.

Gaim Kibreab. 'Eritrean and Ethiopian urban refugees in Khartoum: What the eye refuses to see', *African Studies Review* 1996; 39(3): 131–78.

Gaim Kibreab. 'Forced labour in Eritrea', *Journal of Modern African Studies* 2009; 47(1): 41–72.

Gemund, H. 'From Somalia to Yemen: Great dangers, few prospects', *Forced Migration Review* 2007; 27: 67–9.

Gent, S. and M. Shannon. 'The effectiveness of international arbitration and adjudication: Getting into a bind', *Journal of Politics* 2010; 72(2): 366–80.

Gibney, M. 'Asylum and the expansion of deportation in the United Kingdom', *Government and Opposition* 2008; 43(2): 146–67.

Gilkes, P. *Ethiopia: Perspectives of conflict 1991–99*. Swiss Peace Foundation: Bern; 1999.

Gilkes, P. and M. Plaut. *War in the Horn. The conflict between Eritrea and Ethiopia*. The Royal Institute of International Affairs. Discussion Paper 82. Chameleon Press: London; 1999.

Global Detention Project. 'United Kingdom Detention Profile'. June 2011. Available at: http://www.globaldetentionproject.org/countries/europe/united-kingdom/introduction.html

Global IDP Project. 'Both Eritrea and Ethiopia used mass deportations as a weapon of war (1998–2002)'. 28 October 2003. Available at: http://www.internal-displacement.org/idmc/website/countries.nsf/(httpEnvelopes)/204CCE493 D2236F8802570B8005A7109?OpenDocument

Good, A. 'Expert evidence in asylum and human rights appeals: An expert's view', *International Journal of Refugee Law* 2004; 16 (3): 358–80.

Good, A. *Anthropology and Expertise in the Asylum Courts*. Routledge and Glass House: New York; 2007.

Gray, C. 'The Eritrea/Ethiopia Claims Commission oversteps its boundaries: A partial award?' *The European Journal of International Law* 2006; 17 (4): 699–721.

Greenslade, R. 'Seeking scapegoats. The coverage of asylum in the UK press'. Asylum and Migration Working Paper No. 5. Institute for Public Policy Research: London; May 2005.

Griffith, M. 'Vile liars and truth distorters', *Anthropology Today* 2012; 28 (5): 8–12.

Hamood, S. *African Transit Migration Through Libya to Europe: The Human Cost.* Forced Migration Unit, American University in Cairo: Cairo; 2006.

Hamood, S. 'EU–Libyan cooperation on migration: A raw deal for refugees and migrants?', *Journal of Refugee Studies* 2008; 21 (1): 19–42.

Hathaway, J. A reconsideration of the underlying premise of refugee law', *Harvard International Law Journal* 1990; 31 (Winter): 129–83.

Hayter, T. *Open Borders: The Case Against Immigration Controls.* Pluto: London; 2004.

Healy, S. and M. Plaut. 'Ethiopia and Eritrea: Allergic to persuasion'. Africa Programme AFB BP 07/01. Chatham House: London; 2007.

Hirsch, S. and M. Lazarus-Black (Eds). 'Introduction: Performance and paradox. Exploring law's role in hegemony and resistance', in *Contested States: Law, Hegemony and Resistance.* Routledge: New York; 1994.

Horwood, C. *In pursuit of the Southern Dream: Victims of Necessity. Assessment of the Irregular Movement of Men from East Africa and the Horn to South Africa.* IOM: Geneva; 2009.

Human Rights Watch. *Evil Days. 30 Years of War and Famine in Ethiopia.* New York; 1991.

Human Rights Watch. 'World Report 1999: Ethiopia. Human rights developments'. 1999. Available at: http://www.hrw.org/hrw//worldreport99/africa/ethiopia.html

Human Rights Watch. 'Kenyan government sweep of foreigners puts refugees at risk'. New York; 2002a.

Human Rights Watch. 'HRC general comment on Article 12 of the ICCPR (November 1999)' 2002b. Available at: http://www.hrw.org/news/2002/04/23/human-rights-watch-policy-right-return

Human Rights Watch. 'Eritrea and Ethiopia: The Horn of Africa War. Mass expulsions and the nationality issue (June 1998–April 2002)'. January 2003a.

Human Rights Watch. 'Eritrea'. 2003b. Available at: http://www.hrw.org/wr2k3/africa4.html

Human Rights Watch. 'Stemming the flow: Abuses against migrants, asylum seekers and refugees'. September 2006.

Human Rights Watch. 'Service for life: State repression and indefinite conscription in Eritrea'. New York; 2009. Available at: http://www.hrw.org/reports/2009/04/16/service-life-0

Human Rights Watch. 'Hidden emergency: Migrant deaths in the Mediterranean' 16 August 2012. Available at: http://www.hrw.org/news/2012/08/16/hidden-emergency

Hynes, P. 'Summary of findings: The compulsory dispersal of asylum seekers and processes of social exclusion in England'. ESRC: Swindon, UK; 2006. Available at: http://www.esrc.ac.uk/my-esrc/grants/PTA-026-27-1254/read.

Ibrahim Idris. 'Ethiopian immigration law on the exclusion and deportation of foreign nationals', *RADIC* 1990; 2: 117–28. Available at: http://abyssinialaw.com/uploads/Ethiopian%20Immigration%20Law.pdf

Immigration Advisory Services. 'The use of country of origin information in operational guidance notes'. London; 2009a.

Immigration Advisory Services. 'An analysis of the March 2009 Zimbabwe Operational Guidance Note (extended speaking notes)'. London; 2009b.

Immigration and Refugee Board of Canada. 'Ethiopia: Dedesa and Belaten captive centers: Whether Eritreans were held in those centers, if so, treatment of detainees and whether the International Committee of the Red Cross (ICRC) was involved (1988–2001)'. ETH42979.E. 2004. Available at: http://www.unhcr.org/refworld/publisher,IRBC,,ETH,42df60e41c,0.html

Immigration and Refugee Board of Canada. 'Ethiopia: Procedures that Ethiopian citizens must follow in order to obtain identity documents from consulates or missions in Canada'. ETH103317.FE. 2009. Available at: http://www.irb-cisr.gc.ca:8080/RIR_RDI/RIR_RDI.aspx?id=452714&l=e

Immigration Law Practitioners Association (ILPA). 'The detained fast track process: A best practice guide'. London; 2008.

Independent Chief Inspector of Borders and Immigration. *Asylum: A thematic inspection of the detained fast track*. London; 2011. Available at: http://icinspector.independent.gov.uk/wp-content/uploads/2012/02/Asylum_A-thematic-inspection-of-Detained-Fast-Track1.pdf

Independent Chief Inspector of Borders and Immigration. *An Inspection of the UK Border Agency's Handling of Legacy Asylum and Migration Cases*. London; 2012.

Independent Chief Inspector of Borders and Immigration and HM Inspectorate of Prisons. *The Effectiveness and Impact of Immigration Detention Casework*. London; 2012.

Information Centre about Asylum and Refugees (ICAR). 'Decision-making and the appeals process', ICAR Statistics Paper No. 2. London; 2009.

Ingrams, L. and R. Pankhurst. 'Somali migration to Aden from the 19th to the 21st centuries', *Journal of African and Asian Studies* 2006; 5(3–4): 371–82.

Institute for Public Policy, 'Government is right to consider amnesty for illegal workers', 2006, available at: http//www.ippr.org/press-release/111/2487/government-is-right-to-consider-amnesty-for-illegal-workers

Intergovernmental Committee on Refugees. 'Statelessness and some of its consequences: An Outline'. 1946.

International Centre for Migration Policy Development. 'East Africa Migration Route Initiative'. Gaps and Needs Analysis Project Country Reports. Vienna; 2008. Available at: http://www.anti-trafficking.net/fileadmin/ICMPD-Website/Irregular_Migration/East_Africa_Migration_Routes_Report.pdf.

International Committee for the Red Cross. 'Annual Reports for Eritrea'. Geneva; various.

International Committee for the Red Cross. 'Annual Reports for Ethiopia'. Geneva; various.

International Crisis Group. 'Ethiopia and Eritrea: War or Peace?' ICG Africa Report No. 68. Nairobi; 2003.

International Organization for Migration (IOM). 'Voluntary Assisted Return and Reintegration Programme (VARRP): Frequently asked questions'. 2010. Available at: http://homeless.org.uk/sites/default/files/IOM-VARRP4ppA4.pdf

International Organization for Migration (IOM). *World Migration Report 2011*. Geneva; 2011.

Jacquin-Berdal, D. and M. Plaut. *Unfinished Business: Ethiopia and Eritrea at War*. Red Sea Press: Lawrenceville, NJ; 2005.

Jenkins, R. 'Rethinking ethnicity', *Ethnic and Racial Studies* 1994; 17(2): 197–223.

Jordan, B., B. Strath and A. Trindafyllidou. 'Comparing cultures of discretion', *Journal of Ethnic and Migration Studies* 2003; 29(2): 373–95.

Jureidini, R. 'Women migrant domestic workers in Lebanon'. International Migration Paper No. 48. International Migration Program, ILO: Geneva; 2002.

Kaye, R. 'Blaming the victim: An analysis of press representation of refugees and asylum-seekers in the UK in the 1990s', in R. King and N. Wood (Eds), *Media and Migration*. Routledge: London; 2001.

Kerber, L. 'Toward a history of statelessness in America', *American Quarterly* 2005; 57(3): 727–49.

Khoser, K. 'New approaches to asylum', *International Migration* 2001; 39(6): 85–101.

Kidane Mengisteab and Okbazghi Yohannes. *Anatomy of an Africa Tragedy: Political, Economic and Foreign Policy Crisis in Post-Independence Eritrea*. Red Sea Press: Lawrenceville, NJ; 2005.

Kidane Mengisteab. 'What has gone wrong with Eritrea's foreign relations?', in R. Reid (Ed), *Eritrea's External Relations. Understanding its Regional Role and Foreign Policy*. Chatham House: London; 2009, pp. 45–70.

Klein, N. 'Mass expulsion from Ethiopia: Report on the documentation of Eritreans and Ethiopians of Eritrean origin from Ethiopia, June–August 1998'. Yale School of Law: New Haven, CT; 1998.

Kuhlman, T. *Asylum or Aid? The Economic Integration of Ethiopian and Eritrean Refugees in the Sudan*. African Studies Centre: Leiden and Avebury; 1994.

Lewis, H. *Still Destitute: A Worsening Problem for Refused Asylum Seekers*. Joseph Rowntree Trust: London; 2009.

Liqu Teshome Gebre, P. Maharaj and N. Pillay. 'The experiences of immigrants in South Africa: A case study of Ethiopians in Durban, South Africa', *Urban Forum* 2011; 22: 23–35.

Lonegan, B. 'Immigration detention and removal: A guide for detainees and their families'. The Legal Aid Society; 2004.

Lutterbeck, D. 'Policing Migration in the Mediterranean', *Mediterranean Politics*, 2006; 11(1): 59–82.

Lyons, T. 'The Ethiopia Eritrea conflict and the search for peace in the Horn of Africa', *Review of Political Economy of Africa* 2009; 36(120): 167–80.

Mackenzie, C., C. McDowell and E. Pittaway. 'Beyond "do no harm": The challenge of constructing ethical relationships in refugee research', *Journal of Refugee Studies* 2007; 20(2): 299–319.

Manby, B. *Citizenship Law in Africa: A Comparative Study*. Open Society Justice Institute: Johannesburg and New York; 2009a.

Manby, B. *Struggles for Citizenship in Africa*. Zed Books: London; 2009b.

Massey, H. 'UNHCR and de facto statelessness'. Legal and Protection Policy in Research Series. LPPR/2010/01. UNHCR; 2010.

Matsuoka, A. and J. Sorenson. *Ghosts and Shadows*. University of Toronto: Toronto; 2001.

Mayor of London. 'Into the labyrinth: Legal advice for asylum seekers in London'. London; 2005.

McDonald, I. *McDonald's Immigration Law and Practice* (1st edn). Butterworth: London; 1983.

Migration Observatory. 'Immigration detention in the UK'. 2012. Available at: http://www.migrationobservatory.ox.ac.uk/briefings/immigration-detention-uk

Morris, L. 'Welfare, asylum and the politics of judgement', *Journal of Social Policy* 2009; 39(1): 119–38.

Nader, L. *The Life of the Law: Anthropological Projects*. University of California Press: Berkeley, CA; 2002.

National Audit Office. 'Improving the speed and quality of asylum decisions'. HC 535 Session 2003–2004. London; 2004.

National Audit Office, The Home Office. 'Management of asylum applications by the UK Border Agency'. HC 124 Session 2008–2009. London; 2009.

Nordstrom, C. and A. C. Robben (Eds). *Fieldwork under Fire: Contemporary Studies of Violence and Survival*. University of California: Berkeley; 1995.

Novogrodsky, N. 'Identity Politics', *Boston Review* 1999; Summer. Available at: http://bostonreview.net/BR24.3/novogrodsky.html

Ong, A. *Neoliberalism as Exception*. Durham: Duke University Press; 2006.

Open Society Justice Initiative. 'Discrimination in access to nationality: Review of Eritrea'. Washington, DC; 2009a.

Open Society Justice Initiative. 'Discrimination in access to nationality: Review of Ethiopia'. Washington, DC; 2009b.

Open Society Justice Initiative. 'Statement submitted by the Open Society Justice Initiative for consideration by the UN Human Rights Council at its Sixth Session, on the occasion of its Universal Periodic Review of Eritrea'. 30 November to 11 December. Washington, DC; 2009c

Papadopoulou, A. 'Exploring the asylum–migration nexus: A case study of transit migrants in Europe'. Global Commission on International Migration: Geneva; 2005. Available at: http://www.refworld.org/cgi-bin/texis/vtx/rwmain?page=publisher&publisher=GCIM&type=&coi=&docid=42ce4fa24&skip=0.

Plaut, M. 'Background to war: From friends to foes', in D. Jacquin-Berdal and M. Plaut (Eds), *Unfinished Business: Ethiopia and Eritrea at War*. Red Sea Press: Lawrenceville, NJ; 2005, pp. 1–22.

Polzer, T. and L. Hammond. 'Editorial: Invisible displacement', *Journal of Refugee Studies* 2008; 21(4): 417–31.

Price, P. 'Statelessness in the US: Current reality and a future prediction'. Emory University School of Law Legal Studies Research Paper No. 12-229; 2012. Available at: http://ssrn.com/abstract=2154470.

Rake, A. 'Eritrea: Recent history', in *Africa South of the Sahara*. Europa; 2002, pp. 344–50.

Rake, A. 'Eritrea: Recent history', in *Africa South of the Sahara*. Europa: New York; 2007, pp. 431–38.

Ramji-Nogales, R., A. Schoenholtz and P. Schrag. 'Refugee roulette: Disparities in asylum adjudication', *Stanford Law Review* 2007; 60(2): 295–411.

Refugees International. 'Lives on hold: The human cost of statelessness'. Washington, DC; 2005. Available at: http://www.globalaging.org/armedconflict/countryreports/asia-pacific/hold.pdf

Refugees International. 'Ethiopia–Eritrea: Stalemate takes it toll on Eritreans and Ethiopians of Eritrean Origin'. Washington, DC; 30 May 2008. Available at: http://www.refugeesinternational.org/policy/field-report/ethiopia-eritrea-stalemate-takes-toll-eritreans-and-ethiopians-eritrean-origin

Refugees International. *Nationality Rights for All*. Washington, DC; 2009.

Reid, R. 'Caught in the headlights of history: Eritrea, the EPLF and the post-war nation-state', *Journal of Modern African Studies* 2005a; 43(3): 467–88.

Reid, R. '"Ethiopians believe in God, Shabiya believe in mountains": the EPLF and the 1998–2000 war in historical perspective', in D. Jacque-Berdal and M. Plaut (Eds),

Unfinished Business: Ethiopia and Eritrea at War. Red Sea Press: Lawrenceville, NJ; 2005b, pp. 23–36.

Resoum Kidane. 'What is the underlying reason behind the deportation? Background to the deportation of Eritreans from Ethiopia'. University of Leeds; 1999. Available at: http://www.ehrea.org/DEPORt.htm

Riggan, J. 'In between nations: Ethiopian-born Eritreans, liminality, and war', *POLAR* 2011; 34(1): 131–54.

Rutter, J. 'Counting the uncountable'. Institute for Public Policy Research; 2007. Available at: http://www.ippr.org/articles/56/886/counting-the-uncountable.

Sachs, A. *The Strange Alchemy of Life and Law*. Oxford University Press: Oxford; 2009.

Sawyer, C. and B. Blitz (Eds). *Statelessness in the European Union: Displaced, Undocumented, Unwanted*. Cambridge University Press: Cambridge, UK; 2011a.

Sawyer, C. and B. Blitz. 'Research design and methodology of the country studies', in Sawyer and Blitz (Eds), *Statelessness in the European Union: Displaced, Undocumented, Unwanted*. Cambridge University Press: Cambridge, UK; 2011b, pp. 141–59.

Sawyer, C. and P. Turpin. 'Neither here nor there: Temporary admission to the UK', *International Journal of Refugee Law* 2005; 17: 688–728.

Scheper-Hughes, N. and P. Bourgois (Eds). *Violence in War and Peace*. Blackwell: Oxford; 2004.

Schmidt, C. *Chapters in the Concept of Sovereignty*. MIT Press: Cambridge, MA; 1985.

Schroeder, G. *From the Bullet to the Bank Account: The Economic Empire of the EPRDF. A Preliminary Assessment*. Updated 2006. Copy in author's possession.

Sing'oei, A. 'Citizenship in Kenya: The Nubian case', in B. Blitz and M. Lynch (Eds), *Statelessness and Citizenship: A Comparative Study on the Benefits of Nationality*. Edward Elgar: Cheltenham, UK; 2011.

Smith, A. 'Culture, community and territory: the politics of ethnicity and nationalism', *International Affairs* 1996; 72(3): 445–58.

Smith, E. *Right First Time? Home Office Asylum Interviewing and Reasons for Refusal Letters*. Medical Foundation for the Care of Victims of Torture: London; 2004.

Smock, D. 'Eritrean refugees in the Sudan', *Journal of Modern African Studies* 1982; 20 (3): 451–65.

Somerville, W. 'The immigration legacy of Tony Blair', Migration Policy Institute; May 2007. Available at: http://www.migrationinformation.org/Feature/display.cfm?ID=600

Soucy, A. 'Mixed migration from the Horn of Africa to Yemen: Protection risks and challenges'. Danish Refugee Council; June 2011.

Stevens, D. 'The Nationality, Immigration and Asylum Act 2002: Secure borders, safe haven?' *The Modern Law Review* 2004; 67(4): 616–31.

Taddele S. Teshale. *The Life History of an Ethiopian Refugee (1944–91)*. The Edwin Mellon Press: Lampeter, Wales, UK; 1991.

Tekeste Negash and K. Tronvoll. *Brothers at War: Making sense of the Eritrean–Ethiopian War*. James Currey: Oxford; 2000.

Tekie Fessehazion. 'Eritrean and Ethiopian state of economic relations: A nakfa/birr analysis'. Undated. Available at: http://www.denden.com/Conflict/newscom/com-tek98.htm

Tekle Woldemikael. 'Eritrean and Ethiopian refugees in the US', *Eritrean Studies Review* 1998; 2(2): 89–109.

Terrazas, A. 'Beyond regional circularity: The emergence of an Ethiopian diaspora',

Migration Policy Institute; June 2007. Available at: http://www.migrationinformation. org/Profiles/display.cfm?ID=604

Thomas, L. 'Refugees and asylum-seekers from mixed Eritrean–Ethiopian families in Cairo: "The son of a snake is a snake"', FRMS Working Paper No. 7. Cairo; 2006.

Thomas, R. 'Evaluating tribunal adjudication: Administrative justice and asylum appeals', *Legal Studies* 2005; 25: 462–98.

Triulzi, A. 'Colonial violence and the transfer of memories in the Ethio-Eritrean War (1998–2000)'. (No date) Copy in author's possession.

Tronvoll, K. 'The process of nation-building in post-war Eritrea: Created from below or directed from above?', *Journal of Modern African Studies* 1998; 36(3): 461–82.

Tronvoll, K. 'Borders of violence – boundaries of identity: Demarcating the Eritrean nation-state', *Ethnic and Racial Studies* 1999; 22(6): 1037–60.

Tronvoll, K. 'Human Rights Violations in Federal Ethiopia: When ethnic identity is a political stigma', *International Journal of Minority and Group Rights* 2008; 15: 49–79.

Tronvoll, K., C. Schaefer and Girmachew Alemu Aneme (Eds). *The Ethiopian Red Terror Trials: Transitional Justice Challenged.* James Currey: Oxford; 1999.

Turton, D. 'Refugees, forced re-settlers and "other forced migrants": Towards a unitary study of forced migration', New Issues in Refugee Research Working Paper No. 94. UNHCR; 2003. Available at: http://www.unhcr.org/research/RESEARCH/3f818a4d4. pdf

UK Department for International Development. 'Multilateral Aid Review: Taking forward the findings of the UK's Multilateral Aid Review'. London; 2011.

UK Home Office. 'Asylum Statistics UK 2007 (11/8)'. *Home Office Statistical Bulletin* 2008.

UK Home Office. 'User guide to Home Office immigration statistics'. London; 2012a.

UK Home Office. 'Operational guidance note: The Occupied Palestinian Territories'. London; 2012b. Available at: http://www.ukba.homeoffice.gov.uk/sitecontent/documents/ policyandlaw/countryspecificasylumpolicyogns/occu_pales_terri?view=Binary

UK Home Office. 'Removals and voluntary departures: Data tables, immigration statistics July–September 2012, vol. 3'. London; 2012c.

UK House of Commons Home Affairs Committee. 'The work of the UK Border Agency (April–July 2011): Fifteenth Report of Session 2010–12'. London; 2011. Available at: http://www.publications.parliament.uk/pa/cm201012/cmselect/cmhaff/1497/1497i.pdf

UK Ministry of Justice. 'Annual Reports'. London; various.

UN Development Programme. 'Update on Deportees: 12–19 July 1998'. Report from Designated Official and UN Resident Coordinator, Asmara, Eritrea. PRO/300/OCHA. 1998.

UNHCR. *Handbook on Procedures and Criteria for Determining Refugee Status Under the 1951 Convention and the 1967 Protocol Relating to the Status of Refugees.* HCR/IP4/ Eng/REV/1. Geneva; 1992.

UNHCR. 'Sudan in short'. Global Appeal 2001. Available at: http://www.unhcr.org/publ/ PUBL/3e2c05cde.pdf

UNHCR. *Statistical Yearbook 2002: Trends in Displacement, Protection and Solutions.* Geneva; 2003.

UNHCR. *Statistical Yearbook 2005: Trends in Displacement, Protection and Solutions.* Geneva; 2005.

UNHCR. *2006 Global Trends: Refugees, Asylum-seekers, Returnees, Internally Displaced and Stateless Persons.* Division of Operational Services, Field Information and Coordination Support Section. Geneva; 2007a.

UNHCR. 'Statelessness and issues relating to nationality from the Ethiopian perspective'. The Protection Unit: Addis Ababa; 2007b. [Paper sent to the author from the Addis Ababa office of UNHCR].

UNHCR. *2006 Global Report*. Geneva; 2007c.

UNHCR. 'Refugee protection, and asylum policy and practice in Ethiopia' (non-public). Addis Ababa; 2007d.

UNHCR. 'UNHCR action to address statelessness: A strategy note'. Geneva; 2010a.

UNHCR. *UNHCR Statistical Yearbook*. Geneva; 2010b. Available at: http://www.unhcr. org/4ef9cc9c9.html

UNHCR. 'Funding UNHCR's Programmes', in *UNHCR Global Report 2011*. Geneva; 2011a. Available at: http://www.unhcr.org/4fc8808f0.html

UNHCR. 'UNHCR eligibility guidelines for assessing the international protection needs of asylum-seekers from Eritrea'. HCR/EG/ERT/11/01. Geneva; 2011b.

UNHCR. *A Year of Crisis: Global Trends 2011*. Geneva; 2011c.

UNHCR. 'Ethiopia Refugee Update' UNHCR Ethiopia; March 2012. Available at: http://www.unhcr.org/4f6890d59.pdf

UNHCR and Asylum Aid. *Mapping Statelessness in the United Kingdom*. London; 2011.

UN Security Council. 'Monthly Forecast Report: Ethiopia/Eritrea. Update Report No. 1. 9 November 2005.

UN Security Council. 'Report of the Secretary-General on Ethiopia and Eritrea'. S/2007/645. 1 November 2007.

US Committee for Refugees and Immigrants. 'Annual Refugee Reports'. Various. Available at: http://www.refugees.org/

US Department of State. '2001 Human rights reports: Ethiopia'. Bureau of Democracy, Human Rights and Labor, Washington, DC; 2002.

US Department of State. 'Saudi Arabia: International religious freedom report 2003'. Washington, DC; 2003. Available at: http://www.state.gov/j/drl/rls/irf/2003/24461. htm

US Department of State. '2005 Human rights reports: Ethiopia'. Bureau of Democracy, Human Rights and Labor. Washington, DC; 2006.

US Department of State. '2008 Human rights reports: Ethiopia'. Bureau of Democracy, Human Rights and Labor. Washington, DC; 2009.

US Department of State. '2011 Trafficking in persons report: Ethiopia'. 2011. Available at: http://www.unhcr.org/refworld/country, USDOS,,ETH,,4e12ee7e37,0.html

van Haersoltevan Hof, J. 'The revitalization of the Permanent Court of Arbitration', *Netherlands International Law Review* 2007; 54(2): 395–413.

Vayrynen, V. 'Funding dilemmas in refugee assistance: Political interests and refugee reforms in UNHCR', *International Migration Review* 2001; 35(1): 143–67.

von Mehren, G. and C. Salomon. 'Submitting evidence in an international arbitration: The common lawyer's guide', *Journal of International Arbitration* 2003; 20(3): 285–94.

Weaver, J. 'Sojourners along the Nile: Ethiopian refugees in Khartoum', *Journal of Modern African Studies* 1985; 23(1): 147–56.

Weissbrodt, D. *The Human Rights of Non-Citizens*. Oxford University Press: Oxford; 2008.

Weldehaimanot, S. and E. Taylor. '"Our struggle and its goals": a controversial Eritrean manifesto', *Review of African Political Economy* 2011; 38(130): 565–85.

Wilson, W. 'The deportation of "Eritreans" from Ethiopia: Human rights violations tolerated by the international community', *North Carolina Journal of International Law and Commercial Regulation* 1999; 24 (2): 451–95.

Williams, R. *Keywords*. Fontana: Glasgow; 1976.

Won Kidane. 'Civil liability for violations of international humanitarian law: The juris-prudence of the Eritrea–Ethiopia Claim Commission in The Hague', *Wisconsin International Law Journal* 2007; 25(1): 23–87.

Woolf, H. 'Judicial review: The tensions between the executive and the judiciary', *Law Quarterly Review* 1998; 114: 579–93.

World Bank. *Migration and Remittances Factbook*. Washington, DC; 2011.

Writenet. 'The Ethio-Eritrean Conflict: An essay in interpretation'. 1 November 1998. Available at: http://www.unhcr.org/refworld/country,,WRITENET,,ETH,,3ae6a6b74,0.html

Yintinso Gebre. 'Contextual determination of migration behaviours: The Ethiopian resettlement in light of conceptual constructs', *Journal of Refugee Studies* 2002; 15(3): 265–82.

Yitna G. Yitna. 'Stranded Ethiopian migrants in Bosasso, NE Somali/Puntland'. Field Mission Report. IOM: Nairobi; 2006. Available at: http://www.iom.int/jahia/webdav/site/myjahiasite/shared/shared/mainsite/activities/regulating/ethiopians_stranded_in_bossasso_1106.pdf

Yohannes Anberbir 'Oops! Woyanes won't repay Eritrean expellees as directed', *Ethiopian Review* 24 August 2009. Available at: http://www.ethiopianreview.com/forum/viewtopic.php?f=2&t=14842&p=80215.

Yonas Kibru. 'A bare-faced act of betrayal', *Merkato Blog* 27 May 2009. Available at: http://nazret.com/blog/index.php/2009/05/28/ethiopia_a_barefaced_act_of_betrayal?blog=15

York, S. and N. Fancott. 'Enforced destitution: Impediments to return and access to Sec. 4 "hard cases" support', *Journal of Immigration, Asylum and Nationality Law* 2008; 22(5): 6–22.

Young, J. 'The Tigray and Eritrean Peoples Liberation Fronts: A history of tensions and pragmatism', *Journal of Modern African Studies* 1996; 34(1): 105–20.

Young, J. 'Development and change in post-revolutionary Tigiay', *Journal of Modern African Studies* 1997; 35(1): 81–99.

Zakir Ibrahim. 'The legal aspect of Ethiopia's deportation of undesirable Eritreans'. Ministry of Foreign Affairs: Addis Ababa; 6 November 1998. Available at: http://www.oocities.org/~dagmawi/News/Views_Nov7_Deportations.html.

Zetter, R. with D. Griffiths, N. Sigona, D. Flynn, T. Pasha and R. Beynon. *Immigration, Social Cohesion and Social Capital. What are the links?* Joseph Rowntree Foundation: London; 2006.

Zohry, A. and B. Harrel-Bond. 'Contemporary Egyptian migration: An overview of voluntary and forced migration'. Working paper C-3. Forced Migration and Refugee Studies Program, American University in Cairo: Cairo; 2003.

Zorn, J. 'From erased and excluded to active participants in Slovenia', in B. Blitz and M. Lynch (Eds), *Statelessness and Citizenship: A Comparative Study on the Benefits of Nationality*. Edward Elgar: Cheltenham; 2011.

Index

In this index g. indicates an entry in the glossary; n. indicates a note.